None but the Brave

None but the Brave

THE ESSENTIAL CONTRIBUTIONS OF RAF BOMBER COMMAND TO ALLIED VICTORY DURING THE SECOND WORLD WAR

BY
DAVID L. BASHOW

CANADIAN DEFENCE ACADEMY PRESS

Canadian Defence Academy Press
PO Box 17000 Stn Forces
Kingston, Ontario   K7K 7B4

Produced for the Canadian Defence Academy Press
by 17 Wing Winnipeg Publishing Office.
WPO30415

Cover painting: "Bomb Aimer, Battle of the Ruhr 1944 by Carl Schaefer," CWM 11786.

Library and Archives Canada Cataloguing in Publication

Bashow, David L., 1946-
None but the brave : the essential contributions of RAF Bomber Command
to Allied victory during the Second World War / by David L. Bashow.

Produced for the Canadian Defence Academy Press by 17 Wing Winnipeg
Publishing Office.
Issued by: Canadian Defence Academy.
Includes bibliographical references and index.
ISBN 978-1-100-11551-1 (bound) -- ISBN 978-1-100-11552-8 (pbk.)
Cat. no.: D2-240/1-2009E (bound) -- Cat. no.: D2-240/2-2009E (pbk.)

1. Great Britain. Royal Air Force Bomber Command--History--World War,
1939-1945. 2. World War, 1939-1945--Aerial operations, British. 3. Bombing,
Aerial--Germany--History. I. Canadian Defence Academy II. Canada. Canadian
Armed Forces. Wing, 17 III. Title. IV. Title: Essential contributions of RAF
Bomber Command to Allied victory during the Second World War.

D786 B37 2009   940.54'4941   C2009-980101-9

Printed in Canada.

3 5 7 9 10 8 6 4

Acknowledgements

As is the case with many of life's undertakings, *None but the Brave* has been a cooperative effort from the outset. The book is, in great part, a vastly shortened version of my earlier book, *No Prouder Place ~ Canadians and the Bomber Command Experience 1939-1945*. However, while the earlier work placed the emphasis upon Canada's contribution within the broader Bomber Command effort, this time out, the narrative is much more generic, and it also includes acknowledgement of the synergistic American contribution to the bomber offensive. Over the course of the past several years since *No Prouder Place* was first released, Canada witnessed a heated debate with respect to the efficacy and the morality of the campaign. *None but the Brave* presents an opportunity to build upon my original conclusions, particularly with respect to the evolution of Allied bombing policy and the myriad results obtained by the bomber offensive itself. It will also address some new aspects of this massive effort that surfaced during the course of the debate.

Readers need to understand that *None but the Brave* is, first and foremost, a tribute to the aircrew veterans of this vastly misunderstood bomber offensive. And as was the case in *No Prouder Place*, for those veterans who took the time and made the effort to share their wartime experiences, I extend my profound thanks and gratitude.

I am particularly honoured that Bob Dale agreed to write the foreword to this book, since he is not only one of my personal heroes, but, over the course of the aforementioned debate, we also became friends. In his foreword, Bob modestly neglects to mention that, as a Bomber Command navigator, he won both a Distinguished Flying Cross (DFC) and a Distinguished Service Order (DSO) while completing a very rare three full operational tours of combat. After an initial tour in *Wellingtons* during the very dark early days of the bombing campaign, he later specialized in *Mosquito* operations, completing extremely hazardous duties with the Meteorological Flight, flying unarmed all over Germany and gathering weather data for Bomber Command's daily and nightly efforts. In this role, Bob's experience made him fundamentally irreplaceable. As another Canadian Bomber Command stalwart, Terry Goodwin, recalled: "When Dale completed his 50 trips [of his *second* operational tour – DB], the CO just called him in, told him he was indispensible, and kept him for another 50 trips."[1] Bob's DFC citation, gazetted on 13 March 1942, noted that, "...his ability as a navigator is outstanding and combined with great determination to achieve success, he has inspired the utmost confidence in his crew."[2] The later award of the DSO on 24 October 1944 cited his "...coolness and determination to complete his assignments successfully, which has won great praise."[3]

To all the participants of the bomber offensive, this book is respectfully dedicated.

David L. Bashow
Kingston, Ontario
April 2009

NOTES

1.   H. Terry Goodwin, "Hugh Hay, DSO, DFC – Top Navigator?" in *Airforce*, Vol. 24, No. 1, Spring 2000, pp.36-39.
2.   <http://www.airforce.ca/wwii/ALPHA-DA.html>, p.14.
3.   Ibid.

Table of Contents

Foreword

I enlisted in the Royal Canadian Air Force [RCAF] at the age of eighteen when war was declared in the autumn of 1939, was trained as a navigator under the British Commonwealth Air Training Plan, and was on my way overseas by December 1940.

After operational training, I was posted to 150 Squadron of the Royal Air Force [RAF]. This squadron had been flying Fairey *Battles* in France, had lost all their aircraft in the fierce fighting there, and their surviving personnel had been evacuated through the Dunkirk beaches in June 1940. After a rest period, the squadron was re-equipped with Vickers *Wellington* 1Cs, and the unit was fully operational when I joined them in February 1941.

I arrived in England at a time when the 'Blitz' on London and many of the smaller cities was at its peak, and I witnessed at first hand the terror of these raids and the losses and hardship endured by the British people.

My first tour of operations was carried out during a period when Bomber Command suffered some of its heaviest loss rates. Crews had to contend with intense and accurate anti-aircraft fire in the target area, as well as German night fighters at all times while over enemy territory. Lengthy sorties had to be carried out without the benefit of sophisticated and accurate navigational aids, which did not start to become available until the middle of 1942.

I completed my first operational tour in January 1942, and, after a period of specialist training and staff jobs, I trained on de Havilland *Mosquitos* and joined 8 Group [Pathfinder Force] in January 1944.

I was part of the Special Duty Flight of seven crews, who carried out a variety of operations, including pre-raid weather reconnaissance and post-raid photographic sorties, as well as many interesting missions of a tactical nature.

The demands made upon our group were incredible, particularly during the weeks leading up to D-Day, and I completed my second and third tours of operations by the end of 1944.

FOREWORD

▶ A 426 (RCAF) Squadron *Halifax III* on its hardstand at Linton. Note the Nissen hut in the foreground.

During my operational career, I was personally convinced that Bomber Command was going to have a significant impact upon the outcome of the war. People seem to forget that after the 1940 defeat of the Allies in France and the subsequent withdrawal through Dunkirk, the only way we could strike back at the Germans was through the air. In reality, Bomber Command established a second front that helped pave the way for the eventual invasion through Normandy.

In recent years, the morality of the Bomber Command offensive seems to have become a favourite subject for some historians and for the media, and, sadly, Bomber Command veterans have been forced to defend their proud record in a war that claimed the lives of over 50,000 of their friends in various squadrons. Apparently, it is too easy to forget that in 1941, the United Kingdom stood alone as the only part of Europe still able to hold out against the Nazis and their incredible record of atrocities.

In this book, David Bashow has again set the record straight, and for this, the RAF and RCAF veterans of Bomber Command, along with our American comrades, are most grateful.

Robert G. Dale, DSO, DFC, CD
Squadron Leader
Royal Canadian Air Force [Retired]

Introduction

During the Second World War, Bomber Command of Britain's Royal Air Force (RAF), working in lockstep with the numbered air forces of the United States Army Air Forces (USAAF), played a vital role in bringing about the ruination and collapse of Hitler's Third Reich. However, in the words of the distinguished British historian Richard Overy:

> *Few campaigns have generated more heated argument than the bombing of Germany by the Allies between 1940 and 1945. A great many distortions and illusions litter the popular view of the part RAF Bomber Command played in that campaign. Not the least of these is the view that all Bomber Command ever did was hammer away at German cities regardless of morality or military good sense. Bomber Command did a great deal more than this, and in the process contributed in a variety of ways to the Allied war effort.*[1]

In point of fact, the Allied bombing of the Third Reich and its allies was an integral part of Britain's overall war strategy to take the offensive to the enemy, and to do so as expeditiously as possible. It created a second front that bled off vital resources from the German campaign in the east, including massive amounts of manpower and materiel diverted from the primary German war efforts just to address the threat and the damage it created. The bombing campaign dealt telling blows to Germany's economic and industrial infrastructure, forcing a costly and time consuming decentralization of its war industries. And ultimately, it helped pave the way, through destruction of enemy air defences, oil resources, and transportation networks, for a successful invasion of Germany through northwest Europe in 1944.

First, a brief note on the ranks of the participants mentioned herein. With the exception of some very distinguished principals, the use of ranks has generally either been avoided or they have been recorded as the highest wartime rank attained by an individual. This is due in no small measure to the fact that many of the participants went on to achieve very high rank subsequent to the events chronicled in this book, and thus fall beyond the scope of my mandate.

With respect to sources, extensive use has been made of both primary and secondary material. While there is no formal bibliography, bibliographical data

Credit: DND PL33337

▶ Symbolic of all the participating aircrew, Pilot Officer Jack Ryan, DFC, of Toronto, in front of his 425 Squadron *Halifax, Nobody's Baby*, after flying his last war sortie.

is fully recorded in the extensive endnotes, which are an integral part of each individual chapter.

Chapter One of this three-part study will chart the evolution and refinement of British bombing policy during the Second World War, from its first tentative steps at the commencement of hostilities, to the realization of its most destructive, yet *productive* apex during the last calendar year of the war, operating as it then did synergistically with the numbered air forces of the United States Army Air Force (USAAF) over Europe. Emphasis will be placed upon the relatively little known and frequently misunderstood formative early years of Britain's bomber offensive. Chapter Two will address the human element of the campaign, for this massive, arduous undertaking became a true triumph of the human spirit and a display of sustained courage, prosecuted at times in the face of nearly insurmountable odds. Chapter Three will chronicle the myriad direct and *indirect* contributions of the bombing campaign to ultimate victory in Europe, and its impact upon the Pacific war against the Japanese Empire. In the process, the book will attempt to provide balance and perspective to the criticisms that have been levied against the bomber offensive and its perpetrators over the years, and, hopefully, put paid to some of the more strident, irrational, and ill-founded objections and misconceptions, particularly those that apply to the evolution and development of Britain's wartime bombing policy.

NOTES

1. Richard Overy, *Bomber Command 1939-1945* (London: HarperCollins, 1997), p.11.

Chapter One
THE EVOLUTION OF A HURRICANE

BACKGROUND

Even the pyramids will pale against the masses of concrete and stone colossi which I am erecting... I am building for eternity, for we are the last Germany.

~ Adolf Hitler, 1936[1]

There is no doubt that British bombing policy, as it was conducted during the Second World War, was influenced by the strategic aerial bombardment experiences of the First World War. More than 100 German *Zeppelin* and giant fixed-wing bomber raids on Britain had produced nearly 3500 fatal casualties and had left many more persons injured. Moreover, these raids generated widespread shock, a sense of vulnerability, and a significant disruption of wartime production all out of proportion to the actual damage they inflicted. This widespread disruption included lost time due to the suspension of manufacturing, the upheaval of transportation systems, worker consternation and anxiety, and the diversion of limited human and materiel resources to directly combat these threats.[2] To a much lesser extent, the Independent Force of the embryonic Royal Air Force had conducted a limited strategic bombing campaign against the enemy's core industries towards the end of the war. However, General Sir Hugh Trenchard (later Marshal of the Royal Air Force Viscount Trenchard), the Independent Force's first commander and later the RAF's Chief of the Air Staff from 1919 to 1929, staunchly maintained, throughout the 1920s, that the *psychological* impact of the bombing overshadowed the *material* damage generated by a factor of twenty-to-one.[3] A postwar bombing survey concluded that although the *material* damage had indeed been light, panic had been widely reported in the cities attacked. In attempting to foresee the future efficacy of aerial bombardment, and based upon the bombing results observed in both Britain and Germany, the air staff of Trenchard's day felt that material damage to the enemy would be very secondary compared to the chaos sown by the *moral(e)*[sic] *collapse* of personnel working in the vital public services

Credit: RAF photo

▶ A Bristol *Blenheim* banks for the camera.

sectors, such as water supply, food services distribution, lighting, power, and transportation.[4] Thus, throughout the 1920s and early 1930s, Hugh Trenchard, later reinforced by the British Prime Minister of the day, Stanley Baldwin, and in relative lockstep with parallel doctrine espoused by the Italian general Guilio Douhet and the American general "Billy" Mitchell, essentially helped shape the RAF's conventional wisdom that "...the bomber would always get through," and that determined aerial attacks upon an enemy's war economy "...would produce such crushing damage to both natural resources and civilian morale that the opponent would have to sue for peace."[5]

However, there was a strong countering sentiment to establish a strict set of international rules to govern the use of this new weapon. As Doctor David Hall of Oxford noted: "The 1923 Hague Draft Rules of Aerial Warfare was the first authoritative attempt to clarify and formulate a comprehensive code of conduct, but they were never adopted in legally binding terms. Growing awareness of the military potential of aircraft throughout the 1920s and 1930s ultimately proved too serious an obstacle to reaching an agreement."[6] A significant deterrent to reaching consensus was the inability to establish what constituted a legitimate military target under new conditions of modern total warfare between industrialized nations:

> Factories making armaments and transport bringing them to the battle fronts naturally were included in the category of legitimate targets once the means of attacking them were available. Consequently those civilians in them or dangerously close to them might just have to be equated with civilians in legitimately attacked places. Naval bombardment of ports and towns was an accepted act of war. It was even codified in Article 2 of the Convention on Naval Bombardment, signed at The Hague in 1907. Article 2 stipulated that a naval commander who used his ships' guns to destroy military objectives in an undefended port or town "...incur[red] no responsibility for any unavoidable damage that may be caused by a bombardment under such circumstances." The advent of air power merely increased the opportunity of reaching and destroying such targets.[7]

Noted British historian Richard Holmes has offered further comment on the ambiguity of international law with respect to aerial bombardment at the time:

> Briefly, an attacker is required to exercise discrimination when this does not increase the risk to his own personnel, but the ultimate responsibility for the fate of civilians in a siege lies with the defender, who may at any time put an end to their suffering by surrender, and whose counter measures may reduce the possibility of discrimination, for example by obliging the attacker to bomb from a greater altitude or by night.[8]

CHAPTER ONE

Not surprisingly therefore, when Bomber Command was officially established on Bastille Day, 14 July 1936, the RAF War Manual of that year clearly stated, "...the bomb is the chief weapon of an air force."[9] And the new command was formed within a parent service that had been seamlessly committed to the utility of a strategic bombing policy from that service's conception during the Great War. Further, the perception of the relative invulnerability of the bomber had been erroneously reinforced through acts of indiscriminate area bombardment of civilians during the inter-war years by various totalitarian nations, including the Japanese upon Hankow and other defenceless Chinese coastal ports, the Italians upon native villages in Abyssinia, and, perhaps most notably, by the fascists under Spanish Generalissimo Francisco Franco upon Barcelona, then Guernica, in April 1937. These bombings served chilling notice to the western democracies of a distinct lack of scruples associated with the use of this weapon by the totalitarian regimes; a realization that would be strongly reinforced by the indiscriminate application of area bombing by the Germans against civilians during the early months of the Second World War.

In Britain, during the period of rearmament from 1934 onwards, the role of bombing was defined as follows:

- To assist in the defence of Britain by attacking enemy airpower assets;
- To assist the Army and the Royal Navy; and
- To attack an enemy's economy, but only under circumstances where the government felt that an attack upon enemy civilians could be justified.[10]

The greatest concern rested with Germany, by now regarded as being Britain's most likely future enemy. Late in 1937, the RAF was given the task of deciding what specific economic and military targets it should attack were it required to do so. To that end, the Air Ministry penned the Western Air Plans, a list of 13 specific RAF objectives in the event of war. Contained within these objectives were three that applied directly to Bomber Command:

- Attacks on the enemy's air striking force;
- Direct support of military operations by disabling enemy communications behind the battle front; and
- Attacks on the German war industries, especially those situated within Germany's industrial heartland, the Ruhr.[11]

In September 1937, Bomber Command's second Air Officer Commanding in Chief (AOC in C), Air Marshal Sir Edgar Ludlow-Hewitt, declared himself to be most enthusiastic about the third objective. He believed that enemy air assets would be too widely dispersed and therefore too hard to bomb or located beyond the then-effective range of command aircraft. A similar argument was made for enemy road and rail lines of communication. Therefore, the default viewpoint of Bomber Command's senior staff was that attacks on German industry were more operationally viable and had more strategic utility than the other objectives.

In December, Bomber Command was asked to draw up a list of prioritized targets, a task to be accomplished jointly by Military Air Intelligence and the civilian Targets Sub-Committee. Given a need to target what was believed to be the most critical elements of a complex industrial system, the military planners favoured attacks upon the electrical power grid work, while the civilians promoted attacks on the Ruhr dams, as well as rail and canal transportation lines. In the end, the Joint Chiefs of Staff felt both these directions and their predicted results were excessively optimistic. Therefore, Bomber Command was told to restrict its operations to those against an enemy air force and for the protection of British shipping. Also, for the time being, only clearly identifiable military targets were to be attacked.

However, those in command also recognized that Bomber Command had some very serious capability limitations. The light bombers of the day, such as the Fairey *Battle* and the Bristol *Blenheim*, were altogether unsuitable for longer-range, heavy bombing missions. Even the newer, heavier twin-engine bombers, which were coming on board from 1936 onwards, the Handley-Page *Hampden*, the Armstrong-Whitworth *Whitley*, and the Vickers *Wellington*, could not, with a full bomb load, range much further afield than the Ruhr valley. Defensive armament was at best sparse and of a mere rifle calibre. Electronic aids to navigation were all but non-existent. Targets were often virtually impossible to locate, and bombing accuracy was a joke. The primitive bombsights of the day introduced gross errors in accuracy if even one of myriad release parameters was *conservatively* violated.

Back in 1936, one of the key proponents of a *heavy* versus a *medium* bomber force was Group Captain Arthur Harris (eventually Marshal of the Royal Air Force Sir Arthur Harris), Bomber Command's Deputy Director of Plans at the time. In due course, a new specification was tendered for a bomber capable of

▶ A 408 'Goose' Squadron *Hampden* during an engine run-up at Balderton in Nottinghamshire. It was lost in combat over Denmark on the night of 8/9 May 1942.

flying 3000 miles while carrying a bomb payload of 8000 pounds at 28,000 feet. This would result in the four-engine Short *Stirling* of 1941. However, this aircraft proved to be significantly disappointing with respect to the specified service ceiling and bomb carriage issues, and in 1938, further specifications were issued for a so-called *ideal* bomber, one which also possessed much better defensive armament so that it could cope with the latest generations of enemy fighter aircraft. It was also to have a top speed of 300 miles-per-hour and the ability to carry 12,000 pounds of bombs. These capabilities would eventually be achieved by modifying the designs of two-engine bombers into successful four-engine variants. They would become embodied in the Handley-Page *Halifax* and the Avro *Lancaster*, the mainstay mounts of the command from 1942 onwards.

Just prior to the Munich Crisis of 1938, Ludlow-Hewitt told Prime Minister Neville Chamberlain that Bomber Command was virtually useless in its present state. He offered that his aircraft could only reach the peripheries of northwestern Germany, and that they would incur unacceptably high combat losses against the known German defences. In this extraordinarily frank admission, he maintained that to commit the command to offensive action in its present state would be courting a major disaster. Even more than a year-and-a-half later, when the German *Blitzkrieg* rolled through France and the Low Countries, the command was essentially confined to assisting the land battle on the continent, possessing still nothing but the most rudimentary attack capabilities. Otherwise, Bomber Command was limited to reconnaissance duties, propaganda (leaflet) raids, and sorties against naval targets in the North Sea and on its peripheries. However, it should be noted that public shock and fear of indiscriminate civilian bombardment just prior to the war's commencement in 1939 was by then looming large. Consequently, in April, a joint Anglo-French agreement was signed that was intended to avoid the intentional bombing of civilians, and hopefully, to dissuade Germany from doing so as well. Appropriate instructions were subsequently issued to Bomber Command.[12]

Thus, policy makers made it quite clear that unrestricted aerial warfare was not, at this point in time, considered to be in the interests of Great Britain. The ban on posing a risk to civilian lives would only be lifted the following May, and even then, somewhat tentatively, when Winston Churchill replaced Neville Chamberlain as Prime Minister, and in the wake of the indiscriminate early-war bombings of Warsaw, Rotterdam, and other urban centres by the Germans.

TO WAR

The more darkness in night attacks hinders and impedes the sight, the more must one supply the place of actual vision by skill and care...

~ Scipio Africanus
236-184 BC

British bombing policy was deliberately non-provocative at the commencement of hostilities in 1939, restricted as it was to reconnaissance, leaflet raids, and attacks upon enemy shipping and ports. However, due to the limitations previously mentioned, Bomber Command's daylight raids soon resulted in decimation of the attacking forces and a policy shift to *night* attacks in an attempt to use the cloak of darkness for compensatory protection. Notwithstanding, night attacks were fraught with difficulties and challenges. A series of daylight sorties mounted in strength against the German Home Fleet in November and December 1939 led the pragmatists to conclude that while daylight, precision raids had become prohibitively dangerous, astro-navigation could, at best, get the crews to within 12 miles of a specific target. Nor were electronic navigational beacons, still relatively new and limited, expected to make much of a difference.

Looking to the future, but persuaded that Bomber Command required additional time to build up its strength, the air staff now began to argue that the focus of bombing should shift from producing physical damage, which required sustained and intensive operations and demanded more accuracy than Ludlow-Hewitt could guarantee, to lowering enemy morale, which it wishfully thought could be accomplished by as few as two hundred sorties a week. The idea was to despatch small numbers of aircraft to Germany each night, dispersing them in time and space through as many air defence zones as possible and setting off almost continuous alarms over the whole Reich. This would upset the "nerves and digestion" of the German population and might eventually make living conditions so unpleasant that those employed in the war industries would be "loathe to continue at work."[13]

However, decisive results were not expected from this psychological approach in the short term. In order to inflict *significant* damage, intelligence staffers felt the Axis oil industry needed to be targeted, and concluded that the neutralization of 22 of Germany's facilities, of which 15 were located less than 150 miles from the North Sea (especially in the Ruhr valley), could have a decisive impact upon the German war effort. Thus, on 22 February 1940, the RAF Chief of the Air Staff (CAS), Sir Cyril Newall, approved the oil plan, believing it could get the job done, and Bomber Command began its full conversion to a night bombing force.[14] However, Bomber Command's new helmsman, Air Marshal Charles "Peter" Portal, was not as sanguine, and he told Newall that target identification at night, for *average* crews, was only possible under the best conditions of visibility, and even then, only when the target was on the coast or an enormous waterway, such as the Rhine River, and beyond this, very few *inexperienced* crews "…could be likely to find it under any condition."[15]

The winds of bombing policy change stirred again on 8th and 9th of April 1940, when the Germans invaded Norway and Denmark, and while Pierce continued to implore his superiors to give his command free rein in an air offensive against civilian morale, the senior political leadership remained reluctant as long as Britain had not yet been directly bombed. However, on 15 May, with the Germans pouring west from Sedan and after the decimating bombing of Rotterdam the day before, 'the gloves finally came off,' and Bomber Command was authorized to attack both oil refineries and railroad targets west of the Rhine River.[16] Meanwhile, the Germans were bolstering their defences significantly, including a build-up of the night fighter force, the placement of belts of early warning radars, sound detectors, and searchlights, and the establishment of specific night fighting zones, which would stretch eventually 15 miles deep and unbroken from Holland and the Scheldt Estuary in the south, to the German-Danish border in the north, and into Occupied France. And this formidable electronic fence, within which the *Luftwaffe* night fighters would be positively controlled and directed by radar, blanketed the most probable ingress and egress routes of Bomber Command.

While those in authority struggled to identify and to prioritize the greatest threats and enemy vulnerable areas, including aircraft assembly plants, airfields and aircraft storage areas, oil, barges, troop ships and ports, over the next five months, no less than six separate bombing policy directives had one thing in common; they all provided lists of specific objectives. Nonetheless, in mid-July, Portal and his staff, who frankly were not happy with *any* of the directives, and who remained convinced that command crews were simply incapable of finding and destroying precise targets, specifically asked for authority to make *generalized* area attacks against larger German industrial areas in order to undermine enemy morale, having heard through the Foreign Office that the bombing to date was instilling panic among the German population.[17] Portal believed, along with some of the greyer heads in Britain's highest councils, that an unfettered campaign against the German industrial cities might indeed impact enemy morale significantly and save the United Kingdom from an invasion. And while Portal's request was summarily denied, the Air Ministry insisting that *material destruction* still had to be the primary goal, it would set the stage for future policy shifts that would alter the fates of many German civilians. From 1941 onwards until late-1944, a majority of Bomber Command's sorties consisted of area bombing by night, the chief reason being "...[that] the only target on which the night force could inflict effective damage was a whole German town."[18] The RAF's Official History Branch Narrative has identified this linkage directly with Sir Charles Portal and the more pessimistic yet pragmatic attitude he would bring to future Air Staff deliberations on bombing policy. Ultimately, "... due allowance was made for the inaccuracy of bombing, by ensuring that targets selected were not isolated, but if possible in large centres of population and industry. This was the reason for the initiation of area bombing and the selection of 'industrial centres' instead of factories."[19] This becomes an important point downstream, since Bomber Command's most famous wartime commander, Sir Arthur 'Bomber' Harris, has been the individual wrongly considered most responsible for instituting Bomber Command's area bombing policy, although he did *implement* the policy enthusiastically.

Credit: DND PL19336

▶ A bomb aimer in front of an early-model Handley Page *Halifax*.

The first *major* assault of what would later be commonly referred to as the Battle of Britain took place on 10 July 1940, when a British convoy near Dover was attacked by a force of approximately 20 Dornier Do 17 bombers, escorted by a 'mixed bag' of Messerschmitt Bf 109 and Bf 110 fighters. This attack, and many others to follow, would characterize the first, or 'anti-shipping' phase of the battle. Then, in early August, the *Luftwaffe* switched into its second bombing phase, an all-out assault against the RAF in preparation for Operation *Sea Lion*, the planned invasion of the United Kingdom in September. During this phase, the Germans concentrated upon the service airfields, the aircraft factories, radar sites, and the all-important sector operations centres and other command and control nodes. Then, on the night of 24/25 August, the Germans accidentally bombed London. Churchill demanded immediate retaliation, and the next night, approximately 50 Bomber Command aircraft were sent to Berlin. Although the damage meted out on this occasion was trivial, more effective attacks would soon follow, and on 30 August, the command drew blood with an attack on the city centre near the Görlitzer railway station, ten Berliners being killed. Hitler, in a retributive rage, ordered an all-out assault upon London and other British cities, in what would become known as the 'Blitz,' the third and final phase of the Battle of Britain. While London would bear the brunt, other cities attacked included Bath, Bristol, Liverpool, Glasgow, Merseyside, Portsmouth, Southampton, Manchester, Cardiff, and Coventry.[20] In all, 42,000 Britons would perish from bombing during the Blitz of 1940-1941,[21] and other fatalities would occur during the so-called retributive Baedeker Raids of spring 1942, during various limited attacks and harassment raids, and as a result of the later-war 'V-weapon' attacks. However, the German city bombings in September occurred just in time to spare the RAF's vital airfields and command and control facilities from further specific and concentrated attacks. Arthur Harris, when witnessing the devastation caused by the bombing during the Blitz with Charles Portal, paraphrased the Old Testament (Hosea 7:10) when he stated:

The Nazis entered this war under the rather childish delusion that they were going to bomb everyone else, and nobody was going to bomb them. At Rotterdam, London, Warsaw, and half a hundred other places, they put their rather naïve theory into operation. They have sowed the wind, and now they are going to reap the whirlwind.[22]

Meanwhile, during the early phases of the battle, Bomber Command had been told to conduct attacks against enemy ships and ports its first priority, in anticipation of an upcoming invasion. As combat intensified against the RAF, "… the top priority went to any targets that were calculated to reduce the immediate threat of German air attack – air bases, oil supplies, and any aircraft factories within striking distance."[23] By September, the command's priorities had switched yet again to an anti-invasion role, with concentrated attacks being launched against the barges and transport vessels in the planned invasion ports, including Le Havre, Rotterdam, and Antwerp, until Hitler indefinitely postponed *Sea Lion* on 17 September.

However, as early as 8 July 1940, Churchill had written:

> When I look round to see how we can win the war I see that there is only one sure path. We have no continental army which can defeat the German military power. The blockade is broken and Hitler has Asia and probably Africa to draw from. Should he be repulsed here or not try invasion, he will recoil eastward, and we have nothing to stop him. But there is one thing that will bring him back and bring him down, and that is an absolutely devastating, exterminating attack by very heavy bombers from this country upon the Nazi homeland.[24]

On 9 October 1940, after repeated attacks upon the British cities, *Reichmarschall* Hermann Göring, Commander-in-Chief of the *Luftwaffe*, made public a plan for the obliteration of London and the demoralization of its citizens by bombardment, coupled with the paralysing of Britain's broader industrial and commercial capabilities.[25]

> Inch by painful inch, both British and German policies were slipping from ones aimed at precise objectives to ones of area bombing with psychological overtones. On 2 September, for example, Portal observed that although he was not yet involved in attempts to burn down whole towns, "that stage will come." The next day Churchill asked that Bomber Command "pulverize the entire industry and economic structure" of the German war economy; and, three days later, he called for a series of "minor" but "widespread" attacks on smaller German towns intended to destroy the population's faith in their air defences. Portal responded with a list of twenty such places and urged that it be made public in order to provide a clear statement that, "…as a reprisal for each night of indiscriminate bombing by the enemy, one of these towns would be selected for indiscriminate bombing by the RAF."[26]

Shortly thereafter, Charles Portal was promoted to Chief of the Air Staff, and Sir Richard Peirse, a staunch advocate of area bombing, was made AOC in C of Bomber Command. From now on, Portal's desire to attack the industrial centres as frequently as possible would carry significant weight. And while oil targets carried top priority on clear, moonlit nights when it was darker, Bomber Command was henceforth "…[to] make a definite attempt… to affect the morale of the German people."[27] An interesting letter of the period, written by Secretary of State for Air Sir Archibald Sinclair to the Prime Minister, noted that when piecemeal harassment attacks against the German cities were directed at their railway marshalling yards, the results, confirmed by intelligence reports, were encouraging.[28] Such wartime snippets of intelligence, coupled with a certain application of previous British experiences, played a large part in determining broader policies, such as bombing priorities.

Nonetheless, the new counter-city raids soon came under fire from Churchill for a perceived lack of intensity.

> Peirse then promised, as an example, to pick Berlin targets that were well spaced, in order to ensure broad attack distribution across the city. While this attack policy was certainly grounded in the lack of a precision bombing capability, there was also an emotional component at play. The German attack on Coventry on 14/15 November, followed by similar raids on Bristol and Southampton, drove the planning for Operation *Abigail*, a retaliatory attack upon a selected German city. Due to bad weather, the raid did not occur until 16/17 December 1940 when 134 command aircraft were launched against Mannheim. For the first time, a British raid opened with an incendiary laydown, and subsequent crews were then instructed to bomb on the ensuing fires; an early and rudimentary form of target marking.[29]

The results of this raid, initially reported over-optimistically, proved to be somewhat disappointing, and an *equally* over-optimistic report on the damage inflicted to date on enemy synthetic oil refineries was soon released. Although the accuracy of this second report was soon dispelled, Charles Portal conceded the importance of its theme, and subsequently ordered a campaign against 17 of the Reich's largest synthetic oil plants. The attacks on area targets were to be relegated to nights when weather precluded action against the more demanding, pinpoint refinery targets. Peirse was officially informed, on 15 January 1941, that destruction of enemy oil facilities was deemed to be the "sole primary aim" of the bombers until further orders were received.[30] That said, the War Cabinet was not at this time of a mind "...to discourage ruthlessness by Bomber Command; the feeling was that the British people were entitled to know that they were giving as good as they were getting."[31]

And so, the bombing continued, characterized by generally lacklustre results, tentative initiatives, and a concerted push to accelerate development of some promising electronic aids to navigation and weapons throughout the grim, upcoming year. Meanwhile, the Germans were also making improvements to

Credit: DND PL10457

▶ An early model Handley-Page *Halifax* B. Mk. 1 of 405 (RCAF) Squadron.

their night fighting capabilities, infrastructure, and tactics. Responding to British attempts to skirt the searchlight belts, they developed their *Dunkelnachtjagd*, or "dark night fighting" system, having at its heart eventually a band of 1500 giant *Würzburg* detection, height-finding and gun-laying radars – a quantum leap over the earlier primitive *Freya* radars. Coordinated with the *Freyas* through the control rooms of regionally responsible air divisions, radar fighter controllers vectored the individual night fighters, through tailor-made, coordinated interception guidance, to a killing position on the bombers. This became known specifically as the *Himmelbett*, or "heavenly four-poster bed" method of night fighting, each bedpost representing an essential element of the system; searchlights, ground control, anti-aircraft guns (flak), and night fighters. However, rigid restriction of the individual fighters to specific airspace boxes would prove too confining, and the system was modified in due course to redress this procedural inflexibility.

In Britain, on 9 July 1941, a new policy directive postulated "...[that] the weakest points in [the enemy's] armour lie in the morale of the civilian population and in his inland transportation system."[32] This directive would pave the way for even broader policy changes. Further in July, and again, portending later, broader changes, the practice of blind bombing through cloud on Estimated Time of Arrival (ETA) at target was suspended, and crews were instead given the flexibility to attack any enemy town or built-up area they could see. They were authorized to pick their own aim points, and it was acknowledged that "…these aiming points might include town squares, churches, or municipal buildings, even when, for example, railway marshalling yards or road junctions were the objective of the attack."[33] In point of fact, henceforth, Germany would be bombed more frequently, with greater intensity, and with less target discrimination.

Throughout the first half of the year, although the command's operations continued at a brisk pace whenever weather and opportunity permitted, it was becoming increasingly obvious that the night campaign was not meeting damage expectations. Although new weapons were slowly being introduced, the bombs were generally too small and unreliable. Delivery accuracy was still woefully inadequate, in spite of rudimentary 'fire raising' target marking techniques, first used at Mannheim, being widely implemented. The Germans countered these procedures innovatively by setting alight decoy fires in nearby open fields. By one report, "… in May 1941 over half the bombs dropped by Bomber Command fell in the country, away from villages, towns and cities."[34] Giving voice to this legitimate concern, in August, Frederick Lindemann (later Lord Cherwell), Churchill's chief scientific advisor and trusted confidant, tasked Mr. D.M. Butt of the War Cabinet to examine existing crew bombing photographs to obtain an accurate picture of actual results. They were sobering. Of more than 4000 images recorded in June and July 1941, when the bombing weather was generally optimum, some 650 were singled out for special attention. Only one-in-four showed bombs dropped within five miles of the intended targets. In non-moon periods, this ratio plummeted to one-in-fifteen, and while attacking targets exclusively in Germany, "…the figure was one-in-twenty, and the results over the important Ruhr industrial area were even worse than that."[35] The Butt Report stressed the need to examine bombing techniques and to improve navigational procedures, the only realistic alternative of massive daylight raids being considered just too dangerous.

> Those in authority concurred that it was unthinkable to completely abandon the bomber offensive, since it was at the time the only viable way to strike back at the enemy. The report also included an examination of the effect of bombing on civilian morale, based on the British experience during the Blitz, and concluded that bomb damage to homes, water supply, power sources and the food distribution systems had a greater effect on lowering of morale than did the loss

of friends or relatives. Ultimately, these observations would have an enormous impact on future bombing policy.[36]

In sum, the Butt Report had deemed pathetic the bombing to date with respect to accuracy and the results obtained for the costs incurred. In the near future, in acknowledgement of existing and even anticipated capabilities, less target discrimination would be demanded and more aids to navigation and targeting would be developed. In the months immediately following, Lord Cherwell, a firm believer in the efficacy of area bombing, and in full agreement with the Butt Report, presented a seminal paper to Cabinet that advocated area bombing as the keystone of a concentrated strategic bombing campaign against the Axis forces. The plan proposed attacking deliberately Germany's industrial centres in order to destroy as much working class housing as possible in order to displace the German work force and to disrupt/reduce their ability to work. Although Cherwell's plan was highly controversial from the outset,[37] ultimately, it was approved by Cabinet, since its members believed collectively that it was the only option available at the time to take the offensive directly to Germany, as Britain was not even remotely ready for a land invasion of the European continent, and since the Soviets were stridently demanding pressure relief in some form from the Western Allies for their Eastern Front.[38]

The next major, pivotal bombing policy direction came on 14 February 1942, with the release of Policy Directive #22. Issued by Sir Charles Portal as CAS, and as a direct result of the Butt Report and Lord Cherwell's Cabinet presentation and that body's subsequent approval of the intended strategic direction, Portal mandated that henceforth, the primary objective of Bomber Command was to be "… the morale of the enemy civil population, and, in particular, of the industrial workers."[39] These particular attacks were to be manifested as large raids on selected area targets in the major industrial areas of Germany, and while industrial, military, and infrastructure aim points were always to be identified and specified, collateral damage in terms of "dehousing" the civilian population was considered an acceptable, indeed, a *desirable* adjunct to the bombing. The Ruhr area, especially Essen, as well as Berlin, were considered of primary interest. Further, "…to make sure there was no misunderstanding about what was being called for, the next day Portal told his DCAS [Deputy Chief of the Air Staff] to remind High Wycombe [Bomber Command Headquarters] that 'the aiming points are to be the built-up areas, *not*, for instance, the dockyards or aircraft factories where these are mentioned.'"[40] This last point deserves elaboration, for it acknowledges the command's non-precision capabilities at this particular point of the war, and also the Western propensity for building up sub-urbs around industrial complexes. It also acknowledges that aiming for the hub of an industrial city was likely to at least inflict damage upon key transportation and communications nodes, such as railway stations and marshalling yards, since they tended to be centralized within urban developments. As summarized by the distinguished American historian Williamson Murray, in keeping with the limited navigation, target identification, target marking and overall non-precision weapons delivery capabilities of Bomber Command, exacerbated by the realities of industrial dispersal and residential build-up around industrial sites, along with the centralization of many of the major communications and transportation facilities, Bomber Command inexorably "...came to rely upon the dislocation of the German work force rather than the exclusive destruc-tion of the enemy's industrial plants in order to try to achieve its war aims."[41] This is not to imply that *all* Bomber Command's wartime attacks against the cities were this indiscriminate or standardized. Frequently, *specific* industrial, military, and infrastructure aim points *were* designated and marked, particu-larly later in the war, when electronic aids, tactics, and weaponry were further refined. And while it is probably fair to say that urban centres were the *default* aim point of the command throughout much of the war, it must be emphasized that the industrial city bombing constituted only a portion of the command's efforts. To be precise, of Bomber Command's wartime total 955,044 tons of ord-nance dropped upon the Third Reich and its proxies, only 430,747 tons (45.1 percent) were dropped on the industrial cities. The command became a true 'Jack of all trades,' and not simply a force dedicated to the assault of Germany's economic system.[42]

A NEW HELMSMAN

On 24 February 1942, Arthur Harris replaced Sir Richard Peirse as the AOC in C of Bomber Command, and he would remain the command's helmsman for the duration of hostilities. An uncompromising and pragmatic man, his first priorities were to:

- Overwhelm the enemy defences by putting as many bombers as pos-sible over a given target from a developed bomber 'stream' in a mini-mum amount of time; and
- Improve navigation/target identification capabilities through the in-troduction of new electronic aids and the formation of a specialized target marking force.

Credit: RAF photo

▶ Lübeck cathedral in flames, night of 28/29 March 1942.

Throughout the war, he would remain hostile to the concept of 'panacea' targets, specific elements of the enemy's military, industrial, and infrastructure capabilities and capacities that, if totally eliminated, would destroy its ability to wage war. This was not because they were difficult to hit – and the accuracy of Bomber Command increased remarkably over the course of the war – but because he believed that an enemy economy and social structure could not be dislocated by an attack on just one of its many elements with the prospect of forcing a political decision to capitulate. Electronic aids, such as *Gee*, *H2S*, *Oboe*, and *G-H*, sophisticated marking techniques, stabilized automatic bomb sights, vastly improved weaponry, and highly refined, sophisticated attack tactics would significantly improve delivery accuracies over the course of the war for the Main Force of Bomber Command. However, with the exception of several highly specialized precision attack units, such as 617 and 9 Squadrons flying *Lancasters*, and 106 Squadron (equipped with *Mosquitos*) of the Light Night Striking Force, the bulk of the command was "a blunt instrument," generally incapable of attacking targets with the uncanny precision, accuracy, and reliability of today's forces and munitions. Harris therefore pursued a broader strategy that he believed would use that instrument to best effect, and his dogged obstinacy to reject *all* specific, exclusive types of targets (notably ball-bearings, but particularly oil) would become the main objection to his wartime leadership of the command.[43]

On attacking the enemy work force, Harris believed that bombing out significant numbers of workers meant that vast resources, both materiel and manpower, had to be devoted to their care after the attacks, including repair and reconstruction crews, specialized heavy rescue teams, and special organizations devoted to evacuation and relocation. Collectively, he believed it all added up to a great strain upon resources, and that this whole strategy would affect both war production and civilian morale. The point here is that the *indirect* effects of the bombing, which would constitute one of its *most important* results, were being factored into the equation relatively early in the campaign. While Churchill had by now become somewhat less categorical in terms of enthusiastic support for the bombing, due largely to the disappointing results obtained to this point in the conflict, he was still strongly in favour of bombing the German heartland, telling Sir Archibald Sinclair that while he did not believe that bombing [alone] could decisively end the war, it was better than doing nothing, and it was "… a formidable method of injuring the enemy."[44]

The next pivotal policy determinant was the release of the Singleton Report on 20 May 1942, ten days prior to Operation *Millennium*, the first of several planned 1000-bomber raids, the inaugural operation being one conducted against Cologne. Churchill earlier had asked Cherwell to commission an assessment of the potential value and efficacy of a concentrated area bombing campaign. The result was *The Report on the Bombing of Germany*, written by an independent assessor, Mr. Justice John Singleton. And while Singleton's report played down the view that area bombing could win the war by itself, he believed it would certainly impede the German war effort and it would also provide much-needed relief to the USSR. He asserted that Germany's war efforts could be limited and hampered by attacks upon factories engaged in war work, as well as damage to communications grids and public utility services. Reports of the period coming in from citizens of neutral countries visiting the Third Reich tended to bolster this view. Singleton also believed that significant gains could be realized by the tie-down of enemy resources required to honour the bombing threat, and he opined that enemy morale was also likely to be adversely affected by the bombing. And while endorsing the value of *Gee* as a navigation aid, he was not confident with respect to its utility for target identification. Instead, he saw a need for more sophisticated target identification devices, unaffected by atmospheric conditions, and he also recommended the establishment of a specialized target identification force.[45]

Harris and his planners took great heart from these findings. Accordingly, in August, a specialized target identification and marking unit was officially established as the Pathfinder Force, #8 Group, under the command of the brilliant Australian airman, Air Vice-Marshal Donald C. Bennett. Through trial, error, and the development and implementation of innovative techniques and equipment for target detection and marking, the Pathfinders would enhance significantly the accuracy of the Main Force bombing throughout the balance of the European war.

All the electronic aids to navigation and target finding previously mentioned, along with progressively more sophisticated jammers and radar warning receivers, would now experience accelerated development and conversion into service. But these new initiatives would come at a cost, namely, the electronic 'footprint' or signature emitted by these admittedly useful tools. Once these emission properties were properly grasped, both sides would alternatively exploit those properties, as each developed new equipment, then fielded counters to these initiatives. However, the highly technologically sophisticated game of electronic 'cat and mouse' that evolved would claim the lives of many of the combatants along the way before those electronic footprints were fully understood and appreciated.

On an encouraging note for Bomber Command during late-1942, there was a growing body of evidence that, in spite of the direct damage to German industry caused by the bombing raids, "...the most serious problem confronting the German authorities is that of re-housing the bombed-out population and providing them with clothing and other necessities of life."[46] Again, various source inputs appeared to be providing compelling proof of the validity of the area bombing campaign. Citing a well-placed clandestine source of the period, in close touch with the *Reichluftfahrtministerium* [RLM, or German Air Ministry]:

> ...At the moment the fear of the RAF giant raids is far greater than any anxiety about an invasion. ...These big raids cause mass destruction. In spite of the statements in the *Wehrmacht* reports, the production of war production facilities is fairly considerable. The loss caused by the destruction of food stores and depots is extraordinarily great, as the food cannot be replaced. The effect on the civil population of such raids is not to be underestimated. For instance, in Köln (Cologne) there were between 3000 and 4000 dead [officially only just over 100 were reported], which of course the population of Köln knew very well. They spread the information, and this undermines confidence in the reports of the *Wehrmacht*. In Köln there were at

least 200,000 persons rendered homeless, who for the most part have been evacuated, as in the city itself no new buildings or temporary premises could be erected quickly enough. The problem of the homeless people is the most difficult. There is a shortage of houses and accommodation everywhere, in the country as well as the towns. As a result, wooden hutments have to be erected everywhere...In the RLM there are officers of high rank and influence who seriously fear that the winter will see unrest and demonstrations, unless these mass raids are successfully dealt with. But if the SS has to be used against the civil population, a deplorable situation will arise. According to these officers the great danger is not an invasion, but the systematic destruction of German towns by the RAF.[47]

The importance of bringing forward these source documents is to make the point that the bombing offensive was evolving and developing, based upon *capabilities*, upon *analysis*, and upon *direct feedback* from reliable intelligence sources. Bombing policies were not being developed in a void.

FRIENDS JOIN THE FIGHT

Commencing in July 1942, Britain and the Dominions would no longer find themselves alone in their bombing campaign against the Reich. With characteristic American vigour and enthusiasm, the "Mighty Eighth" Air Force of the United States Army Air Forces had begun a rapid build-up in southern and central Britain. And between the Eighth Air Force and the many stations occupied by Bomber Command, the little island nation was soon transformed into a vast, stationary aircraft carrier. The American contribution to the bombing campaign ultimately would be huge, and from January 1944 onwards, the Eighth Air Force would be joined by heavy bombers of the Fifteenth Air Force operating from bases in North Africa and Italy. By early August 1942, advance crews of the Eighth had been pronounced combat ready, but the British remained highly sceptical of the American daylight-only, massed formation tactics, based upon their own early war experience.[48] "They simply did not believe that the Eighth Air Force could survive daylight missions without crippling casualties. ...It would make more sense, Harris repeatedly told [Lieutenant General Ira C.] Eaker [Eighth Air Force Commander], if the Eighth would reinforce his Bomber Command by joining in the RAF's night missions."[49] On the other hand, Eaker insisted that the heavier armament his B-17s and B-24s carried could beat off the *Luftwaffe's* fighters by flying as a huge defensive entity using

▶ A Short *Stirling* on its takeoff roll with a Famous British Person in the foreground.

massed formation tactics and mutual support to defend itself (ideally a force of 300 bombers or more) to and from targets, largely without fighter escorts. And by bombing 'in the clear' in daylight, "...and using the air forces' super-secret Norden bombsight – the most accurate mechanism of its type yet invented – the US crews would be able to hit specific targets rather than being forced by darkness to dump their bomb loads helter-skelter over the blacked-out cities."[50] As the British had predicted, the blood cost of implementing these tactics would be high, particularly during the first 18 months of combat. But the loss rate would drop significantly during the last calendar year of the European war, following the introduction of the superb North American P-51 *Mustang* for long-range fighter escort to the deep German targets and back in March 1944, and once *relative* air superiority had been obtained over the Germans by that summer.

In spite of British concerns, the Americans were bound and determined to go their own way. And at the Casablanca Conference of January 1943, a working, synergistic bond was formed that would provide the blueprint for the cooperative effort that was essentially to characterize the bomber war over Europe until the end of hostilities. At Casablanca, after Churchill and Roosevelt had reaffirmed their overall "Germany First" plan to defeat the Reich prior to 'finishing the job' in the Pacific, a strategic compromise was struck to carry the war next to Sicily and Italy, thereby postponing a cross-Channel invasion for the time being. Meanwhile, the combined forces of Britain, the Dominions, and the United States would mount a mighty Combined Bomber Offensive (CBO) against targets in the Greater German Reich, the European Axis powers, and Occupied Europe. This campaign would have as its mandate, "…the progressive destruction and dislocation of the German military, industrial and economic system, and the undermining of the morale of the German people to a point where their capacity for armed resistance is fatally weakened." Within that general concept, the primary objectives at that time, subject to the exigencies of weather and tactical feasibility, and in order of priority, were to be German submarine construction yards, the German aircraft industry, transportation targets, oil plants, and other targets within the enemy war industries. Every opportunity was to be taken to attack Germany by day, to destroy objectives that were not suitable for night attack [USAAF mandate], to sustain continuous pressure upon German morale, to impose heavy losses upon the German day fighter force, and to contain German fighter strength and keep it away from the Soviet and Mediterranean theatres of war.[51]

While at Casablanca, Churchill in particular remained highly dubious of the American planned daylight direction. In the end, it may well have been Eaker's utterance of a chance phrase, assessed by Churchill for its dramatic impact and public relations value, that 'made the case' for daylight bombing. According to the American historian Edward Jablonski:

> "If the RAF Bombs by night," Eaker said, "and we bomb by day – bombing round the clock – the German defences will get no rest." Churchill withdrew his objections to the AAF's tactics and shortly after his return to England used Eaker's phrase, "bombing around the clock," in a speech to Parliament. It was the germ of the Combined Bomber Offensive of both day and night raids that soon became official policy and would wreak havoc on Germany in the months head.[52]

Bombing 'around the clock' became an enormous Anglo-American strategic cooperative effort which lasted – with this particular mandate unbroken – for the following 16 months until the spring of 1944, when Bomber Command would be seconded temporarily to Supreme Headquarters Allied Expeditionary Forces (SHAEF) under General Eisenhower, flying in support of the planned D-Day landings in France. The Eighth Air Force would also fly many missions in support of the landings, although the bulk of American participation in this effort would be borne by the twin-engine medium tactical bombers of

General Lewis H. Brereton's Ninth Air Force. And although the two Anglo-American strategic bombing camps would differ somewhat in their respective interpretation of priorities, particularly after Bomber Command was released from secondment to SHAEF in the autumn of 1944, the CBO ranks as one of the most demanding, intense, and prolonged campaigns in modern military history. Even the most conservative of historians concur that, although it may have been somewhat flawed doctrinally, there is no doubt that the CBO and the initiatives that flowed from it during the war's last year decisively influenced the course of the Second World War.[53]

From this point of the war onward, the intent and the implementation of the bomber offensive are much more broadly familiar, openly documented, and better understood, although significant misconceptions still exist. Within the overall broad strategy that had been agreed upon at Casablanca, the two formidable Anglo-American bombing armadas would place their operational emphasis upon different mandated priorities with respect to the enemy's resources at different periods of the campaign, although there was also a great amount of synergism and overlap throughout its duration. Nonetheless, until Bomber Command was seconded to SHAEF in April 1944, it tended to favour attacks upon the broader Axis industrial base, particularly the primary industries and associated infrastructure that *supplied* and *fuelled* the precision manufacturing element, such as production of coal, steel, and pig-iron, and concentration upon transportation nodes, power sources, and mines. By contrast, the Americans preferred direct attacks upon the aircraft manufacturing and ball bearing industries, as well as an earlier *concentrated* emphasis upon enemy oil resources than that which was eventually devoted to it by Bomber Command.

However, the most immediate priority for the Americans was the destruction of the *Luftwaffe*. Accordingly, on 10 June 1943, nearly six months after the Casablanca Conference, the resulting directive was modified to acknowledge the growing strength of the German air defences, and to target specifically the German day fighter arm in a range of bombing options. "The German fighter force was given the status of 'intermediate target,' and its destruction was made the primary goal. The campaign was given the unambiguous codename *Pointblank*."[54] Along with the tasking to American forces, it directed Bomber Command toward:

- The destruction of German airframe, engine and component factories and the ball-bearing industry on which the strength of the German fighter force depend.

- The general disorganization of those industrial areas associated with the above industries.
- The destruction of those aircraft repair depots and storage tanks within range, and on which the enemy fighter force is largely dependent.
- The destruction of enemy fighters in the air and on the ground.[55]

While Bomber Command also felt the stinging power of the German fighter arm, Harris tended, as was his wont, to view the German aircraft industry as 'panacea' targets, and while he would not ignore them, generally he applied his priorities elsewhere, leaving the bulk of the specific *Pointblank* targets to the Americans.

BOMBING TO WIN

Thus commenced in earnest the great, cooperative aerial onslaught against Hitler's *Festung Europa* (Fortress Europe), and before it was over, due to the resounding air superiority that would be attained eventually during the campaign, the Third Reich would become a ruined fortress without a roof. It would result in over *two million tons* of ordnance being dropped upon European Axis targets. However, it would also demand a very high toll in aircrew blood, including over 81,000 total wartime aircrew fatalities from just Bomber Command and the Eighth Air Force.[56] By war's end, the Eighth Air Force alone would have lost 26,000 men aboard nearly 6000 bombers, an overall loss rate of 12.4 percent of the 210,000 US airmen who flew missions out of England between 1942 and 1945, and one-eleventh of all Americans killed during the Second World War. A further 18,000 American airmen from "The Mighty Eighth" were wounded, and nearly 20,000 more were shot down and incarcerated as prisoners of war. During its bloody campaign against the Third Reich, the Eighth would drop over 725,000 tons of bombs on German targets. To these grim statistics must be added those of the strategic bomber crews of the Fifteenth Air Force. As was briefly mentioned earlier, on 1 January 1944, General H.H. "Hap" Arnold, Commander-in-Chief of the USAAF, created a new command, the United States Strategic Air Force – the USSTAF – consisting of the combined strengths of the Eighth and Fifteenth Air Forces under the command of General Carl Spaatz, who would also exercise some command authority over Lieutenant General Lewis Brereton's Ninth (Tactical) Air Force. The hero of the audacious 1942 Tokyo Raid, Jimmy Doolittle, was promoted to lieutenant general and given command of the Eighth, and the Fifteenth was placed in the hands of Lieutenant General Nathan Twining, while Ira Eaker, "much to his

Credit: DND PL4961

▶ A *Stirling* being bombed up for operations. Although rugged, they also had many deficiencies.

open regret," was sent to command in the Mediterranean region.[57] The Fifteenth would suffer a further 2703 aircrew killed, 12,359 either missing in action or captured, and 2553 wounded in combat. It would also lose nearly 3400 aircraft, but would drop over 300,000 tons of ordnance on enemy targets in 12 different countries along the way.[58]

Nonetheless, these losses and loss rates, while huge, pale somewhat in comparison to the blood toll exacted upon wartime Bomber Command. During six years of hostilities, with 364,514 sorties eventually having been flown against European targets, 125,000 aircrew are known to have flown at least one operational sortie with the command. Of that total, 55,573 airmen were killed, 47,268 on operations, and a further 8305 to training, non-operational flying accidents and other causes. Command aircraft losses from all causes totalled 12,330, of which 8655 went down over Germany, Italy, and Occupied Europe.[59] Overall loss rates for the entire war averaged 2.58 percent per raid, which, ironically, would almost provide the '50-50 chance of survival' upon which operational tour lengths would be first codified by the command in May 1943.[60] Furthermore, this grim statistic applied only to a *first* tour of operations, and not to a second tour, which was a command requirement for much of the war. It does not include accidental fatal casualties, 6.64 percent of the wartime force, nor does it include another 3 percent who were seriously injured in these mishaps.

Reduced to round numbers for duration of the *entire* war, of every 100 airmen who joined Bomber Command, 38 were killed on operations, seven were killed in operational accidents or in training, eight became POWs, three were wounded, and three were injured in training.[61] Therefore, only 41 out of 100 escaped unscathed from any of the aforementioned categories, although not necessarily unscathed by all manners of measurement. Only the *Kriegsmarine's* U-Boat arm suffered greater overall casualty percentages on a sustained basis.[62] The violent, dynamic, and wide-ranging nature of the air war was such that many airmen have no known graves, and the skies over northwest Europe remain their only cemetery. In poignant testimony, the Runnymede Memorial in Britain, dedicated in 1953, is inscribed with the names of 20,000 Commonwealth airmen of the Second World War who have no known place of eternal rest. Others are commemorated or buried in locations as diverse as Bournemouth and Berlin.

While the overall Bomber Command losses were indeed grim, an individual aircrew member's chances of survival depended very much upon the time frame during which he commenced and flew his tour of operations, and that applied to the crews of the Army Air Forces as well. In *both* cases, combat tours flown during the last calendar year of the war, wherein the *majority* of the wartime sorties were flown, enjoyed much higher survival rates than in previous years. And while combat survival was never assured, and high loss rates would occasionally occur for various reasons right up until the cessation of hostilities, such occurrences would progressively *punctuate* bomber operations, rather than *dominate* them.

And both the Anglo-American camps experienced particularly arduous specific campaigns or exceptionally costly individual raids during the course of the CBO. The siege of Berlin was gruelling for both air forces, although particularly so for Bomber Command. During the period from 18 November 1943 to 31 March 1944, the command, after three summer exploratory raids, conducted 16 'main event' operations against the Nazi capital, generating 9111 sorties in the process, from which 492 aircraft did not return. This yielded an overall loss rate of 5.4 percent for the entire series, and produced a concomitant dismal predicted aircrew survival rate for an entire tour of 30 operations of just 16 percent.[63] And some aircraft fleets fared worse than others during the Berlin siege. For example, the Short *Stirlings* had been decimated at their lower operating altitudes and were withdrawn from deep attacks, and after the earlier model *Halifax* II/Vs suffered the latest in a string of high loss rates, a soul-destroying 14.9 percent of those reaching the enemy coast on a raid to Leipzig during the Berlin

▶ A *Messerschmitt* Bf 110G, the longest serving combat aircraft in the German night fighter arm.

Credit: Author's collection

series, they too were withdrawn from the deep penetrations into Germany, leaving the deep raids to the *Lancasters* and the later-model *Halifaxes*.[64] The Americans would also shed a lot of blood over the German capital until the P-51 *Mustangs* started providing 'round trip' escort in March 1944. However, during the inaugural American daylight raid on Berlin on 6 March, which ranks as one of the greatest running air battles of the war, the massive attacking force of 660 B-17s and B-24s would lose 69 of their number.[65] Earlier American disasters for very limited gains included a severe mauling on 17 August 1943, when an Eighth Air Force armada of 376 bombers launched a two-prong attack in two separate elements against the ball-bearing factories at Schweinfurt and aircraft assembly plants at Regensburg. Although innovatively planned, " …60 aircraft were shot down on the mission; eleven aircraft were so badly damaged that they had to be written off later, and a further 162 aircraft received battle damage. The overall loss rate, including aircraft written off, was therefore 19 percent. As for the casualties, 482 aircrew members were lost. The Eighth Air Force [had] lost as many bombers on the Schweinfurt-Regensburg mission as it had lost in all its missions between August 1942 and March 1943." A repeat performance to Schweinfurt on 14 October resulted in an additional 60 bombers being shot down. And an earlier raid in September accounted for 45 out of 338 attackers. Even earlier, during multiple raids in a so-called 'Blitz Week' mounted during the last week of July, the Americans would lose over 100 bombers and 1000 airmen, nearly a third of the attack forces available at the time.[66] Indeed, until air superiority could be attained, either through destruction of the enemy's air defences or through provision of 'round trip' fighter escorts, deep penetration daylight raids into the Reich were very high-risk propositions.

And the individual raid losses for Bomber Command over the period were also staggering and demoralizing. A successful night raid on the Baltic coast rocket research station at Peenemünde on 17/18 August 1943 had cost the command 40 of the 596 bombers despatched, producing a seven percent loss rate.[67] Later, on 24/25 March 1944, 72 of 819 bombers sortied against Berlin were downed, nine percent of the attacking force. However, Bomber Command's worst single night of the war occurred on 30/31 March 1944 against Nuremburg. Although the fortunes of Bomber Command were about to change for the better when the force would be seconded to SHAEF the following week, those fortunes would not be realized on this particular raid. Under a bright, clear, cloudless night, aided by a full moon and raging tailwinds, the German night fighters flew up the contrails of the 795 bombers despatched and shot down 95 of them in droves before all was said and done. To make matters worse, the Pathfinders marked the target area inaccurately and the resultant bombing, executed through an overcast, was all for naught.[68] This also marked the end of the Berlin campaign period by Bomber Command's Main Force. Earlier, Sir Arthur Harris had waged what he believed to be a very successful campaign against Hamburg in June 1943, and just prior to that, a concentrated series of attacks against the industrialized Ruhr, the so-called Second Battle of the Ruhr. He continued to be focussed relentlessly in his belief that the German people would crack under the strain of the city attacks, negating the need for a bloody and costly invasion. This mindset was fuelled largely by the results obtained from those bombings, particularly that of Hamburg, which had produced extensive damage, generated an artificial firestorm, and produced an estimated 45,000 fatal casualties. And perhaps due to undue weight being given to a flow of intelligence reports citing civil unrest, which fostered a belief that this would erupt into a popular general uprising, such as had occurred in Italy during the summer of 1943, Harris opined, "We can wreck Berlin from end to end if the USAAF will come in on it. It will cost us between 400-500 aircraft. It will cost Germany the war."[69] This was naïve on a number of counts, particularly with respect to expectations of a popular uprising and the overthrow of a government that ruled ruthlessly by the spur of terror in a total police state, using cruelty to dominate, to subjugate, and to enforce its policies, and to quell any and all dissent and opposition. Furthermore, the USAAF would *not* attack Berlin in earnest until the spring of 1944 and beyond, and although much significant damage had been done to the Nazi epicentre during Bomber Command's siege, the capital had held firm. Harris's gallant crews, while they had persevered steadfastly, had nonetheless been highly demoralized by their long-standing, relentless trail of combat losses. As it materialized, the upcoming secondment to SHAEF, with much fewer deep penetration targets assigned, a progressive rollback and substantial deterioration of enemy air defences, and a significant further build-up of personnel and materiel resources during the secondment period from April to September 1944, would, beyond doubt, become the ultimate salvation of aircrew morale within Bomber Command, and it would also mark a turnabout in its effectiveness.

DIFFERENCES OF OPINION

Another significant point of divergence between Bomber Command and the USSTAF was the importance initially allocated to oil as a priority target. Furthermore, this divergence eventually would lead to a major confrontation between Sir Charles Portal, as Chief of the Air Staff, and Sir Arthur Harris in his role as Bomber Command's helmsman. While an earlier coordinated Transportation Plan, once adopted by Harris, had been waged from April until September 1944 with polite compliance, the counter-oil campaign fared differently. By late-September 1944, once the land campaign had stagnated in northwest Europe and the strategic bomber forces had been returned to the fold of their respective air staffs, Harris sensed that an unrestricted return to his general area bombing campaign of the German industrial heartland was in the wind. However, an Air Staff Directive of 25 September 1944 stated Bomber Command's new targeting priorities as follows:

FIRST PRIORITY

- Petroleum industry, with special emphasis upon petrol (gasoline) including storage.

SECOND PRIORITY

- The German rail and waterborne transportation systems.
- Tank production plants and depots, ordnance depots.
- Motorized Transport (MT) production plants and depots.[70]

Thus, for the immediate future, although counter-air action no longer had any particular priority, relative air superiority having been attained by this time, the generalized city offensive was only to be undertaken when conditions were unfavourable to executing the new priorities. These new priorities certainly suited General Spaatz, since oil, which had been a priority target for the Americans since the summer of 1943, had been placed squarely in the highest position by the British Air Staff, which, by the autumn of 1944, had warmed to the American point of view. Furthermore, Air Chief Marshal Sir Arthur Tedder, Eisenhower's deputy at SHAEF, believed that the plan should be broadened by synergistic linkage to attacks upon all the enemy's means of conveyance, "…to attack *all* communications, railways, rivers and canals as well, thus strangling industry, government control, life itself. Concentrated on such an area as the Ruhr, and linked to a powerful ground offensive, Tedder was convinced this would be decisive."[71] Portal and his staff were in accord with this thinking, and it was once again Harris who appeared to be out of synchronization. To Harris, oil remained the hated 'panacea' he had perceived it to be from the outset, in spite of the Soviet capture of Ploesti and the other Rumanian oil fields in August 1944. According to Harris's biographer, Air Commodore Henry Probert:

> He [Harris] was still deeply suspicious of the prognostications of the Ministry of Economic Warfare; synthetic oil production was spread over many plants, often small, in different parts of Germany, and up-to-date intelligence about them was hard to obtain; the Germans under Speer were adept at dispersal and repair; and effective attacks required a degree of accuracy which he was far from convinced his aircraft could achieve, especially against more distant targets.[72]

During the run-up to Operation *Overlord* in June, and in the weeks immediately following the landings, an overall loss rate of 11 percent of the 832 Bomber Command aircraft despatched against ten synthetic oil plants on a trial basis to the Ruhr industrialized area on three separate operations, including a devastating 27.8 percent loss rate on a 20/21 June operation, had done nothing to convince Harris that these were either sensible or appropriate targets. However, after these exploratory raids, a second round of attacks launched in July was less costly, and by August, the Air Ministry was convinced that oil was a legitimate Number One priority. Nonetheless, personal entreaties by Harris to Churchill led to what Harris believed was qualified approval from the PM for a resumption of the area bombing of the cities, and consequently, Bomber Command devoted only six percent of its bomb tonnage against oil targets in October 1944. That said, the USAAF did little better, contributing only 10 percent of their monthly effort in kind. However, it was at precisely this time that intelligence reports indicated – and they were later proven to be correct – that Germany's

▶ Aircrew enroute to their awaiting *Halifaxes* aboard the ubiquitous bicycles of Bomber Command.

oil situation was at its most desperate juncture. While official historians from the United States, Britain, and Australia have all contended that more ought to have been done against enemy oil during this period, given the 'hitting power' of the Anglo-American forces by this time and the significant weakening of the enemy air defences, the weather during the autumn months was very poor. In fact, the historians also concur that, "…there were few occasions when oil targets could be visually bombed, and not many tactical opportunities were in fact missed."[73] Further, even the USAAF official history states that by the end of November 1944, the weight of effort by Bomber Command against the oil targets was actually exceeding that of the Americans, and they were proving to be both successful and effective. It goes on to say that the results obtained against the oil industry during the last months of 1944 were spectacular, and were "… more effective in terms of destruction than most Allied experts had dared to hope."[74] However, many sharp exchanges would take place between Portal and Harris in late 1944 and continue into early 1945 over the latter's perceived lack of compliance with the Combined Chiefs and Air Staff Directives with respect to oil.[75] Nonetheless, by year's end, Bomber Command would place considerably more weight of effort behind the Oil Plan.[76] Furthermore, while Harris continued undeterred with area bombing, right up until the end of hostilities, *in spite* of perceived differences between Portal and Harris, area bombing would enjoy Portal's support until the very end of the war. As a final word on the oil campaign, Henry Probert sums up the issue with the following comments:

As Harris himself later recognized, oil did prove more critical than he had judged at the time. Influenced by the views of Albert Speer, Hitler's Armament Minister, he wrote in 1947 that in the final weeks of the war all the German armed forces had been immobilized for lack of fuel, rendering the triumph of the oil offensive complete and indisputable. It was the one 'panacea' that actually paid off.[77]

Nonetheless, in spite of the aforementioned differences of opinion and application, the CBO proved to be a highly successful cooperative effort. There is no doubting the ultimate success of the Oil Plan, and it remains an unanswerable question as to just how much the European war could have been shortened had Harris embraced the plan with more enthusiasm at the outset. Further, an earlier joint effort known as the Transportation Plan proved to be a very effective precursor to the Normandy landings. Designed to disrupt rail communications by attacking some 74 key rail centres in France and Belgium as an obvious Operation *Overlord* priority, on 15 April 1944, Bomber Command was allocated 37 of the rail targets, the other half being assigned to the Americans. By the eve of D-Day, some 60 separate attacks had put at least two-thirds of the assigned Bomber Command targets out of action for a minimum of a month. Further, the cost in civilian collateral casualties had been kept well below the 10,000 total that both Churchill and Portal fervently hoped would not be exceeded.[78] So successful was the plan's implementation, "…[that] after the Allied landings had taken place, scarcely any enemy fortifications could be brought into action without lengthy detours or delays, a factor which proved critical during the vital consolidation of the invasion beachheads."[79] And continued, unrelenting pressure by the strategic bombing forces upon Axis road, rail, and waterways from this point onwards until the end of hostilities would yield very tangible results against an enemy transportation network that was already stretched to the limit, due to dynamic and changing operational requirements, and to the tremendous additional burden of forced industrial decentralization, which had been brought about by the bombings.

POUNDING THE REICH

It was during the last calendar year of the war that Bomber Command reached its most productive, albeit destructive apex. Back on 3 November 1942, as a precursor to the Casablanca Conference, Sir Charles Portal, with a major input from Sir Arthur Harris, had presented the British Chiefs of Staff with a blueprint for a joint Anglo-American bombing offensive, which assumed a combined bomber fleet of 4000-6000 aircraft available at all times, upon which to base their bombing strategy.[80] While the top-end of this ultimate goal fell *somewhat* short in reality, although inclusion of Fifteenth Air Force resources brought it close, the last calendar year of the European war was decisive for the strategic bombing campaign, and over two-thirds of the total wartime bomb tonnage was dropped on the Greater German Reich from July 1944 onwards. Also, along with vastly declining German defensive capabilities, due in no small measure to the overrunning of German early warning sites in the land battle for the continent, for Bomber Command, the monthly average number of sorties increased from 5400 in 1943 to 14,000 in 1944, and the average payload-per-sortie nearly doubled. And from the summer of 1944 onwards, once relative air superiority had been attained over northwest Europe, Bomber Command would complement its nocturnal efforts with more and more daylight operations; a trend that would continue for the rest of the war. Furthermore, unlike the manpower shortages that were experienced somewhat by the land forces during the period, both aircrew and aircraft continued to pour into the bomber groups. In the words of the distinguished historian Martin Middlebrook:

> Harris could now regularly dispatch up to 1500 aircraft at any one time, in three or more major raids, dropping 6-7000 tons of bombs. It had taken nearly a year to drop that number of bombs in 1939-40! The introduction of the P-51 *Mustang* as a long-range escort for the American heavies and the need for the *Luftwaffe* to come up into action and attempt to stem the invasion had drawn the night fighter force into daylight action during the summer and reduced its strength. Bomber casualties now fell yet again, to just 1.0% in this period.[81]

At this point, the frequently misunderstood concepts of American *precision* daylight bombing and British night *area* bombing need to be addressed and placed within a proper context. At the end of September 1944, Harris still remained unconvinced that attacks upon the 'panacea' targets of oil, transportation, and the tank industry, for example, could damage the enemy's war making capability as much as broader, renewed attacks upon the industrial cities. Accordingly, and perhaps as a sop or cushion to the blow that had been levied by the aforementioned 25 September Air Staff Directive with respect to targeting priorities, a compromise was struck by the Combined Chiefs that yielded Operations *Hurricane I* and *Hurricane II*. The first was to be a series of concentrated Bomber Command/USSTAF coordinated attacks on the Ruhr area in an attempt to scuttle the enemy's war efforts in a region directly facing the Allied land armies, while the second was to be a generalized reiteration of the campaign against transportation and oil. Although components of *Hurricane II* have already been mentioned, *Hurricane I*, which became a sub-set of the so-called Third Battle of the Ruhr, deserves special mention for its brief intensity and focus. Perhaps the most famous of these raids was a coordinated area attack upon the industrial cities of Duisburg and Cologne on 14/15 October, commencing with a daylight raid on Duisburg by the RAF at dawn, followed by a force of 1251 bombers from the Eighth Air Force against Cologne, and then a night raid by 941 aircraft from Bomber Command against Duisburg. By the time the bombers had finished, extensive damage from area bombing had been meted out to Cologne, and Duisburg had essentially been reduced to rubble, producing substantial damage to the Thyssen and Duisburg-Hamborn mines and coke ovens. And 10,500 tons of bombs had been dropped on Duisburg alone, "… record totals that would never be exceeded in the war."[82]

On the night of 23/24 October 1944, and again the following day, it was Essen's turn to be pounded. The night raid was mounted by 1055 aircraft, including 561 *Lancasters*, 463 *Halifaxes*, and 31 *Mosquitos*.

> Unlike the thousand-bomber raids of 1942, this time no crews from training units had to be included in order to put so many machines in the air. Moreover, all those that participated were four-engined "heavies," so that a greater weight of bombs was delivered. Bombing through cloud, the attackers caused "extensive damage" to a complex of Krupp factories but lost only twelve crews… Thirty-six hours later a daylight raid brought 771 raiders back to the same target. Essen, like many other German cities, was now little more than a heap of rubble.[83]

This concerted effort closed out that mini-campaign known as the Third Battle of the Ruhr. While parts of Essen's steel industry had already been moved to dispersed factories, "…the Krupps steelworks were particularly hard hit by the two raids and there were references in the firm's archives to the 'almost complete breakdown of the electrical supply network' and to 'a complete paralysis.' The Borbeck pig-iron plant ceased work completely and there is no record of any further production from this important section of Krupps."[84]

The late-war *Thunderclap* and *Clarion* plans also merit consideration. The genesis of the *Clarion* plan, eventually an all-out attack on German transportation – railway yards and stations – originated with the original *Thunderclap* plan, an early-

▶ *Oscar*, a *Halifax III* from 424 'Tiger' (RCAF) Squadron, with its famous *Popeye* nose art and an impressive operations tally, taxis for take-off at Skipton-on-Swale, 13 November 1944.

Credit: DND PL41055

August 1944 proposal by the Air Ministry for a massive joint strike on Berlin, "…[in] the hope that it would make Hitler's people see sense; this was shortly after the July bomb attempt on Hitler's life had revealed that support for the Führer was not as solid as people supposed."[85] Essentially, it called for a massive, daylight strike on the German capital by the USAAF, followed up by the RAF with a night raid of equal proportions. Failing the acceptability of this, it called for widespread attacks upon cities across Germany in an attempt to convince the German people that further resistance was futile. The USAAF senior commanders and authorities in Washington rejected *Thunderclap* in its original form on 16 August 1944, but Spaatz was willing to assist *Thunderclap* through precision attacks on Berlin, and by 8 September, he was telling the commander of the Eighth Air Force, General Doolittle, that American forces would no longer plan to hit definite military objectives, but would be ready to drop bombs indiscriminately on Berlin.[86] In fact, by autumn, General Arnold had directed the USSTAF – Spaatz – to prepare plans for an all-out attack upon Germany, "…widespread roving attacks so that all Germans could see the ease with which Allied airpower roamed at will through the airspace of the Reich."[87] Although the German Ardennes offensive delayed this initiative, by January 1945, Spaatz was ready, and "…the all-out attack on transportation [*Clarion*] had been extended to include a smashing blow against Berlin."[88]

On 3 February 1945, just such a "smashing blow" occurred. With Spaatz over-ruling the objections of Doolittle, bombing in clear air over the capital, 937 Eighth Air Force B-17s attacked the Berlin railway system in the belief that the German Sixth Panzer Army was moving through Berlin on its way to the Eastern Front.[89] In the words of the 303rd Bomb Group's official combat mission report, "About three-fourths of the lead squadron[s] bombs hit in the fully built-up central city area with the balance hitting in the compact residential area."[90] While the initial number of civilian casualties was grossly exaggerated at 25,000 fatalities and fed to the world through lurid German accounts to the Swedish press, the actual number of fatalities is now believed to have been not more than one-eighth of that number, between 2500 and 3000, with 120,000 persons "dehoused."[91] Another USAAF area attack on Berlin on 26 February, this time conducted 'blind' through a thick undercast, caused further extensive damage, loss of life, and the 'dehousing' of an additional 80,000 inhabitants. In the words of Charles P. Johnson of the 303rd Bomb Group:

> 26 February 1945 began with an early wake-up call and the briefing that day was for Berlin – the 'Big B' – which the briefing officer assured us was not the formidable target it had been earlier in the war. The real shock came when he told us we were to bomb from the east. We flew east, past Berlin, and then turned 180° in order to bomb into the wind, which, with the strong headwinds, took us over the city at around 35 knots groundspeed, which seemed like an eternity in range of the anti-aircraft guns, but because of the cloud cover and the fact that we bombed from 25,000 feet, we encountered only ineffective flak. The bomb drop was by means of radar and we were unable to observe the result, but since the target was the marshalling yards within the city, we assumed that we accomplished some damage to the enemy.[92]

In point of fact, from late-1944 onwards, both the British and the Americans were area bombing, or 'blind bombing,' as it was referred to in USAAF circles. From the official USAAF history:

> Approximately 80 percent of all Eighth Air Force and 70 percent of all Fifteenth Air Force missions during the last quarter of 1944 were characterized by some employment of blind-bombing radar devices. Without these aids important targets would have enjoyed weeks or months of respite and on several occasions major task forces failed

Credit: Author's collection

▶ The *Frauenkirche* in Dresden, prior to and following the attacks of 13/14 February 1945.

even with radar to reach their objectives because of adverse weather…
In mid-November 1944, operations analysts of the Eighth estimated
that nearly half the blind missions were near failures, or worse.[93]

Richard Overy takes this point even farther.

The US air forces soon abandoned any pretence that they could bomb
with precision, and two-thirds of their bombs were dropped blind
through cloud and smog. A staggering 87 percent of all bombs missed
their target.[94]

In their defence, weather conditions over the European continent were forcing
the blind bombing option upon both camps. It is ironic, however, that while the
USAAF had commenced making area attacks in earnest from late-1944 onwards,
Bomber Command was now making precision attacks, both night and day, upon
specific military and industrial targets.[95] Technological advances abounded. *G-H*
represented a quantum leap in the development of navigation systems, since it
combined levels of accuracy comparable to *Oboe* with the universal applicability
of *Gee*. It had been introduced to service by 3 Group in 1943, and it was used to
effect eventually by other formations. Around the same time, the K-band *H2S*

Mark VI radar was also fielded, and this alleviated some system limitations over poorly defined or obscured targets. Of note, *H2S* became standard equipment for the *Lancaster* fleet in March 1944.

> Bomber Command coupled these new devices with revised tactics. Navigation was now so accurate that decoy fires and spoof raids could be used within a few miles of the actual route. The navigators and bomb-aimers were now sufficiently skilled to use an offset bombing point chosen for its visibility, and to aim their bombs at a given range and bearing from that point.[96]

THE FINAL ROUND

By 1945, Bomber Command was flying regularly during the daylight hours, its flanks now covered throughout operations by hoards of Allied fighters, especially Fighter Command *Mustangs*, *Spitfires*, and *Tempests*. However, command *Halifax* and *Lancaster* crews did not fly in the tight, disciplined, and mutually supportive formations favoured by the B-17s and B-24s of the American air forces. Rather, they flew in relatively loose 'gaggles,' still releasing their bombs by individual aiming upon markers provided by the Pathfinders and other specialist forces. By 1945, marking techniques had reached new levels of maturity and sophistication, including the increasing use of offset tactics. Now, although the Main Force journeymen aimed for a single marking reference on a given target, different approach angles, combined with timed overshoots, provided a number of actual release points on every successful attack. The offset procedure reduced the predictability, and thus the *vulnerability* of the attacking bombers. Also, multiple streams consisting of simultaneous large-scale efforts on different targets were common by 1945, further confusing the defences and further reducing predictability. By this stage of the war, given the predominating weather over the continent, Bomber Command had acquired so much expertise in blind bombing and the innovative use of radar and other electronic aids that its crews were generally as comfortable bombing in obscured conditions at night, with comparable results, as they were when bombing 'in the clear' by daylight. For their part, after the Schweinfurt-Regensburg raids, the Americans accepted that weather, navigation, and target finding were significant problems affecting operations.

> Here again, [they] had the benefit of RAF experience and cooperation. The two air forces had always worked closely together, and this

liaison now paid off. It was accepted that, since European weather was frequently poor, 'blind bombing' was inevitable, even in daylight, and the *Gee*-box and *H2S* – known to the Eighth as H2X or 'Mickey' – were introduced into US aircraft.[97]

Throughout early 1944, the Eighth Air Force continued to rely extensively upon attacking targets by *Oboe* and by *H2X*. In fact, "…on only one occasion in six weeks [during January and early February 1944] were the skies clear enough for visual bombing."[98] And that reliance upon electronic aids would only increase during the rest of the bombing campaign. By early 1945, in a further broad distillation of *precision* bombardment, and a tacit acknowledgement that area attacks had become accepted American strategy, a new crew member known as the 'togglier' frequently replaced the much more extensively trained (and usually commissioned) bombardier within American bomber crews.

[On the Berlin mission 18 March 1945] I was flying as a togglier (enlisted bombardier who threw the switch to release bombs). When the lead bombardier's Norden bombsight released his bombs, two smoke bomb[s] were released from below the chin turret. When the rest of the squadron bombardiers or toggliers saw the smoke bombs released we then hit the *Salvo* switch and released our bombs also. Of course, milliseconds later we would have seen the actual explosive bombs falling from the bomb-bay, but in an attempt to group the bombs on target we needed to release them *almost* at the same time the lead bombardier released his bombs.

~ Hal Province
391st Bomb Squadron,
34th Bomb Group[99]

THE ISSUE OF ENEMY MORALE

Meanwhile, *Thunderclap* had certainly evolved from just being the massive, joint attack upon Berlin that had been initially envisaged. To reiterate and then to elaborate somewhat:

By 1945, the Air Staff considered that *Thunderclap* might well appear to the Germans as an excellent example of close coordination with the Russians, thereby greatly increasing the morale effect. In January

1945, the Joint Intelligence Committee (JIC) played down the possibility of German resistance crumbling, but highlighted the scope for confusion in the movement of reinforcements and refugees if, by implication, critical towns in the infrastructure were attacked.

The JIC report coincided with preparations for the Allied discussions in Malta that were the precursor to the Yalta conference with the Soviets. In the meantime, Churchill had asked the Secretary of State for Air, Sir Archibald Sinclair, what plans he had for "...basting the Germans in their retreat from Breslau."[100]

Sir Charles Portal then advised Sinclair that *Thunderclap*, as it had been conceived months earlier, undoubtedly would be both costly and indecisive, and instead recommended the continued absolute priority of oil targets, the submarine yards, and the jet aircraft factories. However, Portal also endorsed the sentiments of the January JIC report and recommended specific attacks on Berlin, Chemnitz, Dresden, Leipzig, "...or any other cities where a severe blitz will not only cause confusion in the evacuation from the East, but will also hamper the movement of troops from the West."[101] Sinclair then cautiously responded to the Prime Minister, leading with, "You asked me last night whether we had any plans for harrying the German retreat from Breslau." He then said that oil should remain the paramount priority, but that secondary option attacks could be considered against East German cities when poor weather would not permit attacks against oil infrastructure. He reiterated specifically the cities mentioned by Portal, stating that not only were they the main administrative centres controlling military and civilian movements in the region, but they were also the main communications centres through which the bulk of all traffic flowed. Sinclair then closed with, "To achieve results of real value, a series of heavy attacks would probably be required, and weather conditions at this time of year would certainly prevent these being delivered in quick succession. The possibility of these attacks being delivered on the scale necessary to have a critical effect on the situation in Eastern Germany is now under examination."[102] Churchill's particularly testy response to Sinclair is worth quoting in full:

Serial No M.115/5

SECRETARY OF STATE FOR AIR

I did not ask you last night about plans for harrying the German retreat from Breslau. On the contrary, I asked whether Berlin, and no doubt other large cities in East

Credit: DND PMR-71-551

▶ A fine detailed study of *Madam X*, a 428 'Ghost' (RCAF) Squadron *Lancaster X.*, with its likeness of Miss Lace from the Milton Caniff comic strip of the day.

Germany, should not now be considered especially attractive targets. I am glad that this is "under examination." Pray report to me tomorrow what is going to be done.

W.S.C.
26/1/45[103]

The unequivocal tone of this correspondence generated the following immediate response from Sinclair to his Prime Minister:

TOP SECRET

PRIME MINISTER

Your Minute M.115/5. The Air Staff have now arranged that, subject to the overriding claims of attacks on enemy oil production and other approved target systems within the current directive, available effort should be directed against Berlin, Dresden, Chemnitz and Leipzig or against other cities where severe bombing would not only destroy communications vital to the evacuation from the East but would also hamper the movement of troops from the West.

The use of the night bomber force offers the best prospects of destroying these industrial cities without detracting from our offensive on oil targets, which is now in a critical phase. The Air Officer Commanding-in-Chief, Bomber Command, has undertaken to attempt this task as soon as the present moon has waned and favourable weather conditions allow. This is unlikely to be before about 4th February.

A.S.
27th January 1945[104]

Simultaneously, Portal's Deputy Chief of the Air Staff, Sir Norman Bottomley, formally instructed Harris to carry out the specified attacks. A series of meetings between Portal, Tedder, Bottomley, and General Spaatz *reconfirmed* oil as the Number One bombing priority for strategic bombing forces in Britain. This would, in turn, be followed by attacks on Berlin, Dresden, and Leipzig, which included the destruction of communications nodes servicing the respective fronts. Finally, there were the jet aircraft production plants. The Vice-Chiefs in London gave their blessings to these priorities and also added a demand for a more sustained effort against enemy tank production facilities. Thus, that portion of the bomber offensive known as *Thunderclap* was officially carried or born within those other priorities and, in concert with parallel daylight operations by the USAAF known as *Clarion*, it would consist of a series of punishing raids against the remaining industrialized German centres, designed primarily to disrupt enemy communications and transportation capabilities, but also to deal major blows to enemy morale.[105]

The plot now moves to Yalta where the debate over who said what to whom becomes complex. Cold War Soviet propaganda has emphasized that the Russian delegation in the Crimea had no responsibility for the bombing of Dresden. The Allies were unequivocal in their inclusion of Dresden in the target list, in particular with its importance on the Berlin-Leipzig-Dresden railway. The Russian Deputy Chief of Staff, General Antonov, submitted a formal memorandum to the Allies requesting, *inter alia*, that air attacks against communications should be carried out, "...in particular to paralyze the centres: Berlin and Leipzig." The use of the wording "in particular" makes it, at best, disingenuous for the Russians subsequently to suggest that they had not requested action at Dresden. Although the documentary evidence from the Russian perspective is limited, it is highly improbable that informal or non-minuted discussions had left them in any doubt as to Allied intentions. It is worthy of note at this stage that Harris's role had been no more sinister than as a recipient of very high level instructions.[106]

Credit: DND PL44205

▶ *Piccadilly Princess*, a *Lancaster* Mk. X from 424 'Tiger' (RCAF) Squadron. The nose art is a rendition of a Vargas Girl 'borrowed' from *Esquire's* 1944 calendar.

While the justification for the Dresden raids will be discussed in some detail in a later chapter, suffice it to say here that operations by both Bomber Command and the USAAF on 13/14 February resulted in massive destruction and loss of life, although those human losses were grossly exaggerated from the outset. Conditions combined to produce a true firestorm, one of just three that occurred in the European theatre, the others being at Hamburg in July 1943, and then at Kassel in October 1943.

A CERTAIN DUPLICITY

By the spring of 1945, the eddies of public disquiet generated by the bombing of Dresden with respect to Anglo-American bombing policy were certainly swirling. Just six weeks after the February raids, Winston Churchill, perhaps with an eye cast towards his legacy, penned a Minute to Lord Ismay, his military advisor to the Chiefs of Staff Committee, and to the Chief of the Air Staff in particular, which Bomber Command's official historians would later consider "…perhaps the least felicitous," well-expressed, or appropriate of all Churchill's wartime correspondence.[107] The Minute appeared to endorse all the latest public criticism of Allied bombing policy, and it also seemed to shift the blame from the Prime Minister's shoulders to those of the air commanders responsible for implementing the policy. The implication was that Churchill had been misled and that his air leaders were conducting terror bombing on their own initiative, without his knowledge, but both these conditions were patently false.[108]

Serial No D. 83/5

TOP SECRET

GENERAL ISMAY FOR C.O.S. COMMITTEE
C.A.S.

It seems to me that the moment has come when the question of bombing of German cities simply for the sake of increasing the terror, though under other pretexts, should be reviewed. Otherwise, we shall come into control of an utterly ruined land. We shall not, for instance, be able to get housing materials out of Germany for our own needs because some temporary provision would have to be made for Germans themselves. The destruction of Dresden remains a serious query against the conduct of the Allied bombing. I am of the opinion that military objectives must henceforward be more strictly studied in our own interests rather than that of the enemy.

The Foreign Secretary has spoken to me on this subject, and I feel the need for more precise concentration upon military objectives, such as Oil and communications behind the immediate battle zone, rather than on mere acts of terror and wanton destruction, however impressive.

W.S.C.
28.3.45[109]

Sir Charles Portal immediately instructed his deputy, Sir Norman Bottomley, to solicit Sir Arthur Harris's comments. The Bomber Command helmsman's reply was prompt, as well as characteristically blunt and predictable. He pointed out,

> ...that the suggestion that the bomber offensive had been conducted "for the sake of increasing terror, though under other pretexts" was an insult both to the Air Ministry policy and to the crews that had carried it out. Harris went on to highlight the misperceptions over Dresden that would be obvious to any psychiatrist – "...it is connected to German bands and Dresden shepherdesses." Rather, "Dresden was a mass of munition works, an intact government centre and a key transportation point to the East. It is now none of these things." He went on to discuss the policy underlying the bomber offensive, concluding with the warning that such scruples as the Prime Minister was considering would lengthen the war and increase the task facing the army both in Germany and against Japan.[110]

8991

▶ A late-war attack against the German fortifications on Wangerooge Island, 25 April 1945.

Credit: DND PL144281

With equally characteristic flamboyance, Harris also observed that the bombing of the industrialized cities had fatally impaired the overall German war effort and was permitting the land forces to advance into Germany with fewer casualties than expected. He argued that it would be a mistake to totally cease these attacks at the time unless it could be said with absolute certainty that eliminating city bombing would shorten the war and save the lives of Allied soldiers. Then, he made a somewhat insensitive remark, borrowing upon the words the words of Prussia's "Iron Chancellor," Prince Otto von Bismarck: "I do not personally regard the whole of the remaining cities of Germany as worth the bones of one British grenadier."[111] Harris, in his no-nonsense and robust response, when asked his opinions, probably never thought this correspondence, which had been marked at the time both "Personal" and "Top Secret," would one day be made available for public scrutiny and subject to the endless parsings of armchair strategists and moralists. Furthermore, Harris's primary consideration, after getting the job done to the best of Bomber Command's abilities, was to minimize the risks incurred to his aircrews, who had already endured so much hardship during the war.

Churchill also appears to have exercised a conveniently selective memory when he penned the offending Minute, choosing to ignore the various telephone conversations, memos, and directives to Sir Archibald Sinclair in January, which had urged bombing attacks upon the eastern cities.

> Churchill was well aware that the RAF was going to attack Dresden and the other eastern cities; the decision to do so had originated in Cabinet and had his full support. To deny it now did him no credit and was clearly an attempt to distance himself and his government from the political fallout among the neutral countries and in the USA. The comment, "The Foreign Secretary has spoken to me on this subject" is a pointer in this direction.[112]

Also, the Prime Minister's enthusiasm for using bombing as a punishment had led to excesses in rhetoric from time to time, as we have already seen. These remarks occasionally required others, including Harris, to set Churchill's moral compass straight. The repeated considerations of reprisal raids in response to the German razing of Lidice, Czechoslovakia in 1942, and the *Crossbow* campaign against the V-weapons in 1944, constitute proof of this trend in the PM's behaviour.[113] It should be noted here that Churchill was inconsistent in his pugnaciousness with respect to bombing policy throughout the course of the war, but particularly towards the end of European hostilities, when he was undoubtedly considering both his legacy and his political future. For example, detractors of the campaign have made much of his "Are we beasts?" remarks made at Chequers on the night of 27 June 1943, when viewing a film showing the bombing of German centres. Aside from the fact that the remark may well have been exacerbated by the consumption of alcohol, as was the prime minister's wont, both Churchill and Sir Arthur Harris were prone to excesses of rhetoric on occasion. It was, quite simply, part and parcel of the flamboyant nature of both these exceptional wartime leaders.

At any rate, Portal enthusiastically endorsed Harris's views on this occasion. And the Prime Minister's Minute had so shocked the Chiefs of Staff that Portal, backed wholeheartedly by Sir Archibald Sinclair, asked Churchill to withdraw it. In fairness, Churchill recognized the validity of the arguments and concerns

Credit: DND PL42872

▶ A Canadian *Halifax* III at rest by the base bomb dump.

of his chiefs, and on 1 April 1945 he approved the substitution of a considerably more guarded and restrained note. What follows is the formal request for removal of the offending first Minute and the replacement correspondence.

D.89/5

TOP SECRET

OFFICE OF THE MINISTER OF DEFENCE
PRIME MINISTER.

After yesterday's Staff Conference, you said you would withdraw your "rough" minute, No.D.83/5 of 28th March, to the Chiefs of Staff Committee and C.A.S. about the bombing of German cities, and you instructed me to redraft the minute in less rough terms.

1. A redraft is submitted herewith for your consideration.

2. Meanwhile all copies of your previous minute are being withdrawn.

H.L. Ismay
30 March 1945[114]

Serial No. D.89/5

TOP SECRET

PRIME MINISTER'S
PERSONAL MINUTE

GENERAL ISMAY FOR C.O.S. COMMITTEE
C.A.S.

It seems to me that the moment has come when the question of the so-called "area bombing" of German cities should be reviewed from the point of view of our own interests. If we come into control of an entirely ruined land, there will be a great shortage of accommodation for ourselves and our Allies: and we shall be unable to get housing materials out of Germany for our own needs because some temporary provision would have to be made for the Germans themselves. We must see to it that our attacks do not do more harm to ourselves in the long run than they do to the enemy's immediate war effort. Pray let me have your views.

W.S.C.
1.4.45[115]

The revised Minute contained no reference to either "terror" attacks, or, specifically, to the raid on Dresden. Nevertheless, the damage had already been done, and in spite of Lord Ismay's assurances to the contrary, the first Minute also remained on file, and the effects of public scrutiny and analysis of it in future would be far-reaching.

WITH A VIEW TO THE FUTURE

As the spring of 1945 continued to unfold, the Prime Minister's newfound determination to put an end to the bombing of the German cities took effect rapidly. The fundamental guidance contained in the revised 1 April Minute had promptly been acted upon by the Air Staff. That same day, Sir Charles Portal recommended the termination of the area bombing offensive, other than that portion needed to support the land and sea campaigns. The Air Staff recommendations were subsequently approved up the chain of command, and Sir Arthur Harris was so informed on 6 April.[116] However, before arriving at this recommendation, Portal very clearly articulated the purpose of, the justification of, and the caveats under which area bombing could still be conducted, if necessary. Portal has been frequently cited, like Churchill, as having an eye to the historical record and to distancing himself from Harris and from Bomber Command's campaign against the industrialized cities. However, in spite of the aforementioned disagreements with Harris, and the degree of emphasis the latter placed upon the city attacks at times, Portal staunchly defended Harris to those in higher authority, and he made it very clear that area bombing still had its place. He remained convinced that it was useful under certain circumstances, even at that late stage of the war. He also made it very clear that the command's precision attack capability was relatively newfound, and that, even with all the technological and tactical advances, it certainly had its limitations and precision bombing capabilities were still not widely practiced by the bulk of the Main Force. Portal's document outlining these considerations is thus heavily excerpted here:

TOP SECRET

AREA BOMBING

NOTE BY CHIEF OF THE AIR STAFF

- It is only in recent months that the development of night fighting technique has enabled us successfully to undertake the night attack of particular industrial plants or relatively small objectives. By day, the successful bombing of these objectives requires clear skies over the target, conditions which occur on few occasions in the year. For these and other reasons, it has been an essential part of our policy, in order to extract from our bomber forces the maximum continuity and weight of attack of which they are capable, to attack important concentrations of German war industry by means of area attack.

- The objects of attacking industrial areas have been:

    1. To destroy important industrial plants and to disorganize essential services and labour.

    2. To disrupt communications vital to the maintenance of order and the smooth and efficient working of the military supply organization to the areas immediately behind the enemy's fighting fronts.

    3. To disorganize and disrupt the Nazi organization.

4. To force the enemy to employ in defence, repair and rehabilitation measures, resources and manpower which would otherwise be used both in war production and in strengthening the offensive power of his armed forces.

- In spite of recent advances in our ability to make precise attacks at night, the operational considerations which have in the past necessitated area attacks still exist. Nevertheless, it is recognized that at this advanced stage of the war no great or immediate additional advantage can be expected from the attack of the remaining industrial centres of Germany, because it is improbable that the full effects of further area attacks upon the enemy's war industries will have time to mature before hostilities cease. Moreover, the number of targets suitable for area bombing is now much reduced as a result of our past attacks and of the rapid advance of the Allied armies. For these reasons, and since Allied superiority in military resources is already overwhelming, the effort of the Strategical [sic] air forces is being directed primarily to secure the most immediate effect upon the enemy's ability to resist the Allies' advance into Germany. This is being achieved by disrupting communications vital to the armies as necessary.

- There may still be occasions, however, when the disintegration of enemy resistance can best be brought about through the medium of area bombing. These may arise in the following circumstances.

  1. If resistance should stiffen on the Western Front or fail to disintegrate on the Eastern Front, attacks on built-up areas immediately behind the fronts holding reserves and maintenance organizations, and engaged in handling military supplies, may be as effective in the preparation for an assault as they have proved in the past. Such situations may occur when the Russians approach nearer Berlin and the industrial areas of Saxony, or when we advance into Central Germany from the West.

  2. It may become a military requirement to attack the communication systems of Central and Southern Germany, over which the enemy may attempt to move forces between the two fronts, or to withdraw to the redoubt in Southern Germany. The time factor

may not always allow us to await precise bombing
conditions and area bombing will then prove a necessity.

3. There is strong evidence that the German High
Command, its attendant staffs and Government De-
partments and the Party Organization are to be
established in a number of Thuringian towns for
the purpose of directing continued resistance. The
destruction of these towns by means of area attack
may then become a military requirement.

4. The German Navy has been forced by territorial
losses to withdraw from the Eastern Baltic and
to concentrate in the Western Baltic and North
Sea ports, especially at Kiel. Here some eighty
commissioned U-Boats and a large number of enemy
naval vessels are congregated. The attack of this
target which is already ordered may well involve
widespread devastation in the town of Kiel with
results which will approximate those of an area
attack.

• We appreciate the importance of refraining from the
unnecessary destruction of towns and facilities which
will be needed by our own troops or for Allied reconstruction purposes. If, however, we were to restrict
our bomber forces to visual precision attack we should
certainly reduce the contribution which they can make
towards hastening the collapse of the enemy. It is
considered that area attacks are still justified stra-
tegically, insofar as they are calculated to assist in
the advance of the Allied armies into Germany or in
shortening the period of war. Any incidental further
destruction of the German cities which is likely to be
involved in the time remaining will certainly be small
in comparison with that already accomplished.[117]

Accordingly, Washington was advised of the intended British change in direction of their strategic bombing policy, an initiative that the Americans soon
fully endorsed.[118] However, in a sequel to this strategic sea-change, the city of
Potsdam was heavily bombed on 15 April 1945, which prompted the following
terse Minute from Churchill:

Serial No. M/362/5.

PRIME MINISTER'S
PERSONAL MINUTE

SECRETARY OF STATE FOR AIR
C.A.S.

What was the point of going and blowing down Potsdam?

W.S.C.
19.4.45

Ref: Cabinet War Room Record No. 2051 for the 24 hours ending 0700, 15th April 1945, Para 8 (513 aircraft despatched to Potsdam).[119]

This, in turn, generated the following response from Portal. Clearly, the Air Staff were quite prepared to exercise their new limited mandate for area bombing when they felt the war situation clearly dictated it, even in Germany's 'twelfth hour.'

TOP SECRET

PRIME MINISTER

Your personal minute No. 362/5 of yesterday. The Joint Planning Staff and the J.I.C. (Joint Intelligence Committee) have drawn attention to the importance of Potsdam in an attack on the German Government machine.

• The J.I.C. have pointed out that the control centre of the G.A.F. operational Headquarters has been evacuated to the Potsdam area as also have the O.K.L. (i.e., Air Ministry).

• The object of the Bomber Command attack was the destruction of such control centres, of the communications leading West from Berlin through Potsdam, and of the barracks housing military and Nazi personnel.

• The attack of this target was discussed and agreed at the Air Commander's meeting at S.H.A.E.F. on the 12th April.

- In accordance with your decision on the recommendation of the Chiefs of Staff, we have already issued instructions to Bomber Command that area bombing designed solely with the object of destroying industrial areas is to be discontinued. The attack of Potsdam, however, was calculated to hasten the disintegration of enemy resistance.

C.P.
20th April, 1945
C.A.S.[120]

Within two weeks of Portal's reply to the Prime Minister, hostilities in Europe would be concluded, but a vast amount of unfinished business still remained in the Pacific theatre. Strategic bombing had truly come of age in the European theatre of operations, and many of the bloody lessons learned there would soon be applied to telling effect against the Empire of the Sun.

> *"Gebt mir funf Jahre und ihr werdet Deutschland nicht wieder erkennen."*
> *("Give me five years and you will not recognize Germany again.")*

~ Adolf Hitler
circa 1936*

*Sign posted in the rubble-strewn streets of Mainz, Germany, close to the war's end.

NOTES

1. Adolf Hitler to Hans Frank [Reich Minister Without Portfolio and later Governor General of Occupied Poland], circa 1936. Transcribed from Hans Frank, *Im Angesicht des Galgens*, in Joachim C. Fest, *From the Face of the Third Reich* (New York: DaCapo Press, 1999), p.203.
2. The German fixed-wing bombing raids against Britain are often collectively referred to as the "Gotha Raids." However, the *Gothaer Waggonfabrik AG*, which produced a series of these successful bombers, was not the only manufacturer of these types. Other successful heavy bombing aircraft were produced by the *Zeppelin* (the *Staaken* series) and *Friedrichshafen* firms. Nigel Smith & Peter Hart, *Tumult in the Clouds* (London: Hodder and Stoughton, 1997), pp.262-284.
3. Overy, p.13.
4. John Terraine, *The Right of the Line – The Royal Air Force in the European War 1939-1945* (London: Hodder and Stoughton, 1985), p.11.
5. Brereton Greenhous, Stephen J. Harris, William C. Johnston, and William G.P. Rawling, *The Crucible of War 1939-1945 ~ The Official History of the Royal Canadian Air Force – Volume III* (Toronto: University of Toronto Press, 1994), p.528.
6. David Ian Hall, Arguments For and *Against the Strategic Bomber Offensive: The Contrasting Views of Wing Commander T.D. (Harry) Weldon and RAF Chaplain L. John Collins*, an essay presented by Dr. Hall of Linacre College, University of Oxford, for the Bomber Harris Trust Essay Competition, 30 June 1997, p.5.
7. Ibid.
8. Richard Holmes, *Battlefields of the Second World War* (London: BBC Worldwide, 2001), p.179.
9. Overy, p.16.
10. Ibid., p.24.
11. Ibid.
12. Air Ministry 'Instructions Governing Naval and Air Bombardment,' dated 22 August 1939 (PRO Air 8/283), as quoted in Overy, p.30.
13. Greenhous *et al*, p.535.
14. Ibid.
15. Portal to Newall, Ibid., p.536.
16. Ibid., p.544.
17. Special Distribution and War Cabinet Report from Switzerland, Memo No. 529, 28 July 1940, in Public Record Office (PRO) Premier 3/11/1, p.35.
18. Sir Charles Webster and Noble Frankland, *The Strategic Air Offensive Against Germany*, Vol. 1 (London: Her Majesty's Stationary Office, 1961), p.233.
19. AHB(Air Historical Branch)/II/117/1(B), p.122.
20. Coventry was hit by a number of raids, the most devastating being on the night of 14/15 November 1940, in an attack codenamed Operation *Moonlight Sonata* by 515 German bombers, complete with a dedicated Pathfinder marking force. Bombing was accurate. The raid destroyed or damaged around 60,000 buildings in the centre of the city, and is known to have killed at least 568 civilians. <http://en.wikpedia.org/wki/Coventry_Blitz>, accessed 15 January 2008.
21. Overy, p.202.
22. Harris to Portal, September 1940, reprinted in Arthur Travers Harris, *Bomber Offensive* [First Edition] (London: Collins, 1947), p.52. The essence of this statement would be repeated in a well-known and extensively referenced radio broadcast by Harris in 1942.
23. Henry Probert, *Bomber Harris – His Life and Times* (Toronto: Stoddart, 2001), p.54.
24. Sir Martin Gilbert, *Finest Hour – Winston Churchill 1939-41* (London: Heinemann, 1983), pp.655-656.
25. Roy Conyers Nesbit, *The Battle of Britain* (Thrupp, UK: Sutton Publishing, 2000), p.217.
26. Lord Portal, as quoted in Greenhous *et al.*, p.539.
27. Air Ministry Guidance to Sir Richard Peirse, 25 Oct 1940, PRO Air 9/132, as quoted in Ibid.
28. Sinclair to Churchill, 7 Oct 1940, in PRO Premier 3/11/11A, p.515.
29. David L. Bashow, *No Prouder Place – Canadians and the Bomber Command Experience 1939-1945* [1st Edition] (St. Catharines, ON: Vanwell Publishing, 2005), p.36.
30. Terraine, p.276.
31. Ibid.

32. Greenhous *et al.*, p.544.
33. Senior Air Staff Officer Bomber Command Memorandum to Groups, 3 July 1941, in PRO Air 14/232.
34. Various Bomber Command sources, as referenced by Greenhous *et al.*, p.550.
35. Martin Middlebrook, "Bomber Command's War – The Turning Points," Pt. 2, in *Flypast*, No. 206 (September 1996), p.80.
36. Bashow, p.65.
37. Frederick Lindemann (Lord Cherwell) was a scientist and academic, and a true *eminence* grise as Churchill's great friend. But his influence often extended beyond his expertise, and he was not a military man. "Cherwell also used his position to promote particular strategies and tactics, even if it meant distorting the scientific evidence." David Zimmerman, *Britain's Shield – Radar and the Defeat of the Luftwaffe* (Stroud, UK: Sutton, 2001), p. 231. Not only did such incursion into military purviews place Cherwell at loggerheads with many senior uniformed members, his distortion of scientific and technological capabilities to suit his policy initiatives occasionally earned him the contempt of his scientific colleagues, notably, Sir Henry Tizard. However, his influence upon Churchill was profound, and the Prime Minister would often side with him on issues, whether his ideas had merit or not. Ibid., p. 232. In this particular case, the greatest element of controversy swirled around the assessment of the impact upon the morale of British citizens due to the German bombing during the Blitz, and using those observations as a predictor of German behavior under like circumstances. Also in contention were Cherwell's estimates of British bomber production and predicted bomb damage upon the Axis. Lord Cherwell quoted in Holmes, p.183.
38. Probert, p.139.
39. Charles Webster and Noble Frankland, *The Strategic Air Offensive Against Germany*, Vol. 4, Appendix 8 (London: Her Majesty's Stationary Service, 1965), p.144.
40. Air Historical Branch (AHB) Bomber Command Narrative, IV, p.130, DHist (Canada) File 86/286; Bottomly to Baldwin, 14 Feb 1942, quoted in Webster and Frankland, SAO, Vol. 4, Appendix 8, pp.143-145. Portal to Bottomly, 15 Feb 1942, quoted in Webster and Frankland, SAO, Vol. 1, p. 324, all in Greenhous *et al.*, p.576.
41. Williamson Murray, *Strategy for Defeat – The Luftwaffe 1933-1945* (Secaucus, NJ: 1986) p.105.
42. <http://www.nucleus.com/twright/bc-stats/html/>, accessed 15 May 2005. Richard Overy's research closely mirrors these findings and acknowledges the diversified effort in many other areas. "Between February 1942, when Air Marshal Arthur Harris became Commander-in-Chief, and May 1945, some 43 percent of Bomber Command tonnage was directed at industrial centres in Germany, while over 40 percent was devoted to support for land operations, long range reconnaissance, mining, supporting resistance operations, attacks on communications and airfields, and the war at sea." Overy, p.51. Other command taskings included designated precision attacks, propaganda (leaflet) raids, electronic warfare support, and humanitarian relief missions towards the end of hostilities. Bashow, p.459.
43. Overy, p.80.
44. Churchill to Sinclair, 13 Mar 1942, Portal Papers, Folder 3, in Probert, p.133.
45. John Singleton, "Report on the Bombing of Germany to Prime Minister Churchill," 20 May 1942, in PRO Premier 3/11/4, p.124.
46. Air Intelligence Result of Recent RAF Attacks Report to Prime Minister, 23 Sept 1942, in PRO Premier 3/11/12, p.621.
47. Air Intelligence Report No. 346 to CAS, 22.9.42, in PRO Premier 3/11/12, pp.627-629.
48. Winston Churchill, policy note to War Cabinet, 16 Dec 1942, in PRO Premier 3/11/6, pp.179-182.
49. Edward Jablonski, *America in the Air War* (Alexandria, VA: Time-Life Books, 1982), p.56.
50. Ibid.
51. Webster and Frankland, *Strategic Air Offensive*, Vol. 4, Appendix 8, Directive xxviii, pp.153-154.
52. Jablonski, p.65.
53. Mark W. Wells, *Courage in Air Warfare – The Allied Aircrew Experience in the Second World War* (London: Frank Cass, 1995), p.210.
54. Overy, p.111.
55. *Pointblank* Directive, 10 June 1943, in Webster and Frankland, *Strategic Air Offensive*, Vol. 1, pp.158-160.

56. Ibid., p.2.

57. Robin Neillands, *The Bomber War ~ The Allied Air Offensive against Nazi Germany* (Woodstock & New York, NY: The Overlook Press, 2001), p.293.

58. Ibid., p.379. Philip Kaplan, *Bombers ~ The Aircrew Experience* (London: Aurum Press, 2000), p.225.

59. Overy, p.204.

60. <http://www.nucleus.com/~lwright/bc-stats.html>, accessed 17 December 2007.

61. The earlier years were proportionately much more dangerous overall. For example, in 1942, the average loss rate per operation was 4.1 percent. By 1944, this had diminished to 1.7 percent, and by 1945, to .9 percent, and the majority of the total wartime tonnage was dropped during the last calendar year of the war. Overy, p.204.

62. Of the 1169 operational wartime U-Boats, 821, or 70.23 percent, would be lost due to enemy action or marine accidents, and of the 41,000 personnel attached to this arm of the service, more than 27,000 (66 percent) would forfeit their lives. Roger Sarty, *Canada and the Battle of the Atlantic* (Montreal: Art Global, 1998), p.160.

63. Terraine, p.554.

64. DHist 74/250, in Greenhous *et al.*, p.771.

65. Jablonski, p.104.

66. Neillands, pp.255, 272.

67. Ibid., p.257.

68. Bashow, pp.306-308.

69. Quoted in Webster and Frankland, *Strategic Bomber Offensive*, Vol. 2, (London: Her Majesty's Stationary Service, 1963), p.190.

70. Webster and Frankland, *Strategic Bomber Offensive*, Vol. 4, p.172.

71. Terraine, p.673.

72. Probert, p.306.

73. Ibid., p. 07.

74. Various official British and American sources, including W.F. Craven and J.L. Cate, *The Army Air Forces in World War II* (Chicago: University of Chicago Press, 1958), Vol. 3, p.670.

75. Webster and Frankland, *The Strategic Bomber Offensive*, Vol. 3, pp.81-94.

76. During the four effective months of European combat in 1945, Bomber Command would drop 181,000 tons of bombs, which constituted nearly one-fifth of the aggregate for the entire war. Considering the multiplicity of "diversions" placed upon the command, even at this late stage of the war, and that 66,482 tons (36.6 percent of the effort) was devoted to attacks on the cities, it is commendable that a full 47,510 tons or 26.2 percent of the total effort for the period was devoted to oil targets. Terraine, pp.678-679.

77. Probert, p.312.

78. Ibid., p.292.

79. During the two months of the Transportation Plan's implementation, more than 42,000 tons were dropped by Bomber Command on 33 of the 37 assigned railway centres. During the same period, USAAF forces delivered 11,648 tons on 23 of their assigned targets. John D.R. Rawlings, *The History of the Royal Air Force* (Feltham, Middlesex, UK: Temple Press, 1984), p.146.

80. Sir Charles Portal, Memorandum for British Chiefs of Staff, 3 Nov 1942, in PRO Air 14/739A.

81. Martin Middlebrook, "Bomber Command – The Turning Points," in *Flypast*, No. 209, (Dec 1996), p.85. By April 1945, the command had 1600 operational heavy bombers at its disposal all the time. Probert, p. 306. By way of contrast, in June 1944, the Eighth Air Force *alone* had an effective daily combat strength of 1855 heavy bombers, and that number would rise further in 1945. Williamson Murray, *Strategy for Defeat – The Luftwaffe 1933-1945* (Secaucus, NJ: Chartwell, 1986), p.178.

82. Neillands, p. 340; Bomber Command Diary (online), at <http://www.raf.mod.uk/bombercommand/diary/diary 1944_1.html, p. 7>, accessed 14 January 2008.

83. Brereton Greenhous and Hugh A. Halliday, *Canada's Air Forces 1914-1999* (Montreal: Art Global, 1999), p.118.

84. Bomber Command Diary, October 1944, p. 1.

85. Neillands, p.337.

86. Ibid.

87. David R. Mets, *Master of Airpower: General Carl A. Spaatz* (Novato, CA: Presidio Press, 1997), p.269.

88. Neillands, p.341.

89. Paul Addison and Jeremy A. Crang, *Firestorm* (London: Pimlico, 2006), p.102.

90. 303rd BG [H] Combat Mission No. 311, 3 February 1945, at <http://www.303rdbg.com/missionreports/311.pdf>, accessed 10 March 2008.

91. *Bombing of Berlin in World War II*, at <http://en.wikipedia.org/wiki/Bombing_of_Berlin_in_World_War_II>, accessed 10 March 2008, and Frederick Taylor, *Dresden – Tuesday, February 13, 1945* (New York: HarperCollins, 2004), p.354.

92. Neillands, p.370.

93. Craven and Cate, *The Army Air Forces in World War II*, Vol. 3, p.6.

94. Richard Overy, *Are We Beasts?* A review of *The Fire: The Bombing of Germany 1940-1945*, by Jörg Friedrich, and *Inferno: The destruction of Hamburg*, by Keith Lowe, in *Literary Review*, March 2007, at <http://www.literaryreview.co.uk/overy_03_07.html>, accessed 7 March 2008.

95. Neillands, p.339.

96. Bill Swetman, "Avro Lancaster," in Jeffrey L. Ethell (ed.) *The Great Book of World War II Airplanes* (Tokyo: Zokeisha Publications, 1984), pp.417-418.

97. Neillands, p.255.

98. Ibid., p.293.

99. This assumes, of course, that the lead bombardier 'got it right' in the first instance. Reaction times would further increase bomb impact dispersion, as would the normal spread formation of a bombing squadron. *Major Deceptions on Contrails Unmasked*, at <http://goodsky.homestead.com/files/deception5.html>, accessed 12 March 2008. Of note, of the 39 B-17s of the 303rd Bomb Group that bombed Berlin on 3 February 1945, 23 were crewed by toggliers versus bombardiers. <http://www.303rdbg.com/missionreports/311.pdf>, accessed 10 March 2008.

100. Group Captain Peter W. Gray, "Dresden 1945 – Just Another Raid?" *Royal Air Force Airpower Review*, Vol. 4, No. 1 (Spring 2001), p. 5. Considering the train of events which was to follow at Dresden, Churchill's choice of the word "basting" was imprudent, to say the least. While he undoubtedly meant it to mean "to thrash" or "to beat soundly," his famous ruthless bellicosity and choice of inflammatory rhetoric resulted in another connotation associated with roasting. This may well have added to the emotional denouncement of the Dresden raids over time, as well as of those who sanctioned their prosecution.

101. Quoted in Webster and Frankland, *Strategic Bomber Offensive*, Vol. 3, p.101.

102. Sinclair to Churchill (Top Secret), 26 January 1945, in PRO Premier 3/12, p.37.

103. Prime Minister's Personal Minute to Sinclair, 26 January 1945, in PRO Premier 3/12, p.34.

104. Sinclair to Churchill (Top Secret), 27 January 1945, in PRO Premier 3/12, p. 33.

105. Gray, "Dresden 1945," p.6.

106. Ibid.

107. Quoted in Webster and Frankland, *Strategic Air Offensive*, Vol. 3, p.112.

108. Neillands, p.373.

109. Minute (Top Secret) Churchill to Ismay *et al*, 28 March 1945, at PRO Premier 3/12, p.23.

110. Gray, "Dresden 1945," p. 9.

111. Quoted in Probert, p.322. The paraphrased remark of Bismarck's, made at the Congress of Berlin in 1878, reads as follows: "The whole of the Balkans is not worth the bones of a single Pomeranian grenadier."

112. Neillands, p.372.

113. This is a very interesting area of study. The first case involves entreaties from Eduard Beneš, the exiled President of Czechoslovakia, to Churchill following the razing of Lidice in the wake of the Reinhard Heydrich assassination on 29 May 1942. Churchill asked Bomber Command to consider retribution against comparable German towns, but Harris was able to deflect this initiative tactfully from the PM. Examined in Bashow, pp.91-93, and Notes 68-72, especially Letter and Minute in PRO Premier 3/11/12, p.667, Letter Beneš to Churchill, 15 June 1942, in PRO Premier 3/11/12, p.669, and Letter Harris to Churchill, 15 June 1942, in PRO Premier 3/11/12, p. 666. The *Crossbow* experience involved the Prime Minister, this time asking the Chiefs of Staff to consider reprisals against the German people for the V-weapon attacks upon Britain. These considerations ranged from exploring the pros and cons of threatening to use poison gas against the Germans [Prime Minister's Minute No D. 217/4, 5 July 1944, and COS Minute to Prime Minister 1126/4, 5 July 1944, both in PRO Premier 3/12, pp.81-83], to retaliatory attacks on selected German towns by Bomber Command. With respect

to the gas initiative, when he was informed of it, an exasperated General Dwight Eisenhower actually waded in with the following response: "Let's, for God's sake, keep our eyes on the ball and use some sense." Lord Tedder's Memoirs, quoted in Terraine, pp. 652-653, and R.V. Jones, letter to *Daily Telegraph*, 11 June 1981. Concerning bombing the towns, the Air Staff defused the initiative, claiming that with respect to indiscriminate bombing, "We have hitherto always maintained consistently in all public statements regarding our bombing policy that it is directed against military objectives and that any damage to civilians is incidental to our attack on the German war machine. This is a moral and legal point of great importance, both now and in the Maintenance of our position after the war, and it would be greatly weakened should we now for the first time declare that we intended deliberate attacks on the civilian population as such." Examined in Bashow, pp.341-344, and Notes 75-78, particularly War Cabinet Conclusions, Minute 4, 3 July 1944, in PRO Premier 3/12, p.92, and Note by Air Staff, "Crossbow – Consideration of Retaliation," in PRO Premier 3/12, pp.85-89.

114. Minute D. 89/5 (Top Secret) Ismay to Churchill, 30 March 1945, at PRO Premier 3/12, p.23.

115. Attachment (Top Secret) to Minute D.89/5 (Top Secret) Churchill to Ismay *et al*, 01 April 1945, at PRO Premier 3/12, p.22.

116. Probert, p.325.

117. Note (Top Secret – undated) by Sir Charles Portal, at PRO Premier 3/12. pp.18-21.

118. Additional correspondence contained at PRO Premier 3/12, pp.7-17.

119. Churchill to Sinclair and Portal, 19 April 1945, at PRO Premier 3/12, p.3.

120. Portal to Churchill, 20 April 1945, at PRO Premier 3/12, p.2

Chapter Two

A TIME FOR FORTITUDE

~
THE HUMAN ELEMENT

"Bearing enormous loads of bombs and petrol, these heavy aircraft, both because of their weight and on account of the need to conserve fuel for the long hours of endurance, travelled, by comparison with the German night fighters, very slowly, making an airspeed of perhaps 180 knots on the way out and 210 knots on the way home. Though they could perform the famous "corkscrew" manoeuvre by which they sought to evade or at least to present a more difficult target to the fighters, their manoeuvrability was, nevertheless, far inferior to that of their smaller and more speedy opponents. Restricted to .303-calibre machine-guns, they were substantially outshot and completely outranged by their cannon-equipped enemies. Their armour-plating was progressively removed, until little remained, to increase their bomb-lifting capacity. Belching flame from their exhausts as well as radar transmissions from their navigational and fighter warning apparatus made them all too apparent to those who hunted them. Once engaged in combat, they had little chance of victory and not much of escape, while the large quantities of petrol, incendiary bombs, high explosives and oxygen with which they were filled often gave spectacular evidence of their destruction. Outpaced, outmanoeuvred and outgunned by the German night fighters and in a generally highly inflammable and explosive condition, these black monsters presented an ideal target to any fighter pilot who could find them, and it was the night fighters which caused the overwhelming majority of the losses sustained by Bomber Command..."

~ Sir Charles Webster and Noble Frankland[1]

By the summer of 1943, Bomber Command had matured into a technologically and tactically sophisticated weapon, engaged in an all-out, relentless campaign, night after night, against the European Axis states. That mighty co-operative effort known as the Combined Bomber Offensive was now in full stride, and it would become one of the most focused and demanding prolonged campaigns in modern military history. As punishing as this massive air

Credit: DND photo PL33941

▶ A typical Bomber Command pre-operation briefing.

offensive would be to the Germans and, to a lesser extent, the Italians, it would not come cheaply to the Allies. At *peak* periods of the bomber offensive, such as the Second Battle of the Ruhr and the Berlin raids of 1943/1944, for every 100 airmen who joined an operational training unit, 51 would be killed on combat operations, nine more would be killed in non-operational accidents and twelve would become prisoners of war. Three would be wounded or injured badly enough to be removed from operations, and one would successfully evade capture in enemy territory. Only 24 of the original 100 would emerge unscathed from these arduous periods of combat.[2] But while Bomber Command's morale faltered on occasion, it never imploded. No other broad element of the western Allied combatants suffered the same enormous casualty rates over a sustained, long-term campaign, nor did they face "...the mathematical certainty of their own deaths so routinely and so unflinchingly."[3] Specifically, less than 1 percent of the participants suffered debilitating combat stress that rendered them unable to carry on operations against the enemy, and significantly less were categorized in one form or another with a shortage of moral fibre or resolve.[4] We will now explore the human dimension of this epic aerial struggle. Since the number of combat stress related casualties was considered by most in the organizational hierarchy to be surprisingly small, given the highly detrimental conditions involved, it is certainly as important to highlight the reasons for this vast demonstration of psychological resolve as it is to mention the reasons for the relatively infrequent failures.

What caused the crews to prevail so steadfastly overall? Bomber Command aircrew, like their American counterparts, were motivated to join the war effort by a wide range of emotions, including patriotism, righteousness, and a sense of duty. All were volunteers. For the British, who had witnessed the ravaging of their island from the air earlier in the war, that patriotic sense of duty was probably more pronounced than it was for the men from the Dominions, who "...were far from their homes, and many did not feel the personal sense of commitment to the war that was possible for Englishmen."[5] Other compelling draws were the lure of flight itself and the thrill of service in a dimension considered glamorous by the aviation-minded public of the day. On the whole, these were fit, specifically and rigorously selected, well-trained young men who at least commenced their operational tours secure in the belief that they were vital cogs in the war effort, and that their contributions would be both necessary and meaningful, and their cause just. The RAF and the Dominion air forces did a superlative job of fostering the elite status of the crews through distinctive brevets or flying badges, decorations, and achievement awards, such as the operational tour wing and the Pathfinder badge, and the flyers were fiercely proud of these marks of distinction. However, the grim realities of air combat, especially the random nature of the bomber casualties, eventually dispelled a lot of the more glamorous notions. As the unrelenting, bloody, and depressingly-random nature of the casualties incurred during the bombing campaign unfolded, crew motivations for continued engagement of the enemy had much less to do with patriotism and much more to do with pragmatic considerations, ranging from self-esteem to simple survival. "Like the airmen of all nations, they were concerned about pay, privilege, rank and prestige to some extent. But ultimately their morale... depended to a great degree on the quality of their equipment, the length of time they were kept in combat, the results they obtained and the rate of attrition."[6] Douglas Harvey, a distinguished Canadian *Lancaster II* pilot and Distinguished Flying Cross (DFC) winner with 408 Squadron, has argued that while the military elite was preoccupied by lofty goals, such as the strategic war aims, those of the aircrew flying the missions were generally much more narrowly focused, exemplified by the following comment in reference to Sir Arthur Harris:

> At the time I knew nothing of Harris's grand design or of the horrible ordeal that lay ahead of me. His goal was the total aerial destruction of Germany. My goal, like that of other kids in Bomber Command, was quite simple: to carry out thirty raids, the magic number that constituted a tour of operations.[7]

However, crew solidarity, a sense of shared danger, and an exceptionally strong motivation not to do anything to jeopardize the other members of their aircrew team or family went a long way in mitigating the effects of combat stress. Many aircrew prevailed in the face of formidable obstacles simply because they would rather perish than let their fellow crewmembers down. Bomber crews, in many ways, became classic examples of small unit cohesiveness. Loyalty, and the strength they derived from these loyalties, is a major reason why most of them were able to prevail in the face of such daunting adversity.

> We were intensely preoccupied with our own crew and very strongly motivated not to let it down. Apart from our commanders and three or four other crews that were close contemporaries, we knew few other aircrew on the station as more than passing acquaintances.[8]

THE DANGEROUS SKY

In order to understand the extent of the human contribution, one must first grasp the environment and the challenges that were presented to the crews. In essence, flight itself is conducted in what is, for all intents and purposes, a potentially hostile environment, and combat airmen are sustained in this environment by artificial means. "Thus, airmen, more than any other wartime combatants, had to deal not only with the direct challenges of combat, but also faced the life-threatening hazards of their surroundings."[9] Those hazards constituted a very real element of friction in the airman's world, and they did so from take-off until landing. In the words of American historian Mark Wells, "...the sky itself magnified what arguably might be considered the 'normal' physical and mental stresses placed on any combatant."[10] Many day-to-day hazards associated with air operations combined to take a vast toll upon the Main Force and also upon the American daylight raiders. While many veterans, particularly over a cool ale or two, will wax nostalgically with respect to the flying characteristics of their *Lancasters, Halifaxes, Stirlings, Fortresses,* and *Liberators,* these aircraft were all exceptionally difficult to fly at times, especially when overburdened by volatile fuel loads and high explosives on take-off from chronically-short runways, or when returning from arduous raids with extensive battle damage and/or wounded crew members. Systems failures were commonplace, and routine operations at maximum permissible performance settings left precious little room for error. For example, a single engine failure on take-off, even on four-engine aircraft, normally constituted a death sentence for a hapless crew so afflicted. Also, the gruesome pyrotechnic effects of 2000 gallons of high octane fuel and 10,000 pounds of high explosive ordnance igniting were both spectacular and unnerving to other crews awaiting departure, adding further to the psychological stresses at play.

> Pilot skill was the difference between life and death for a crew at all times, not only when attacked, [but] never more so than on takeoff when loaded with tons of explosives. It was an inescapable moment of dry-mouthed tension for all on board and, unlike enemy action, it was experienced on every sortie. One pilot recalled the drill: 'Right hand on the throttles, thumb advancing port outer to stop her swinging, stick forward to get the tail up, deft use of rudder to keep her straight, the needle creeps up to 90 knots marking the point of no return.' The flight engineer acted as co-pilot and a mistake on his part could be no less fatal...[11]

Weather is notoriously unreliable and inconsistent over Britain and northwest Europe, even with today's enhanced predictive assets. Structural damage, including catastrophic airframe failures due to turbulence and icing, were common during the war. As late as 5 March 1945, 20 6 Group aircrew were killed, just in take-off accidents, in one night aboard seven crashed aircraft. The raid, an operation to Chemnitz, started disastrously when crews later reported that "...during the climb, they encountered varying degrees of icing near Linton. The icing was particularly bad in one area where cumulus cloud had apparently developed within the stratocumulus layers. During their climb from Tholthorpe, three *Halifax* crews encountered icing so severe that the pilots could not maintain control of their aircraft and ordered their crews to bail out."[12] Pilot Officer Jimmy Waugh of 420 Squadron, an intrepid gunner who would be awarded both a Distinguished Flying Medal (DFM) and later a DFC for his wartime exploits, was one of the lucky survivors that night:

> ...on the 5th of March 1945 I was involved in what I believe to be one of the worst aircraft accidents that had ever happened in England to that date. While flying as a spare mid-upper gunner, with our aircraft loaded with petrol and high explosives, we climbed to 10,000 feet where we encountered severe icing and the pilot was unable to control the aircraft. At 7000 feet we were ordered by our pilot to "Jump! Jump!" but due to difficulties with the engineer, I did not get out until [the] base of cloud, which was [at] approximately 1200 feet. At approximately 800 feet the explosion of [the] aircraft upon impact

Credit: DND PL10811

▶ Time to go. Boarding the crew bus outbound.

caused me to become severely tangled with my parachute. Finally at about 300 feet I managed to untangle [the] shroud lines, etc., from my parachute harness and alight with slightly more than normal impact. The remaining six members of the crew did not jump and were all killed in the explosion. No trace of the bodies could be found. The largest piece of the aircraft that could be found was no larger than a normal sized wash basin.[13]

Other hazards to flight abounded. Major performance limitations or design flaws handicapped some of the bomber fleets, such as the *Stirlings* and the earlier models of the *Halifax*. However, engines were notoriously unreliable *generally,* and instruments and control surfaces frequently froze or otherwise failed. By way of example, Murray Peden recalls his early operations piloting Main Force *Stirlings*:

Even when most equipment was working well, it was almost a given that on every operation something would malfunction. Between the "routine" action of dodging flak at our modest level, it was not uncommon, for example, to have one engine start to run hot, which posed an unpleasant problem in a *Stirling*, already well below the height of the bulk of Main Force. Or an intercom point would start acting up, very serious if it was a gunner's; or someone would start having difficulty with his oxygen supply, and even in a *Stirling*, this could be serious if it were protracted. Compasses were prone to be affected by well-charged clouds, and their verification and the re-setting of the gyro directional indicator was a near-constant chore.[14]

Supplemental oxygen systems failed and fatally incapacitated crew members, usually without warning, and life-sustaining oxygen was a vital requirement at the altitudes most raids were conducted. During the Second World War, these systems, especially the regulators and the connectors, were unreliable, and the effects of hypoxia or oxygen starvation were generally not well known. That said, an alert crew could occasionally make a life-or-death difference, while many others were probably not so lucky. In late-1943, a *Halifax* crew from 429 Squadron flying out of Leeming was very fortunate:

> It was on one of these high-level daylight exercises across Scotland that the pilot, Flying Officer Les Thompson, called up the flight engineer, Flight Sergeant Stan Fisher, on the intercom and asked him if he could see the black cat walking across the wing between the two engines. The crew all woke up on hearing this and Flight Sergeant Budgen, the wireless operator, found the pilot's oxygen line was disconnected. He quickly coupled it up before he [the pilot – DB] could pass out.[15]

Air traffic control was primitive at best, and air traffic congestion was enormous. For example, the traffic patterns at the 6 Group stations had significant overlapping, and with only the most rudimentary navigational aids, mid-air collisions and ground impacts due to spatial disorientation were commonplace. Also, "...with thousands of young, relatively inexperienced airmen at the controls of complex, multi-engine aircraft, there were a huge number of crashes very likely due simply to pilot error."[16] RAF Bomber Command had nearly 6000 airmen killed *in training accidents alone* during 1943 and 1944, and for the entire war period, accidents would kill nearly 12 percent of the combatant force.[17]

Airfield control was generally *procedural* rather than *technological* at the time. Individual aircraft were 'funneled' into a landing sequence, assigned a numerical priority, and provided with a time separation from a preceding aircraft. Control was normally exercised by visual means, and under conditions of poor visibility, it broke down frequently. Murray Peden recalls:

The problem, more often than not, was not finding your way back to base, but finding the visibility there safe for what you had in mind, namely getting down and climbing into the crew bus. When the weather clamped, and you were diverted to another drome, it was usually along with the aircraft from half a dozen other dromes that had also been taken off the board by fog or morning mist. Even with reasonable visibility at the new stopping place, the circuit was over-filled with tired crews, often running short of juice, and anxious to get down PDQ. They often produced some of the more hair-raising incidents of the night just by bad flying and a touch of irresponsibility. Air traffic control separation, at these times, was as good as one could expect under such abnormal circumstances.[18]

Readers should note that aircraft returning with unserviceable or malfunctioning radios, and there were many, were equipped with recognition flares and briefed on specific 'colours of the day,' to ensure that the airfield controllers and ground defences did not mistakenly consider them as German intruders, who were a routine threat. The use of *Gee* as a vectoring device to home stations was a widespread and preferred recovery option, and many Bomber Command navigators became particularly adept at getting their crews home to within a fraction of a mile through skilled use of this valuable equipment. That said, navigators, like all crew members, were not infallible, as *Halifax* pilot and DFC winner Bob Pratt from Toronto, who flew his operational tour with 434 Squadron, later recalled. On one occasion, low on fuel, Pratt was informed by his navigator, Willie, that they had successfully completed their return trip and were now overhead British soil. After acknowledging this, Pratt let down through clouds, spotted an airfield and started an approach; the idea being that he would land, get fuel and his bearings, then continue on to his home base. However, on final approach, the airfield defences opened up on the hapless *Halifax*. The same thing happened after an orbit and a second approach, when Pratt fired the flare colours of the day. After Pratt fired a second round of identification flares, the airfield defences ceased firing. Bob Pratt then asked his navigator to re-confirm that they were, in fact, over Britain. His navigator then asked Pratt to head generally north while he took an astro-navigation shot for verification. Pratt, flying in pouring rain, sardonically observed that in that weather they would not even be able to see a single star, let alone to obtain an accurate positional plot. He then asked his wireless operator to try to get an electronic vector from Britain. This was immediately successful, and they were then informed by anxious British controllers that they had been attempting to land on a German airfield! Pratt urgently retracted his landing gear, headed north to England, and eventually landed at a coastal fighter base without further incident. His subsequent reaction to his navigator's performance and to that of the posting authorities is priceless:

> We got home, and I said to Willie, "That's your last trip with me." So they gave him his commission and sent him home, as a navigation instructor...[19]

Several new approach aids were being introduced to service late in the war. The SCS 51 system, developed initially in the USA, was introduced to Britain early in 1944, and it provided azimuth direction, localizer, and glide path information to the user through a system of tone modulation discriminations. This was a great advance over the earlier beam approaches, as it provided a continuous indication of deviations from course. The civilian version of this equipment would become famous as the Instrument Landing System (ILS). Also developed late in the war was the Ground Controlled Approach (GCA), which consisted of extremely high precision microwave radar, which provided the position of a 'target' aircraft in azimuth, range and elevation. By this means, the position of a landing aircraft relative to a predetermined approach path was displayed on a ground scope, whereby a skilled operator could provide directions to 'talk the aircraft down.' This equipment was, however, in a very neophyte stage of utilization during the war years. Similarly, the use of short-range microwave Airfield Control Radar (ACR) for directing the flow of aircraft in the vicinity of airports was pioneered at several Bomber Command stations during the war years, and much valuable experience was gained for future applications.

As an approach aid, *when* it was used, the most common means of positioning for landing in bad weather was the Standard Beam Approach (SBA). Although it had been introduced into service in 1939, it had not achieved widespread popularity. This was due partially to the unreliability of the equipment, but also because considerable practice was required to retain a high level of skill in its use. Its inherent weaknesses were that it was slow and time-consuming, there were vagaries in radio reception on the dedicated frequencies, and it lacked glide path and continuous range information to touchdown. During the latter years of the bomber offensive, when the Main Force was equipped broadly with VHF radios, as pioneered by Guy Gibson and 617 Squadron on the Ruhr Dams Raid of May 1943, a standby Direction Finding (DF) or homing service was provided to aircraft whose normal aids to navigation had been put out of action.

Credit: DND PL4958

▶ An early-war shot of a navigator at his work station.

However, the RAF knew it needed an approach option for returning aircrew that would permit them to penetrate the last few hundred feet of fog and low cloud in conditions that totally obscured the ground. To that end, an innovative chain of emergency landing fields with long, wide runways was constructed, primarily along the coastal approaches, to provide sanctuary to the returning bombers. They were also equipped with a system designed by the Fog Investigation Dispersal Organization (FIDO), consisting of elevated pipes paralleling the length of the runway, which warmed the air and burned off the fog with a double row of burners that were fed with gasoline under pressure and distributed by pipeline. Fearsome in appearance, they were very effective and saved many lives, although they were extremely costly to construct and to operate. One such base in the chain, equipped with a 9000 x 700 foot runway, was opened at Carnaby on the east Yorkshire coast in March 1944, and it saved many aircraft and crews, particularly those from 6 Group. At Carnaby alone, over 1500 operational landings utilizing FIDO were recorded during the European war.[20]

The aerial battlefield over northwest Europe was replete with dangers. American tactics in daylight dictated tight formations for optimum use of massed defensive firepower and offensive bombing accuracy. However, many hours of close formation and vigilant visual scanning of the aerial battlefield, exacerbated by vibration, noise, extreme cold, and the forces of gravity, were physically debilitating in the extreme. At night, Bomber Command did not face as great a fatigue factor from flying extremely close formation in the bomber stream, but "... the gloomy conditions of cloud cover and darkness increased the chances for mid-air collisions or navigation errors."[21] In fact, mid-upper gunners undoubtedly saved more lives by warning their pilots of impending collisions than they did by firing their guns, especially on the climb-out to the altitude prescribed for joining the bomber stream on any given night.

A MATTER OF LUCK

In spite of the generally-excellent preparatory flight training received by the crews, chance played a major role in determining their fate. Although experience was a useful tool in isolation for extending aircrew survival, casualties were often depressingly random, and various system malfunctions often claimed many crews who were at the peak of their experience, confidence and productivity. Also, it was frequently just a matter of luck if a particular aircraft was singled out for attack by an enemy fighter, or if a shell from an anti-aircraft barrage exploded lethally close.

> The raw crew who arrived one morning only to be posted missing a few days later were not always victims of their own lack of experience: our casualties were evenly distributed. The old hands, now few in number, would react quicker to a situation but in the thickly concentrated bomber stream chance played a big part. The will to fight on when attacked, to use every trick and turn to defeat the enemy fighter, to stay with the aircraft when there was the least possibility of getting the crew home was strong in all the young captains and it often paid dividends.[22]

However, the crews strongly held to some beliefs that could hasten their fates beyond randomness. For Bomber Command airmen, aircraft illuminated by fires, bright moonlight, or the dreaded radar-controlled searchlights, often became fatal statistics. That said, as the crews became increasingly aware of this random nature of aerial death and the heightened importance of luck, many responded with a form of fatalism, often glumly calculating their odds against survival. Others did everything they could to improve their chances, including the cultivation of teamwork, diligent training, and painstaking attention to even the smallest details. And good luck charms and mascots were everywhere, with Saint Christopher medals, rosaries, and rabbits' feet being seen as frequently as sextants, flashlights, parachutes, and escape kits. "Jock Wilson carried a little yellow duck with 'Berlin or Bust' written on it. In addition he packed a small towel and soap 'to wash my feet with in the dingy.' One of our pilots, a short chap named Jackson, used to carry a large panda and tuck it behind his seat."[23] John Lewis, a distinguished Canadian navigator who flew a total of 46 operations with 426 Squadron and then later with 405 Squadron as a Pathfinder, winning a DFC and Bar along the way, also recalls some of the ritualistic behavior:

> Believing it would help stave off disaster, some would don their flying gear only in a specific order; some would urinate on the tail wheel of the aircraft; others would carry talismans of various shapes and sizes. Some would insist on boarding the aircraft first, second, third, etc.; others pledged they would not launder their white-wool submarine sweaters until they were through with ops. As we were rolling down the runway on take-off, I would silently repeat the Lord's Prayer...[24]

Others showed somewhat contemptuous disdain for such beliefs, and some even dealt with the mathematical odds in a rather lighthearted manner. Bert Houle was a distinguished Canadian veteran, and although his war service was with the fighter community, the sentiments and the logic could certainly be applied to bomber operations:

> Many pilots built up their courage with a philosophy that went something like this. "There is only a 25 percent chance that I'll get shot at, and if I am there is only a 25 percent chance that my aircraft will be hit. If the aircraft is hit there is only a 25 percent chance that the hit will be serious. If it hits a vulnerable spot there is only a 25 percent chance that I will be hit. If I am hit there is only a 25 percent chance that it will be fatal. With odds like that, why should I worry?"[25]

Once a bomber was mortally hit, the crew usually only had seconds to react in order to save their lives. If they survived the crippling attack, abandoning a disabled bomber brought with it all its own perils, including exposure to fire, the structural failure of aircraft components, the inability to reach escape hatches, especially in the *Lancaster*, the less-than-perfect reliability of parachutes, and subsequent exposure to oxygen deprivation, frostbite, and perilous landing conditions. Sadly, moving more than a few feet in a wildly-gyrating stricken bomber was often impossible. This condition applied particularly to those Bomber Command aircrew obliged to negotiate the notorious main wing spar of the *Lancaster*, which was imbedded deep within the fuselage. While the following comments are American in origin, they are also certainly applicable to Bomber Command operations:

> ...of that horrible plunge to earth; this is what unnerved even the bravest. The parachute did not always promise succor. There were ships that were torn in half, or had a wing blown loose to flip-flop crazily through space, while the bomber whirled in a tight spin, and centrifugal forces pinned the men inside helplessly, like flies smashed against a wall. How long does it take to fall 25,000 feet inside the blasted wreck of a *Flying Fortress*? Whom is there to ask?[26]

Individuals, like aircraft, were also blessed or cursed with good or bad luck. A very few survived four operational tours, while many more were felled on their first combat mission. At least one aircrew member survived the experience of being pinned inside his spinning bomber by gravitational forces, only to be blown clear to safety when it exploded. Wireless operator Harry Lomas described his emotions at the time in *One Wing High*: "Having accepted it was physically impossible to escape, I felt no urgent need for despairing frenzied effort. The end would be sudden and painless, and the fear was suddenly expunged. There came no flashbacks of my past life. All I was conscious of was a feeling of resignation and intense sadness that all was going to end like this."[27]

TAIL-END CHARLIE

Of all the bomber crew stations, the most dangerous, the least survivable, was held by the man in the rear turret. His was the coldest and most detached position of all. Bundled in extra garments, including electrically-heated suits to ward off the - 40° C outside air temperatures, exacerbated by the deliberate removal of Perspex panels on their turrets, (the so-called Granston Lodge modification, adopted to facilitate the early spotting of German night fighters), his lot was miserable. Since space was extremely limited in the turret, the rear gunner's parachute had to be stored in the aft fuselage. Thus, in time of dire need, the gunner had to exit the turret, don the parachute, then rotate the turret door to the stern of the aircraft in order to bail out. In reality, the turret, for one reason or another, frequently jammed, trapping the gunner inside. At

▶ Getting there was often an adventure in itself. To England via troop ship.

Credit: DND PL4881

any rate, this method of escape was not recommended in the *Lancaster*, since *all* crew members, *including* the rear gunner, were advised, time and circumstances permitting, which they rarely did, to exit through the emergency hatch in the extreme nose of the aircraft. An egress during flight via the rear fuselage crew entry door on the *Lancaster* was also fraught with risk during many flight conditions, most notably from impact with the horizontal tail surfaces. However, for the rear gunner, encumbered with extra garments and the greatest distance to travel to safety, exit through the front door hatch was particularly problematic.[28] The odds against this gunner surviving were certainly lengthened by the manufacturer's rather callous disregard for his emergency egress route. Few *Lancaster* rear gunners survived a mortal hit on their bomber, and they were occasionally seen to be defiantly firing their weapons right up to the instant of ground impact, rather than attempting escape.[29] While the other crew members were huddled together in the nose section in relative security, comfort and mutual physical and psychological support, 'Tail-End Charlie' lived, and frequently *died*, in an isolated and lonely world of his own. Kenneth McDonald was a Canadian born in Bristol, England, who served as a pilot with 78 Squadron in 4 Group, winning the DFC in the process. His is a touching tribute to the rear gunners in general, and to his own in particular.

> It is the rear gunner who is alone, aft of the tail surfaces, in the slipstream of the four Merlins, from the take-off, when he is first off the

ground as the tail lifts with the *Halifax's* gathering speed, until six or seven or eight hours later he sees the ground coming closer, the approach lights flash by, and the tail wheel hits the runway. All that time, the equivalent of a normal day's work that he has put in at the end of a normal day, he has been on his own in the dark; cold, poised at the levered end of a 71 foot fuselage, his head never still, searching, searching, for the moment when one of the shapes he has learned to recognize appears below, or above, or to one side, and he alone must decide whether its pilot has seen the glow of the *Halifax's* eight stub exhausts, or is tracking another *Halifax*, or a *Lancaster*, that the gunner can't see. He has already alerted the pilot. If the shape turns, or climbs, or noses down, toward his own aircraft, he does two things at once: he calls "Corkscrew left (or right), go," the moment he fires his four Brownings at the shape, and keeps firing as the turret is dragged down and twisted and pulled up in the stomach-wrenching attitudes of the corkscrew.

It took a special kind of courage to fly as a rear gunner, the "two o'clock in the morning courage" that Napoleon said he had very rarely met. Mac McCoy was like that. He didn't say much. In fact, no-one spoke except to deliver a message, such as change of course, a wireless transmission from base, the bomb-aimer's instructions, or an aircraft sighting. He never complained. On the Turin trip, when he was in cloud most of the way, bumped about and half-frozen, I doubt it occurred to him that he might have left his turret for the less-cold fuselage while we were in cloud. But the cloud might have broken, or a fighter might have found its way to us by radar, so he kept his post.

...The next time we saw each other after Linton was in 1947, when I drove up to the gate at Trenton and there was Mac, raising the barrier. He had left at the end of the war, didn't care for civilian life, and re-enlisted as the Leading Aircraftman he then was, grinning at me, with his air gunner's brevet and his DFM. We lost touch after that but I still feel closer to him than even the others...[30]

DEFENSIVE EQUIPMENT AND TACTICS

In terms of defensive capabilities, American bombers were much more heavily armed generally, although *some* heavier guns would be fitted to some

Bomber Command aircraft later in the war. Relying upon their massed fire-power, most B-17 *Fortresses* and B-24 *Liberators* had at least ten .50 calibre flex-ible machine guns, and when arranged in group formations of multiple combat boxes, they produced a truly formidable volume of protective fire. By contrast, Bomber Command emphasized stealth by night for self-defence, trading speed and increased bomb load for defensive armament. Woefully under-armed, the standard machine gun was the Browning .303 calibre weapon, which, although they dispensed significant volumes of lead, lacked the range and destructive power of the heavier guns. Further, ventral turrets were generally removed on Bomber Command aircraft from 1943 onwards to make room for the *H2S* radar dome. This lack of defensive coverage from below would make Sir Arthur Har-ris uneasy in the extreme, and he encouraged both formal and localized initia-tives to redress this shortcoming. As it materialized, he had legitimate cause for concern. The elimination of the ventral guns allowed the Germans to capitalize on the situation and field a formidable, innovative, and deadly weapons system, known as *Schräge Musik*, consisting of pairs or multiples of 20 mm or 30 mm cannon, mounted in oblique-vertical positions in the fuselage, aimed through a sight mounted on the roof of the glass canopy, and designed to fire *up* at the bombers from the blind cone below the target aircraft.

In order to foil the attacking night fighter's gun tracking solution, Bomber Com-mand crews developed the 'corkscrew' manoeuvre. The corkscrew was taught as a 'last ditch' defensive tactic, either to force the flight path overshoot of an attacking enemy night fighter, or to deny him a stabilized tracking solution for his guns if he was already within lethal attacking range. This manoeuvre was practiced assiduously by the bomber crews on routine affiliation exercises with Fighter Command aircraft, and it was also briefed extensively and repeatedly prior to operations. In a nutshell, if performed correctly, it allowed a bomber to continue on a course while presenting the attacking fighter with an extremely difficult firing solution. On being warned about a threat from astern, the pilot 'firewalled' his throttles while simultaneously banking at 45 degrees in a diving turn to port or starboard, depending upon the exact location of the threat and guidance from the gunners, losing 1000 feet of altitude in just six seconds. Dur-ing the manoeuvre, the bomber would normally accelerate to approximately 300 miles-per-hour. After 1000 feet of descent, and still in the banked turn to port, if that was the initial direction of turn, the pilot pulled his bomber up into a climb. Then he reversed the turn to starboard, bleeding off his airspeed sharply and hopefully forcing a flight path overshoot of the attacking enemy fighter. Upon regaining his original altitude, and with the airspeed now down to around 185 miles-per-hour, and still in the starboard turn, the bomber pilot pushed the aircraft down in another dive. Again picking up speed, he descended through 500 feet before commencing another turn reversal to port. If the enemy night fighter had been particularly tenacious, and had remained 'camped at 6 o'clock' to the bomber throughout the evasive action, the bomber pilot was forced to repeat all or a portion of the manoeuvre. The physical effort required to 'horse' a heavy bomber of the period around in these extreme conditions was debilitating, and it has been compared by some to the labour required from a skilled oarsman pulling hard during a competition boat race.

The flak was either of the barrage variety, which simply attempted to saturate a given patch of airspace with lead, or it was radar-directed, as were the master searchlights. Barrage flak was extremely difficult to counter, unless areas of known concentrations could be seen and/or avoided. From 1943 onwards, the Pathfinders, and later, elements of the Main Force, were actively using flight avoidance countermeasures against the radar-directed guns from known sites. The rough rule of thumb, as worked out by the 8 Group Tactics Officer, was to change headings randomly by at least fifteen degrees in either direction every twenty seconds, or vary the altitude by 500 feet every twenty seconds. This would usually cause the radar-directed flak to 'lag' the bomber's flight path, although it did nothing to mitigate the possibility of a hit on following aircraft. Once on the final bomb run, and once the aim point had been positively identified, the aircraft had to be held straight and level for the bomb-aimer, no matter how intense the gun defences over the target. This period of time, which undoubtedly felt like an eternity, normally lasted about two minutes.[31] However, once the Mark XIV gyro-stabilized bombsight was brought into extensive service, more manoeuvring in the target area could be routinely permitted, and, in a limited manner, right up to the moment of bomb release. After that final run-in, however, there was still a short period of time that the aircraft had to be held steady in order for the photoflash, the photographic proof of the accuracy of a bomb drop on target, to activate.[32] This vulnerable period, when the bomb-aimer was still in control of the aircraft, was an extremely tense time, since it was during this stage of operations that most aircraft were lost to the radar-directed flak and searchlights. The searchlights were terrifying in their own right, as their intense brightness was extremely disorienting, and this often caused pilots so captured to make fatal flying errors, or to lose their nerve and attempt to dive out of the light source, and into the range of the massed lighter guns clustered below. Being 'coned' by searchlights was both dramatic and unnerving. Many crews did not survive the experience, as described by one who did:

Turning back was quite out of the question, we therefore flew steadily onwards and, as we did do, we found that we were skillfully handed over from one group of searchlights to another. There was nothing we could do in that nightmare situation; it was impossible to see outside our aircraft to any worthwhile degree because of the dazzle, and all sensation of speed seemed to vanish. The world had disappeared and we felt as if we were hanging motionless in space.[33]

Jimmy Sheridan, a 426 Squadron pilot who would later win a DFC flying *Halifaxes*, recalls getting coned and the manner by which he got the searchlights to break their deadly lock upon him:

The Ruhr valley was one of the most heavily defended areas in Europe, with hundreds of flak guns, searchlights and fighters. As one highly-decorated, experienced wing commander put it, "A target in the Ruhr strikes fear into the heart of *any* pilot." It had been stated that if one was coned over the target area, it was impossible to get out of the lights. Hundreds of searchlights and flak guns would converge upon the hapless bomber, creating a cone miles wide. However, fighters *also* converged. Then, all the flak guns would fill the cone with shells, or a fighter would swoop in for the kill.

I was coned one night on a run into target in the Ruhr. I started corkscrewing at full throttle in a shallow dive. In doing so, I noticed that a cloud had formed over the burning target thousands of feet below. I thought that if I could position myself over the cloud, it might break those searchlight beams. By the grace of God, I got there and it did so. I then dropped my bombs and flew home without further incident.[34]

Thus, the very nature of the bomber offensive was fraught with risk, both from the inherent dangers of flight and from enemy combat capabilities. Murray Peden provides an excellent analogy as to the effect the repeated confrontation with these myriad risks could have upon the crews, knowing as they did that killers were lurking in the darkness, poised to strike them at any time during their bomber's long journey in harm's way:

Compared with the armament they are carrying, you are virtually defenceless. Moreover, you must carry a pail of gasoline and a shopping bag full of dynamite in one hand. If someone rushes at you and begins firing, about all you can do is fire a small calibre pistol in his direction and try to elude him in the dark. But these killers can run twice as fast as you, and if one stalks and catches you, the odds are that he will wound and then incinerate you, or blow you to eternity. You are acutely aware of these possibilities for every second of the five or six hours you walk in the darkness, braced always, consciously or subconsciously, for a murderous burst of fire, and reminded of the stakes of the game periodically by the sight of guns flashing in the dark and great volcanic eruptions of flaming gasoline.[35]

GUESTS OF THE THIRD REICH

While the odds were stacked against Bomber Command's crews surviving a mortal wound to their aircraft over enemy territory, especially in the *Lancaster*, many men *did* successfully abandon their stricken aircraft. In all, 9784 Bomber Command aircrew and 54 groundcrew became prisoners of war of the Axis nations, and 138 of them perished in captivity.[36]

Although most prisoners were treated quite fairly and correctly during their forced stay in the Third Reich, as mandated by the rules of the appropriate Geneva Conventions, particularly when compared to prisoner treatment at the hands of the Japanese and the reprehensible dichotomy of what was taking place in the concentration camps, some prisoners found themselves situated outside of this generalized protection. In Germany, the *Luftwaffe* was responsible for the incarceration of air force prisoners and their care was generally fair and humane, in spite of erratic and inconsistent supplies of food and basic needs, particularly towards the end of hostilities. During that period, even the parcels from the International Red Cross, which bolstered the rations supplied by the Germans, were no longer being distributed systematically, although this was somewhat understandable, given the chaotic conditions of the time.

As the war waged on into late-1944 and 1945, and the bombing became even more widespread, Joseph Goebbels fanned up resentment against the *Terror-fliegers* amongst an increasingly frightened, disenchanted, and embittered civilian populace, much as Ilya Ehrenburg had done for the Soviets. Day-to-day life in Germany was becoming increasingly tumultuous and unpredictable, the breakdown of order and restraint progressively more routine. Resistance to the Nazi regime was officially viewed as being even more intolerable than ever. The search for escaping prisoners of war placed an additional manpower

> ▶ Good luck charms abounded in wartime Bomber Command. Note the panda on the navigator's shoulder.

Credit: DND PL43740

burden upon a system now stretched to the breaking point. Accordingly, new laws and policies were promulgated with respect to escaping prisoners. Airmen parachuting into Germany were often assaulted and beaten, and occasionally lynched upon landing, the fury of their captors' response largely dependant upon who seized them, and when and where the seizure occurred. In the immediate wake of the February 1945 Dresden raid, Goebbels suggested to Hitler that several thousand Allied prisoners should be executed in reprisal. This suggestion was welcomed by Hitler, Jodl, Keitel, and other members of the Nazi ruling elite, but it was totally opposed by Hermann Göring.[37]

However, these initiatives had official, albeit secret sanction under the terms of the *Kugel Erlass* – the 'Bullet Decree' – of 1944. This directive called for captured aircrew, particularly those who were re-captured after attempting escape, to be transported to the Maulthausen concentration camp near Vienna, where they were either to be immediately executed or worked to death by hauling rocks up the staircase to the quarry located there. "More than 40 American, British and Dutch officers were so treated within a few months – the latest in a long series of German actions against captured soldiers, ranging from the notorious Commando Order of 1942, which led to the murder of many British Commando soldiers, to the execution of 50 RAF [and Allied – DB] officers captured after the 'Great Escape' from *Stalag Luft III* in March 1944."[38] Other aircrew were murdered by fanatics or by the *Gestapo* in the course of escape attempts or upon re-capture. It is worth emphasizing that, while he was guilty of many other crimes against humanity, Hermann Göring, along with many other soldiers and German civilians, was totally opposed to these atrocities. In point of fact, "Göring offered Allied aircrew his personal protection, and the *Luftwaffe* and *Wehrmacht* soldiers generally took no part in reprisals against Allied flyers, frequently rescuing them from beatings or murder at the hands of Nazi Party members or the mob."[39]

Nonetheless, the new 'top down' direction with respect to the treatment of POWs came boiling to a head as the result of the escape of many air force prisoners from *Stalag Luft III* at Sagan, some 160 kilometres southeast of Berlin in Upper Silesia, on the night of 24/25 March 1944. This mass break-out from two of the original three superbly-engineered and innovative tunnels yielded 76 escapees before the stampede was detected and curtailed. Hitler, incensed, ordered all those re-captured to be summarily executed. However, he eventually calmed down, and upon advice given by Heinrich Himmler that the execution of *all* of them could pose a credibility problem downstream, agreed that more than half of those re-captured were to be shot and cremated. Accordingly, the subsequent directive was teleprinted to *Gestapo* headquarters under Himmler's order, and a list of 50 subsequently was culled from the 76 escapees by General Nebe and Dr. Hans Merton. Upon re-capture, these men were taken away singly or in small groups by representative agents from various *Gestapo* field districts or regional headquarters.

> The *Gestapo* groups submitted almost identical reports that 'the prisoners, whilst relieving themselves, bolted for freedom and were shot whilst trying to escape.' This famous expression has now passed into history as a euphemism for cold-blooded murder.[40]

Of the 76 escapees, fifty were murdered, 23 were eventually returned to prison camps, and three escaped to freedom via either neutral Sweden or Gibraltar. Postwar trials in 1947 and 1948 resulted in the execution or imprisonment by the western Allies of many of the perpetrators, while the Soviets disposed of others. Still more committed suicide rather than face legal accounting for their crimes, while others were killed accidentally or in combat during the Third Reich's final hours.[41]

Association with Resistance forces in the occupied territories, either by contrivance or by happenstance, could generate dreadful repercussions for Allied airmen, as Ed Carter-Edwards, a wartime member of 427 "Lion" Squadron flying *Halifaxes* out of Leeming, recalls. Carter-Edwards had dreadful experiences, and his words are all the more chilling for having been written in his minimalist style:

> Completed 21 ops. Shot down on #22 – 8 June 1944 at 1:30 AM, west of Paris. Target – Acheres but we never reached it – bailed out from our burning *Halifax*. Assisted by French Underground but betrayed to the *Gestapo* by a collaborator. I was classified as a spy and saboteur and threatened with execution. Then, I was horribly beaten and thrown into Fresnes, a civilian prison run by the *Gestapo* and those sadistic SS (Death's Head) forces. Eventually, I was taken by French cattle cars (80-90 per car) to the Buchenwald concentration camp to be executed. Here, we witnessed and also experienced sadistic, barbaric acts of inhuman indecency inflicted upon innocent prisoners. After 3½ months in Buchenwald, we were taken to *Stalag Luft III* on a death march in January '45. Then, by box car to Marlag-Milag. Then, another march in April '45, and eventual liberation near Lübeck on the 5th of May, 1945...[42]

THE ELECTRONIC WAR

Deliberately offsetting stealth, speed, and increased bomb carriage capacity for reduced self-defence capabilities, Bomber Command placed a great amount of faith in electronic deception, warning and jamming equipment, as well as associated techniques. *Window,* tinfoil strips cut to the enemy's radar wavelengths and then dispensed as bundles of foil chaff, which had been so enormously successful at Hamburg, was supplemented by *Mandrel*, which was an electronic method of jamming the early warning radars. However, the Germans eventually countered with *Freya-Halbe*, *Mammut*, and *Wassermann* radars, all with various anti-jamming properties. And the Germans also had their own jammers. *Heinrich* and *Bumerang*, to deal with *Gee* and *Oboe* respectively, *Naxos* and *Naxburg* to home on *H2S*. As a counter to the AI *Lichtenstein* radar and the infrared detection device known as *Spanner*, which homed on a bomber's hot engine exhausts, Bomber Command brought on board *Monica*, a warning radar designed specifically to cover the bomber's vulnerable stern area. German countermeasures to *Monica* followed, notably the *FuG 22 Flensburg*, which homed upon this British

▶ A Vickers *Wellington* at dispersal.

▶ A 419 'Moose' (RCAF) Squadron *Wellington* over England.

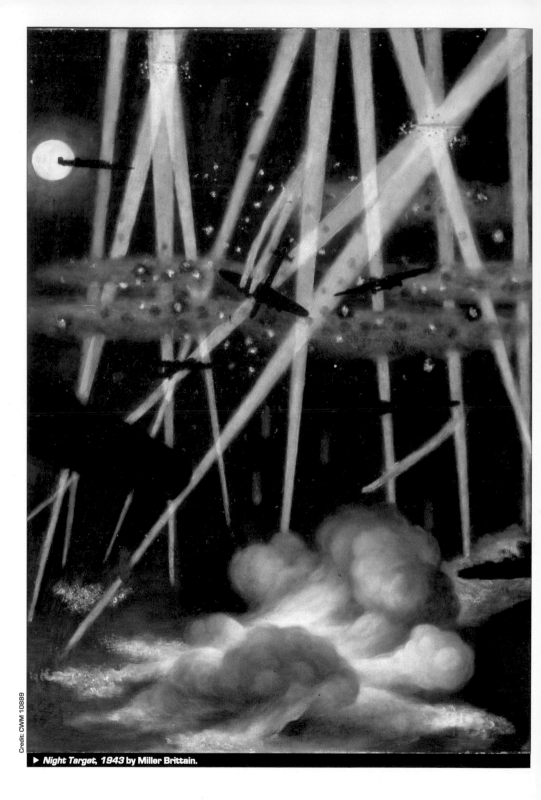

▶ *Night Target, 1943* by Miller Brittain.

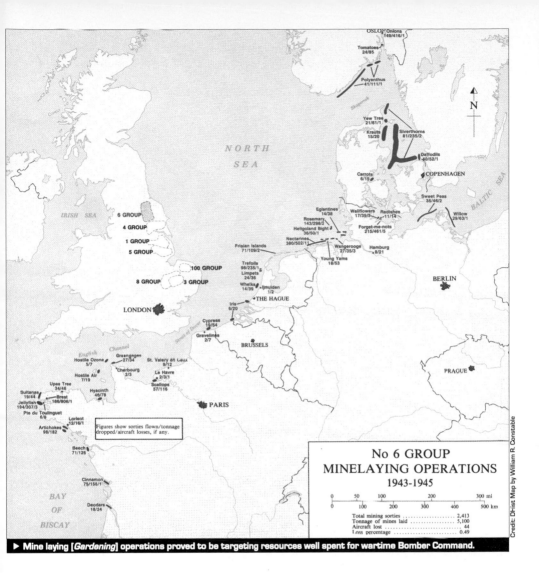

OSLO Onions
149/416/1

Tomatoes
24/95

Polyanthus
41/111/1

Yew Tree
21/61/1

Krauts
15/20

Siverthorns
81/235/2

Daffodils
40/52/1

Carrots
6/15

COPENHAGEN

Sweet Peas
36/46/2

NORTH
SEA

IRISH SEA

6 GROUP

4 GROUP

1 GROUP

5 GROUP

100 GROUP

8 GROUP   3 GROUP

LONDON

Eglantines
14/38

Wallflowers   Radishes
17/39/3   11/14

Willow
29/63/1

BALTIC SEA

Rosemary
143/298/5

Heligoland Bight
36/50/1

Forget-me-nots
215/461/5

Nectarines
380/502/11

Friesian Islands
71/109/2

Wangerooge
27/35/3

Hamburg
8/21

Young Yams
16/53

BERLIN

Trefoils
98/235/1

Limpets
24/36

Whelks
14/39   Ijmuiden
1/2

Iris
6/20   THE HAGUE

Cypress
19/54

Gravelines
2/7

BRUSSELS

English Channel

Strait of Dover

Hostile Ozone   Greangages
5/7   27/34

St. Valery en Caux
9/12

Cherbourg
2/3

Le Havre
2/3/1

Hostile Air
7/19

Scallops
57/116

Upas Tree
34/46   Hyacinth
46/78

Sultanas   Brest
19/44   165/806/1

Jellyfish
194/307/3

Pte du Toulinguet
6/6

Lorient
12/16/1

Artichokes
98/182

PARIS

PRAGUE

Figures show sorties flown/tonnage
dropped/aircraft losses, if any.

Beech
71/128

Cinnamon
75/156/1

Deodars
18/24

BAY
OF
BISCAY

N

No 6 GROUP
MINELAYING OPERATIONS
1943-1945

0	50	100		200		300 mi
0		100	200	300	400	500 km

Total mining sorties 2,413
Tonnage of mines laid 5,100
Aircraft lost 44
Loss percentage 0.49

▶ Mine laying [*Gardening*] operations proved to be targeting resources well spent for wartime Bomber Command.

▶ A *Wellington* crew member getting ready for a trip to Axis Europe.

NO. 6 GROUP BOMBING TARGETS
1943 - 1945

```
0      50    100           200              300 mi
0      100   200    300    400    500 km
```

(Neutral)

COPENHAGEN

IRISH SEA

NORTH SEA

BALTIC SEA

(Neutral)

6 GROUP
4 GROUP
1 GROUP
5 GROUP

100 GROUP

8 GROUP   3 GROUP

Bergen
123/571/1

Peenemünde
63/155/12

Heide/Hemmingstedt
299/1078/3
Heligoland
110/328/2
Wangerooge
190/902/4
Kiel
688/2335/9
Norden
1/2
Wilhelmshaven
304/924/5
Stettin
116/349/4
Emden
139/380
Hamburg
1298/4666/43
Bremen
95/323/1
Oldenburg
6/14/3
Hannover
575/1764/29
Berlin
1070/2573/84

BERLIN

LONDON

V-1 sites
2152/8014/5
Brussels/Melsbruck
98/478
Soesterberg
102/528/1
Osnabrück
284/1033/4
Brunswick
111/442/9
Magdeburg
228/675/29

Calais
655/3176/1
Pas-de-Calais
THE HAGUE
Wesel
2/5
Münster
293/1090/3
Hildesheim
87/382/2
Dessau
81/260/3
Cap Griz Nez
162/815
Le Clipon
42/151
Domburg
33/160
Dorsten
96/3141/16
Leipzig
406/1137/27
Boulogne
514/2336/3
St-Omer
12/30
Volkel
101/459
Goch
43/134
Soest
186/726/2
Kassel
155/402/17
Merseburg
156/567/3
Böhlen
110/253
Dresden
66/20
Somme
972/3726/1
Gheel
220/999
Bourg-Leopold
149/505/3
Julich
197/613
Cologne
1138/4248/14
Zeitz
242/711/14
Chemitz
286/748/9
V-1 sites
Lens
153/782/1
Courtrai
46/258
Louvain
89/324/5
Montzen
63/241/10
Wesseling
150/598/1
PRAGUE
Neufchatel
69/275
Lille
53/239
St. Ghislain
106/528/2
Bonn
96/460
Pilsen
26/65/4
Au Fèvre
118/444
St. Valery en Caux
105/479
Arras
96/300/6
Utaine
72/325/6
St-Pierre
62/175
St. Vith
Aachen
205/703/10
Troisdorf
146/510
Frankfurt
545/1292/36
Aulnoye
160/714
Valenciennes
8/20
Schweinfurt
193/570/3
Longues
24/77
Le Havre
226/1074
Cambrai
98/505
Laon
240/193/1
Somain
112/507/1
Wiesbaden
60/277/2
Hanau
586/1621/23
Rüsselsheim
33/119/1
Coutances
125/463
Caen
515/2243/4
Thiverny
89/437
St-Leu d'Esserent
Mainz
264/1021
Ludwigshafen
Worms
111/349/6
Nuremberg
290/689/17
Schwandorf
118/492
Brest
35/171
Ile de Cezembre
187/909/1
Nucourt
64/300
Amiens
181/658/11
Chantilly
190/706/1
Metz
97/290/7
Mannheim
586/1621/23
Karlsruhe
195/670
Conde-sur-Noireau
112/385
Meulen
60/280
Saarbrücken
139/370
Zweibrücken
192/755
Stuttgart
782/2120/33
Augsburg
58/113/6
Mayenne
80/282/1
Merville
136/526
Trappes
117/565
Vaires
74/310/1
Connantre
99/351
Pforzheim
50/189
Gablingen
17/45
Munich
69/174/5
Falaise
258/1166
Achères
94/345/5
Le Mans
391/1614/2
Trouville
54/180
Noisy le Sec
137/646/4
Friedrichshafen
19/55
Donges
99/296
Versailles
114/418/4
Villeneuve St. Georges
243/1033
St. Nazaire
213/475/3
Forêt de Montrichard
99/343

English Channel

PARIS

RUHR

Lorient
441/993/6

BAY OF BISCAY

La Pallice
130/468

Montlucon
63/117/2

Le Creusot
39/98/1

(Neutral)

Modane
48/107/1
Milan
48/120/1
Turin
14/42

ADRIATIC SEA

Cannes
20/50

(Neutral)

MEDITERRANEAN SEA

Figures show sorties flown/tonnage
dropped/aircraft losses, if any.

RUHR inset

Gladbeck
95/340
Scholven/Buer
47/225/2
Kamen
109/364/1
Bottrop/Welheim
172/735
Castrop-Rauxel
398/1434/4
Sterkrade
334/1149/13
Wanne-Eickel
197/1344/5
Dortmund
900/3141/16
Oberhausen
244/995/6
Bochum
587/2050/26
Duisburg
1312/4903/25
Witten
83/253/3
Mülheim
41/102/6
Gelsenkirchen
296/1114/9
Hagen
333/1389/6
Krefeld
58/145/6
Essen
1117/3594/22
Düsseldorf
719/2739/35
Wuppertal
111/349/6
Neuss
220/948
Mönchen-Gladbach
83/207/3
Remscheid
32/80/2
Grevenbroich
134/355
Opladen
146/631/2
Leverkusen
121/303/4

```
0    5    10 mi
0    10    20 km
```

(Neutral)

RUHR

▶ **Representative bombing targets of #6 (RCAF) Group, 1943-1945.**

"Men with a Purpose"

Join the
ROYAL CANADIAN AIR FORCE

▶ RCAF recruiting poster, circa 1942.

BATTLE OF GERMANY

JOIN AN AIR CREW

HOLMES

► The bombing offensive enjoyed widespread wartime public support.

▶ Air Vice-Marshal Clifford M. 'Black Mike' McEwen (right) and Wing Commander Bill Swetman in front of a Canadian *Lancaster II*.

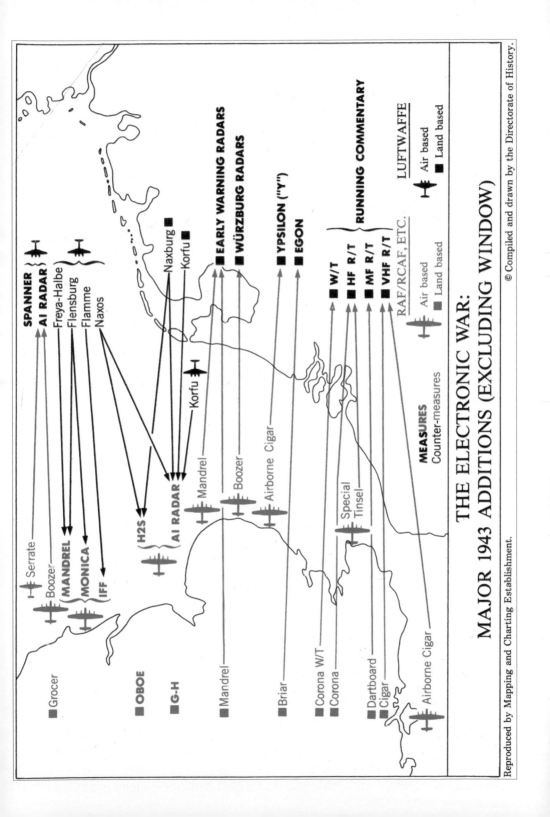

THE ELECTRONIC WAR:
MAJOR 1943 ADDITIONS (EXCLUDING WINDOW)

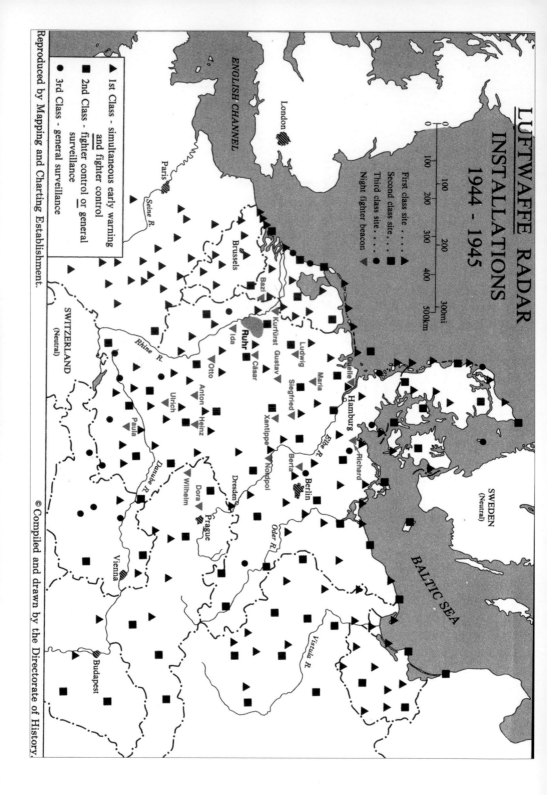

LUFTWAFFE RADAR INSTALLATIONS 1944 - 1945

First class site . . . . . ▶
Second class site . . . . ■
Third class site . . . . . ●
Night fighter beacon . . ◀

▶ 1st Class - simultaneous early warning and fighter control

■ 2nd Class - fighter control or general surveillance

● 3rd Class - general surveillance

▶ The Canadian Warplane Heritage Museum's magnificent tribute Mynarski *Lancaster* over southern Ontario.

▶ de Havilland *Mosquito*.

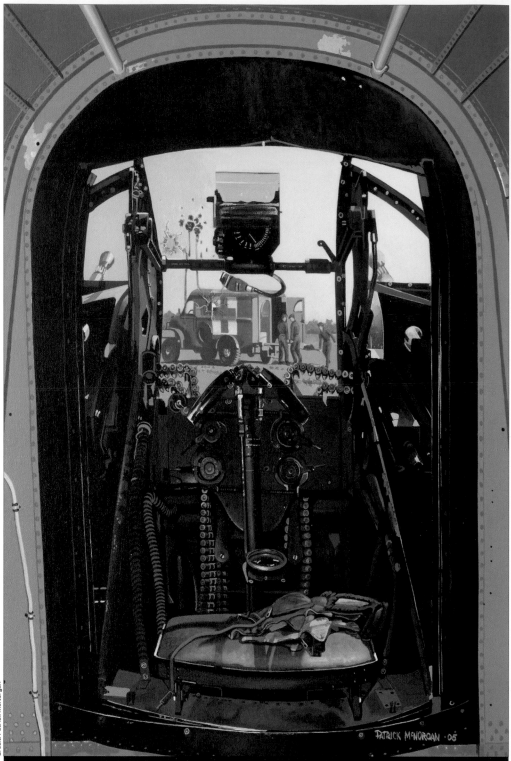

▶ *Stained Glass Window*, by Patrick McNorgan. A tribute to the air gunners. Here, the artist has drawn inspiration from the great film director, Alfred Hitchcock, who was well known for showing his audience the aftermath of violence, but not the action itself.

► A 434 'Bluenose' (RCAF) Squadron *Lancaster* Mk. 10 photographed late in the war.

► *Girl from the North Country,* by Patrick McNorgan. A Lancaster Mk. X from 431 'Iroquois' (RCAF) Squadron unloads a 4000 pound 'cookie' on a German target as an enemy night fighter overshoots.

▶ *Marshalling of the Hallies*," by Paul Goranson.

▶ *Marshalling Lancasters against Stuttgart*, by Carl Schaefer. While discerning viewers will note that the artist has depicted earlier-variant *Lancasters* in this painting, the potential energy and the moodiness of the scene certainly also applied to later-war operations.

▶ 'Big Joe' McCarthy (centre) and his distinguished crew of 'Dambusters' from 617 Squadron. McCarthy was an American serving in the RCAF, and on his immediate right is Pilot Officer Donald Arthur MacLean, DFM, from Toronto, McCarthy's talented navigator.

▶ de Havilland *Mosquitos* of the Light Night Striking Force.

► A youthful 23-year-old Group Captain 'Reg' Lane and his Yorkshire lass Barbara 'tie the knot.' Theirs is representative of many wartime marriages between British women and visiting servicemen. St. John's Church, Moortown, Leeds, Yorkshire, 3 December 1945.

innovation. Naturally, the command soon introduced counter-countermeasures. However, one lesson, briefly mentioned earlier, that was only slowly and painfully learned by *both* sides was that most of this sophisticated new technology left an electronic footprint, thus providing an unintentional marker as to a particular transmitter's whereabouts. Many aircraft were lost from both fighting camps due to this new phenomenon. Bomber Command's myopia with respect to electronic signatures started as early as the spring of 1942. At that time, a widespread yet irrational belief, fostered by a few incredible coincidences, prevailed that the electronic cycling of the Identification Friend or Foe (IFF) equipment prevented bomber acquisition by enemy radar directed searchlights and flak. So widespread was this misguided belief that the Air Ministry actually approved for a time a modification to the IFF called the "J - Switch," which allowed the aircraft to electronically radiate continuously for one-half second every twelve seconds in a highly predictable manner. As it transpired, this misguided procedure was also providing an excellent homing beacon to the Germans.[43]

Bogus radio transmissions from England to German night fighters, code named *Drumstick*, *Fidget* and *Jostle*, later supplemented by the airborne *Tinsel* transmissions, further served to confuse and deceive the German defences.

> All these exotic tools and techniques came into play incrementally, spread over the length and breadth of the bomber offensive, each with its own grotesque identifier – *Cigar* and *Airborne Cigar, Corona, Dartboard, Grocer, Piperack, Perfectos* and *Shiver* on one side, *Donnerkell, Dudelsack, Erstling, Flamme, Laubfrosch, Lux* and *Sagebock* on the other.[44]

Yet, while most of these innovations leant progressively more accuracy, efficiency, and sophistication to the bomber war, it was the undisputed, sustained courage of the crews, volunteers all, who brought these new technologies to the combat arena, night after night, that made the campaign a distinct if costly success. In the words of Canadian historians Brereton Greenhous and Hugh Halliday: "The bomber offensive of 1942 - 43 and the first months of 1944 was the Second World War's equivalent of the First World War's Somme and Passchendaele."[45]

NEW WORLD MEETS OLD WORLD

Crew structuring was significantly different between the American and British bomber forces, and the formality of rank was often much more

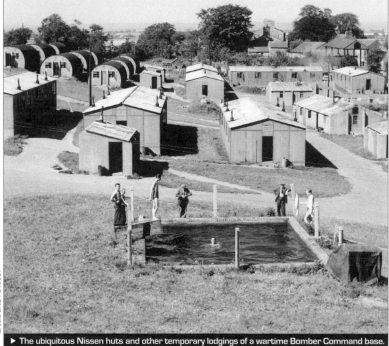

Credit: DND PL45597

▶ The ubiquitous Nissen huts and other temporary lodgings of a wartime Bomber Command base.

blurred in the American military. Essentially, Bomber Command consisted of two air forces; the pre-war, largely-commissioned, upper-middle class, public school Regular force, and the vast augmentation of largely non-commissioned volunteers from the lower-middle and working classes. Class structure was still very much an element of British military society during the Second World War, and senior leadership harboured grave concerns with respect to the dilution through battle casualties of their public school, upper-class core element. Regular force officers and senior NCOs were often exasperated by the appearance and conduct of many of the temporary officers and NCOs. This mindset is important, since it helps explain the relatively Draconian approach the RAF would later adopt in dealing with those who could no longer face combat, particularly the NCOs. Roger Coulombe, a pilot with 426 Squadron, would become famous as "The Berlin Kid," flying in a record twelve of the nineteen major attacks against that city during the August 1943-March 1944 time period. He would also be commissioned and win a coveted 'Immediate DFC' along the way. Coulombe recalls the early days of his tour at Linton, conducted initially as a sergeant pilot, his first commanding officer, and relations with the British administration staff generally:

I got along fine with the three British 'blokes' in my crew, but I didn't like the British administration officers all that much. We sure had to march stiff and straight in what they called the "attention area," that is, near the administration buildings, especially so if you were a non-commissioned officer. Otherwise, some English administration officer would open his office window and order you to get close so that he could get your name and reprimand you right on the spot. I never found them very sympathetic, except for Wing Commander Crooks, who was a wonderful and very sympathetic person, and he was British. We were blessed with good leadership in 426 Squadron during my tour of operations. Wing Commander Leslie Crooks, DSO, DFC, was the commanding officer when I arrived on squadron. He had done a first tour on *Wellingtons* but unfortunately, was shot down and killed during the raid on Peenemünde: the very first raid of his second tour while flying a *Lancaster* Mark II.[46]

In the American system, the pilot, co-pilot, bombardier, [except for the late-war toggliers] and navigator were almost always commissioned officers, while the flight engineer and the five gunners were virtually always sergeants in various grades. Under the British system, while the gunners and the flight engineer were usually not commissioned, particularly until later in the war, the pilot, navigator and the bomb-aimer may or may not have been officers. Since both the American and the British hierarchies felt that the pilot was the logical aircraft captain and crew commander, the British inconsistency of rank with respect to crew positions often led to awkward situations and additional stress if a junior pilot was attempting to discipline or coordinate senior crew members. Under the American system, although officers and NCOs slept in separate quarters, they usually ate and frequently socialized in All Ranks Messes, and their chain of command actively encouraged mixed-rank activities. In the British system, NCOs and officers, echoing the class system, were messed in strict segregation, although mixed crews often socialized in off-station venues. However, the British Executive frowned somewhat upon this practice, and, especially, upon any formally organized mixed-rank functions. In fact, a 1943 report on personnel issues went so far as to *attack* the practice of holding All Ranks dances at bomber stations. This reinforcement of social claims was frequently frustrating to the more egalitarian aircrew from the Dominions who were under RAF control, since their shared social values were much more akin to those of the Americans than those of the British:

The Commonwealth aircrew, especially, believed that it was their very intimacy with their crews, their indifference to rank, that often made them such strong teams in the air. An Australian from 50 Squadron cited the example of a distinguished young English ex-public school pilot who was killed in 1943. This boy, he said, was a classic example of an officer who never achieved complete cohesion with his crew, who won obedience only by the rings on his sleeves and not by force of personality. "He simply wouldn't have known how to go out screwing with his gunners in Lincoln on a Saturday night." In his memoirs, Harris argues that the English made the best aircrew, because they had the strongest sense of discipline. It was a difference of tradition.[47]

Whether the sentiment was widespread or sustained throughout the RAF that the 'Colonials' lacked discipline appears to be a matter of debate, but the observations of historian Max Hastings along this line are interesting, and perhaps they help explain why men from the Dominions were not frequently given command positions in Bomber Command outside their national formations, in *spite* of the fact that their proportional representation merited more of them. Thus, one is led to suspect that there was some cultural and social bias by the British Executive coming into play:

> To survive, brilliant flying was less important than an immense capacity for taking pains, avoiding unnecessary risks, and maintaining rigid discipline in the air. Canadians were highly regarded as individual aircrews, but incurred intense criticism as complete crews, as squadrons, as (eventually) their own No. 6 Group, because they were thought to lack the vital sense of discipline. A 50 Squadron gunner who was sent one night as a replacement with an all-Canadian crew came home terrified after circling the target while they sang "Happy Birthday to You" down the intercom to their 21-year-old pilot. Later in the war, 6 Group became notorious for indifference to radio-telephone instructions from the Master Bomber over the target.[48]

On top of the aforementioned dissatisfactions, the British occasionally exacerbated problems by infringing upon the jealously-guarded free time of the citizen-aircrew 'temporaries,' saddling them with extraneous disciplinary responsibilities for which they were neither trained nor inclined to accept. Again, quoting from the 1943 personnel report:

Aircrew are becoming more and more divorced from their legitimate leaders, and their officers are forgetting, if they ever learnt them, their responsibilities to their men. Aircrew personnel must be disabused of the idea that their sole responsibility is to fly... and to do this, their leisure hours must be more freely devoted to training and hard work.[49]

The problem here was that the old, Regular force pre-war RAF, just like the Regular force echelons of the other services, was applying its professional expectations to these 'citizen airmen,' who were, by and large, only planning to serve 'for the duration of hostilities.' Those same unrealistic expectations certainly also held true within the Canadian and American services, between the Regular force cadres and the militia types, the reservists, and those only in uniform for wartime service.

At this point of the story, readers need to be aware that for every man from the Dominions who had a wartime run-in with British authority, another has provided a specific example of British fairness, and generous acts of compassion and kindness to them abounded. Many felt that the multinational RAF squadrons were the absolute best way to serve, while others yearned to be exclusively with their own kind, governed by Canadian national regulations and policies. It appears, like so many of life's experiences, to have been very much an individual perception, driven in no small measure by the personality and the character of the officers under whom they served.[50]

A 1947 report by British psychologists Charles P. Symonds and Denis J. Williams on wartime psychological disorders in flying personnel discussed extensively the importance of leadership in helping airmen to accept and to carry the load of operational flying. Symonds and Williams found "... no exception to the opinion that good leadership was vital, and many thought it was the most important factor of all."[51] Canadian veterans, serving with both their national squadrons and with RAF formations, have emphasized that the wartime leadership was of a particularly high calibre generally, and that having the backing of the British citizenry was a formidable boost to their spirits.

LIFE AMONG THE BRITISH

Living conditions in wartime England also had an impact upon aircrew morale. The RAF, as part of the host nation, and its Canadian members therein, operated generally from at least somewhat established facilities, such

▶ The loneliest job. *Lancaster* rear gunner Pilot Officer Nuncie 'Nick' Leone from Toronto in his turret. Killed in action over Brunswick 14/15 January 1944.

Credit: DND PL26157

as those in Yorkshire and Lincolnshire. However, the accommodation on the expansion bases was frequently dingy and barren in the extreme. This state of affairs certainly also applied to most of the American bases, located largely in East Anglia. Jimmy Sheridan recalls his wartime quarters in Britain, and provides the reader with a precursory view of the food situation:

> I had a mixture of quarters. On some bases we lived in pre-war buildings that were like hotels – solid buildings. Others were Nissen huts which were adequate but usually uncomfortable – hot in summer – cold and damp in the winter. They were heated by stoves burning coke, which nobody seemed to know how to light or to keep going.

The occupants of the hut had to look after the stoves themselves, and with different flying hours, there was no one there to keep them properly stoked. This meant that coming in from night flying during the winter there was no heat in the hut, which resulted in damp sheets for the bed. I got chilblains in both heels at this camp. Went to the Doc and he more-or-less said, "Tough. Walk on your toes." I just toughed it out without losing any flying. It was at this camp we had a cement block building for a bath house – unheated in winter – snow on the ground – bath tub with wood pallet for a floor but hot and cold water. On a day off I would get to the nearest town and rent a hotel room to have a decent warm bath and bedroom.

As for food, it was adequate but of poor quality, but it was the best they could do, no doubt. It was then I learned beef could be cut paper thin. As for mutton, it came to be abhorred by all. But we survived. When listed to fly an operation, we were allowed one whole egg cooked any way we wished – the only time we saw an egg – otherwise it was powdered egg all the way.

Once I got on squadron, we got a pre-war building, which was great. Three officers to a room with shared bath facilities – good lounge rooms and dining room, too. We even had batman and laundry services...[52]

Jim Northrup of 415 Squadron similarly recalls life at East Moor, from where he flew his tour of operations:

Life on the squadron was pleasant. You were out of the petty crap of Training Command and things were much more relaxed. We trained continuously on abandoning an aircraft, dingy drill in the pool, fighter affiliation and cross-country trips for the newer crews. The food was not the greatest but you could survive on it and we could always get a decent meal in York. However, to this day, I don't eat liver, lamb or Brussels sprouts. Aircrew on ops always had bacon and eggs before and after a trip. They would only serve powdered milk as the local milk was unpasteurized. When I was on OTU in the Midlands, a very pretty girl of about sixteen had a little stand set up beside the farm house where she sold glasses of fresh milk for a shilling. We had to walk by her on the way to the airdrome and everybody would have a glass. She must have done very well as most of us gave her two shillings, one for the milk and one for the smile. Our barracks were about a mile from the Mess, dispersed in the trees. They were fairly cool in winter, each room having a little round stove, and the amount of heat generated depended upon your ability to burn the 'clinkers' they called coke. Power was turned off at 10:00 PM, and if you were up at 3:00 AM for a daylight op, it was quite an art to be able to shave in the dark. On a normal day, you got up at 7:00 AM and reported to the flight commander by 9:00 AM as to the status of your crew. This was then given to the CO, so he knew how many crews were available for operations. If ops were on that night, the crews selected would know by 9:30 AM so that they could check their aircraft and then rest until briefing time. Those not flying would have some training laid on. The station was then closed to anyone leaving the station, which in some ways was silly, as often when we were in York whooping it up, the taxi drivers would come into the pubs and the dance hall and loudly announce that all aircrew were to return to their stations as ops were on.

Your laundry was something you had to look after yourself, and I found a lovely lady in Sutton-on-the-Forest to do mine. I thought of her as being quite old, but she probably was only forty or so...

Our transport on the squadron was limited to a canvas-covered stake truck and one old bus. In 1986, I started to organize a function to put up a marker at East Moor, and a ground crew type wrote me from Quebec, asking me if I remembered the beautiful red-haired girl who drove the bus. He then went on to say he had married this girl and could never understand why none of the aircrew had made a play for her. I wrote and congratulated him on his good fortune and explained that on the way out to our aircraft our minds were fully occupied on the operation, and on returning, we were initially too tired to do much thinking about girls. Actually, I remembered her very well as she was not only very pretty, she was very pleasant. Our ground crews worked very hard and a Yorkshire winter is not a pleasant thing. They built a small shelter by the dispersal pens so they could get out of the weather and warm up. I had the same ground crew all during my tour of operations. They were a hard working bunch and my aircraft was always ready to go. They kept it clean and there were never any oil streaks around the engine cowlings. To them, it was their aircraft and their crew that was flying it. Once a month I took them to *The Blacksmith's Arms* for beer and lunch. The pub always put up a splendid spread for us and the boys really appreciated it...[53]

The aircrew were not always housed on base, and although billeting on the economy could be somewhat charming, it also brought its own problems, as Roger Coulombe recollects from his time at Linton:

As sergeant pilots with 426 Squadron, I was billeted in an old peacetime manor, a couple of miles from the station, that had been requisitioned for the aircrew. We were quartered two to a very small room with very narrow bunks that had three separate 'cookies' for a mattress, and a sort of a round pillow that looked like part of the trunk of a tree, and was as hard. On getting up in the morning, we had stiff necks and would often find we were lying on only one of the cookies, the other two having shifted about. We also had no sheets, just a gray wool blanket.

Apart from the uncomfortable sleeping accommodation, the worst threat to our night's sleep and health was the enormous quantity of rats. During the time I resided in Aldwark Manor, I slept every night holding a fire poker in one of my hands to fight the rats in case of attacks. I even saw a big rat eating one of my chocolate bars, which was lying in a chair just inches from my face. My presence in bed did not seem to disturb him one bit. The rats were running up and down the stairs as you entered the main entrance at night. They could be in the bathroom eating soap where you went to shave in the morning. You had to chase them away if you wanted to be able to shave. I know of at least one gunner of a crew who was bitten on a foot by a rat who had gotten under the blanket in his bunk.

There were so many rats in the basement that, if you ever had to go there, you could see them running all over the water pipes, even in twos. I had nightmares about being attacked by rats for several years after the war, and they only eventually stopped after six or seven years...[54]

The austere quarters were, however, for the most part, just a place to 'crash' between operations, wartime leave policy was as generous as possible to the combat

Credit: Author's collection

▶ Two stellar German night fighter aces, *Major* Heinz-Wolfgang Schnaufer and *Oberstleutnant* Hans-Joachim Jabs in front of a Messerschmitt Bf 110G.

crews, and the local distractions were plentiful, the host citizens, generally warm and generous. Howard Ripstein, a wireless air gunner on 426 Squadron, recalls:

> Operational aircrew were granted one week of leave out of every six and Lord Nuffield paid for rail travel anywhere in the UK. Generally we went to London. Personally, I went to visit a Canadian family in Minchinhampton, Gloucestershire, for R and R after about three days of the hectic life in the Big City. ...Locally, York was a fun place and the ladies one met in *Betty's Bar* and the *De Grey Rooms*, a dance hall, were delightful and frequently easy lays. While in London, and while I was and always have been a great believer in inter-service co-operation, I was never interested in any liaison with *The Piccadilly*

Commandos, who, for about two pounds, would do the naughty deed and likely give one a dose of the clap...[55]

Generally similar sentiments were expressed by Ron Cassels, a wartime navigator on 428 "Ghost" Squadron, and they echo the feelings of the vast majority of Canadians who served in Britain:

> The war gave many of us the opportunity to see the beautiful British Isles and see many places with historic significance. We had the opportunity to meet the local people, many of whom invited us into their homes. The ordinary folk had the habit of going to their pub at night and having one or two beers, playing some darts and having a restful sociable evening. We were young and taking part in a bitter conflict. On our nights off we went out to the local pubs. There is no doubt that we took them over and in the course of doing so we drank too much. The regulars never complained. They sat back in the corner with their pint and kept quiet while we used their dart board, and sang our dirty and boisterous songs. Our noisy behavior must have been most annoying but I never heard them complain. When we went on leave we crowded on the trains and didn't care what compartment we were in. Tourist tickets were as good as first class until the conductor made you move, which was very seldom. The British made us welcome and used their limited rations to give us tea. I often think of the poor farmer whose farm yard was just behind our dispersal. Every time old "Z" for Zombie started, he had a hurricane across his yard. We did our flying at all hours and it must have been next to impossible for him and his family to get a good night's sleep. The British people treated us very well. [But] there were a few that regarded us as colonials. We were not from the upper class or the right school and therefore should not be officers or leaders...[56]

Along with regular leave, special leave of several days was given as frequently as was possible operationally. Headquartered in London, the excellent Lady Ryder Leave Organization placed Commonwealth aircrew as honoured guests in many stately British homes, as well as with other Britons from all walks of life and social standings. These specific wartime acts of generosity and hospitality are still remembered with great affection by many surviving veterans, and numerous long-term friendships formed this way in wartime have withstood the test of time.

CHAPTER TWO

FOOD, GLORIOUS FOOD

While quartering was largely a 'luck of the draw' situation, the Americans were decidedly better off in provisioning matters than their British and Commonwealth counterparts. It must be emphasized that there were many, many food shortages in wartime Britain, and the lot of the aircrew, particularly those on operations, was decidedly better than the average citizen, who accepted their austere wartime conditions generally with stoicism, grace, and good humour. Although with respect to content, the British were providing as best they could for their Commonwealth and Allied wartime guests, there is no doubt that British wartime food was particularly galling to the men from the Dominions, who, like the Americans, were conditioned to generally much better fare in terms of both quantity and quality. A key difference here was that the Americans provided their troops with foodstuffs imported direct from North America, whereas the Canadians were provisioned mostly from British stocks through the British messing system. For the Canadians, the dissatisfaction started early, usually on the troop ship crossings to Britain, and it maintained a generally predictable level thereafter. Sometimes, however, the Atlantic crossing was particularly unpleasant:

> It was the most distasteful messing ever encountered in my Service life. One could taste sand grit in all the greens served which, to top it all, were boiled to a 'glop' soup in a large open kettle from which the contents were ladled by an enormous cook who refused to wear anything but a singlet. The weather was warm and at each bend of his bountiful body, sweat droplets would fall in the soup making ringlets on the greasy surface. Finally, this reached all proportion of decency and I therefore contacted our medical officer, one Dr. Rankin, who applied his authority. Conditions improved, but not totally.[57]

> We now eat with the RAF. The technical name for this unseasoned pig-swill we're fed is 'plain wholesome food.' The lunches are edible but uninteresting. The other meals aren't big enough to keep a canary in good voice. And the Mess stinks to high heaven, a greasy lavatory smell that is enough to kill the finest appetite, mother. You may think I'm joking, still, this is the plain, simple truth – *we're hungry all the time*. I'm speaking for myself and Rusty and for every other Canadian on this accursed station.[58]

At one training station in England, the Orderly Officer was a real 'pukka' type, complete with handle-bar moustache. One day, we were served tripe, and when the Orderly Officer asked for complaints, my buddy stood up. Over marched the Orderly Officer and the Orderly Sergeant. "Yes? What is it?" the officer demanded. Pointing at the tripe, my friend asked, "Is this to be eaten or has it already been eaten?" He got twenty-one days Confined to Barracks.[59]

The food was bloody awful on the station. I haven't eaten a Brussels sprout since 1945. The coffee was weak so we drank tea, of some unidentified blend. The sausages were 80 percent bread, and the eggs powdered. Decent steaks were not available. Were it not for the Black Market and parcels from home I would have starved on the RAF rations. After an operation we got real fried eggs and good bacon with rum-laced coffee, which I can still taste. Once, a dietician decided that we should be served poached eggs, which almost caused a riot.[60]

However, as the saying went at the time, "There's a war on, you know!" That reality appeared to forgive a lot of transgressions and shortcomings, and most airmen soldiered on with resignation and a sense of being in it together, grumbling about food being, at any rate, the serviceman's universal prerogative. Roger Coulombe remembers the food at Linton, but puts the situation in perspective:

The food in the Sergeants Mess was minimal. Of course, many supply ships were sunk by U-Boats coming across the Atlantic Ocean. Therefore, a lot of the food destined for us went to the bottom of the sea. However, the English civilian population was no better off. They made great sacrifices and they were very brave and cheerful in spite of their miseries. I think the civilian population was admirable. And the civilians we met at the pubs were always very pleasant and sympathetic. They seemed to like us Canadians.[61]

However, occasionally, Canadian airmen caught a glimpse of how their American counterparts were faring, and it certainly provoked a certain amount of nostalgic envy. Sid Philp recalls:

Most of 6 Group's airfields were located in the Vale of York where, during the winter months, it was not uncommon for fog to descend during the early morning hours and obscure the whole countryside.

If that occurred, as it frequently did, when bombers were returning from a night mission, they had to be diverted to other airfields in the south. One such night (or morning) we had to land at Bury St. Edmonds, an American bomber station. What an eye-opener! What generosity! I had been in England for about a year-and-a-half and had become accustomed to good, but not great, RAF food with its rationed amount of rabbit stew or sawdust sausages and Brussels sprouts or powdered eggs. The first thing I noticed when I entered their dining hall was a sign saying, "Take all you want but eat all you take." Then the first meal served up was frankfurters and sauerkraut. For me, at that time, that was a veritable delicacy! But the best was yet to come; for dessert we had real fresh fruit salad with, if we wanted, ice cream. Wow! Later, we were sitting around the Officers' Mess just shooting the breeze; the Americans thought we were strange because we stayed away from the bar. Then they discovered that we were not supposed to take cash with us on our operations and we were virtually penniless. At that, they told us that the bar was open to us and we could have whatever we wanted for as long as we wanted. We didn't over-partake of their hospitality, but we weren't terribly annoyed that the weather kept us there for three days...[62]

Others had positive recollections of the wartime British food, and like so many things in life, experiences appeared to depend upon specific circumstances. Reg Patterson, a late-war stalwart flying with 101 Squadron, recalls his situation, and also some convenient denial exercises on the part of his navigator:

The food in general in our Officers' Mess was very good. Our sergeant-cook had been a chef at the Trocadero in London before the war. He certainly did his best with what he had. We always had what was called an operational meal last thing before we went down to briefing and thence off to the aircraft. It usually consisted of an egg and some sandwiches. Aircrew were the only people that got eggs. It almost seemed like a bribe. The sandwiches were quite often large ham sandwiches. My navigator was a Jewish boy from Windsor, Ontario, Flying Officer Morley Ornstein. He was a big fellow with an even bigger appetite. He would dig into those sandwiches and grin all around, saying, "I don't know where they get their chickens from around here, but they sure are good." As a navigator, he was superb...[63]

For the crews of Bomber Command, the full risks associated with combat flying generally were not fathomed until operations commenced. Relatively early in the bombing campaign, the RAF determined that "... an average casualty rate of five percent per mission was considered to be the most that the bomber crews could bear without faltering over any prolonged length of time."[64] Also, experience gained from the Western Front during the Great War had driven home the value of front-line rotations, followed by periods of rest from combat. "If men were going to be able to sustain themselves during night after night of arduous and extraordinarily dangerous flying, some sort of rotation policy was necessary."[65]

Prior to the spring of 1943, the *generally* accepted first operational tour length was approximately 200 cumulative flying hours on combat operations, followed normally by a minimum of six months service in a training or related staff billet, followed by a second and roughly-equal operational tour. The 200 hours of combat flying time would equate *roughly* to thirty operational trips.[66] Aircrew were removed from combat operations by death or severe injury, by enemy incarceration, at the request of higher authority, or at the discretion of the member's commanding officer. This latter, highly subjective category was meant to determine when an individual had done enough, one who did not fit within the earlier boundaries, but needed a respite from combat. However, this practice was frequently held hostage by Service needs, and it occasionally lacked the application of even-handed common sense, a quality that was not uniformly demonstrated throughout Bomber Command, especially during the early war years. There is also little doubt that an element of favourable bias, particularly when applied to commissioned or pre-war Regular force aircrew, was at play occasionally. The system cried out for standardization. And so, as was briefly mentioned in Chapter One, it was decided that operational flying needed to be broken up into manageable portions of time, from which there must be a reasonable chance of survival. "It was generally accepted that it should be drawn at a point which offered a '50-50 chance.' "[67] It should be noted, however, that the actual odds against survival were held somewhat in confidence by the Executive of the RAF during the war years.[68] That said, as we have seen, those odds varied considerably at various times throughout the bombing campaign. Some individuals have maintained that losses and loss rates were deliberately withheld from the public during the war, while countering claims have been made that the Executive was totally transparent about the losses. As often happens, the truth lies somewhere in the middle. While the RAF did not go out of its way to routinely report losses and loss rates to its aircrew, there is no evidence of a deliberate attempt by authority to deceive the crews that the odds of survival

▶ Life goes on. Scratch baseball on the flight line in front of a taxiing *Halifax III*.

Credit: DND PL28521

were actually better than perceptions or reality dictated. For one thing, in a re-flection of the *usual* transparency of British war policy, the BBC Home Service accurately broadcast individual raid losses on a routine basis, and the crews would have known roughly how many aircraft had participated in any given operation. Also, the overall strength and compositions of various raids were made public, at least, on occasion, and they would have been briefed routinely to participating crews.[69] Thus, loss rates, although not dwelled upon, would have been easy to calculate. Kenneth McDonald elaborates:

> We knew what the chances were from personal experience on squad-rons, from the numbers reported missing each day by the BBC, from word of mouth accounts of casualties elsewhere within 4 Group, and obviously from passage through the Heavy Conversion Units of course after course of aircrew to squadrons.

> What we knew instinctively was confirmed many years afterwards when the "Diaries"[70] published the mathematical chances of a crew surviving fifty operational flights at various rates of loss. At the high-est rate shown, four percent, out of 100 crews, thirteen would survive. Also cited is that "The casualty rate during the coming period, that of the opening operations of the Pathfinder Force (which was when we

started operating), would be 4.6 percent." We didn't know this at the time, but the average loss rate on the trips we did in that same period was 5.7 percent.[71]

With respect to codifying a tour length, Harris and his staff had grave concerns with respect to the possible perception that a contractual agreement was being entered into with the airmen under his command, and these concerns were not without substance. However, on 8 May 1943, Bomber Command codified operational bomber service into two combat tours of thirty sorties and a maximum of twenty sorties respectively for the Main Force, with an intervening staff or instructional tour of duty of normally not less than six months. Other operational tour lengths were established in the other commands at the same time. Concurrently, Sir Arthur Harris also reduced another significant source of anxiety to his crews by curtailing operational flying in clearly unsuitable weather, a policy turnaround which undoubtedly saved many lives and aircraft from needless accidents. "The tour of operations, with its definite promise of relief, was a sheet anchor of morale in Bomber Command. It made the unbelievable endurable."[72] However, the vision of the average aircrew member was extremely short, and few grasped at the time that their operational flying would not be completed after the first tour, until late in the war, when trained manpower surpluses for the most part eliminated the need for a second tour of operations. This frame of mind was undoubtedly a psychological defence mechanism.[73]

THE STRESS OF SUSTAINED COMBAT

Inevitably there were some, not many overall, who could not face the continued stress, and these occurrences usually were associated with periods of extensive operations and high combat losses. The spring of 1943 and the winter of 1943/1944, which corresponded with pitched, concentrated battles for the Ruhr and Berlin respectively, proved to be particularly problematic.[74]

It is fair to say that the unique characteristics of the strategic bombing campaign placed extraordinary strains upon the participating airmen. The challenges often appeared overwhelming, and the pressure to prevail was relentless. For many, the only meaningful goal was survival, and personal experience coupled with the grim mathematical statistics often compounded to warn that survival was doubtful at best. Small wonder that aircrew were rendered highly vulnerable to both the physical and the mental symptoms of stress.

In their initial report on RAF psychological disorders, Charles Symonds and Denis Williams noted particularly the impact of physical fatigue when added to heightened levels of anxiety.[75] The combat mission itself imposed many stresses on the crews. Operational conditions, such as weather, duration of the operation, the nature and the intensity of the defences and the frequently hazardous return trip certainly contributed to the stress.[76] However, most aircrew found "... the anticipation of a raid as great a load as the raid itself, unless it happened to be unusually hazardous."[77] Other qualified observers echoed these findings, and both the American and the British camps cited briefings, cancellations, especially *late* cancellations, as having pivotal, even disastrous effects upon morale.

> No one who saw the mask of age which mantled the faces of these young men after a period of continued standing by, punctuated by inevitably false alarms, is likely to forget it. Their pallor, the hollows in their cheeks, and beneath their eyes, and the utter fatigue with which they lolled listlessly in chairs about their Mess, were eloquent of the exhaustion and frustration which they felt. In ten hours they seemed to have aged as many years.
>
> ~ Dr. D. Stafford-Clark
> Wartime Bomber Command Medical Officer[78]

Other factors were cited as contributing to stress, including the alternating nature of the air war, and crews recall the unreal contrast of returning to a peaceful, pastoral England after spending agonizing hours over Germany in the most horrific conditions:

> Life on the squadron was seldom far from fantasy. We might, at eight, be in a chair beside a fire, but at ten, in an empty world above a floor of cloud. Or at eight, walking in Barnetby with a girl whose nearness denied all possibility of sudden death at twelve.[79]

One common denominator of stress to the airmen was the recurring jolt brought about by suddenly empty living quarters and dining facilities; mute testaments to the sudden and violent passing of friends:

> Their attitude to losses and the deaths of friends was particularly striking. It was one of supreme realism, of matter-of-fact acceptance of what everyone knew perfectly well was inevitable. They did not plunge into outspoken expression of their feelings, nor did they

display any compromise with conventional reticence about the fact of violent death. They said, "Too bad... sorry about old so-and-so...Rotten luck." Their regret was deep and sincere, but not much displayed or long endured. They were apt and able to talk of dead and missing friends, before mentioning their fate, just as they talked of anyone else or themselves. It took the loss of particular friends or leaders, flight commanders or squadron commanders, to produce a marked reaction among a squadron. Then they might feel collectively distressed, have a few drinks because of that, go on to a party and feel better.

~ Dr. D. Stafford-Clark[80]

During the late evening on December 3 1943, a new crew arrived from nearby Topcliffe having just been posted to 429 Squadron. Duly reporting to the Orderly Room for 'billets,' they were informed the NCOs' aircrew billets were all filled and they would have to bunk in the Airmens' Quarters for the night. They were then cheerfully informed that an 'operation' was in progress that night and that there would be plenty of space for them in the morning. This shook them up, especially when they saw all the NCO aircrew queued up to get their 'operational supper' that night at the Sergeants' Mess, all looking very serious and grim, with no horseplay or joking.[81]

Perhaps one of the most profound stressors of the bombing campaign, both to aircrew and to ground crew, was the psychological impact of battle-damaged aircraft returning with dead or wounded on board. At RAF Station Woodbridge, *which was only one of the RAF's master emergency airfields*, 516 killed or wounded airmen were returned in 1720 aircraft in a one-year period from January 1943 to January 1944.[82] The following excerpt, although taken from an American airman's diary, typifies the carnage involved in these occurrences:

B-17 *Tinkertoy* ground-looped just off the runway. *Tinkertoy* had her nose shot out and the pilot had his head blown off by a 20mm cannon shell. There was hardly a square inch of the entire cockpit that was not covered with blood and brain tissue. One half of his face and a portion of his cervical vertebra were found just in front of the bomb bay. The decapitation was complete.[83]

Symonds and Williams also concluded that there were "... three critical periods in which men are likely to show the effects of stress, as well as a critical period

▶ Group Captain 'Johnnie' Fauquier when commanding 617 'Dambuster' Squadron late in the war, posing beside an enormous 22,000 pound *Grand Slam* earthquake penetration bomb.

Credit: DND PL44700

after exceptional strain has been experienced." These were identified as being after the first few trips, when the enormity of what an individual was up against had been digested, around the twelfth-to-fourteenth mission, when the individual felt he had used up his quota of luck, the tour-end was still far off, and he could not go on, and within a few operations of tour completion, when men generally acquired a renewed sense of hope that they might actually survive.[84] Many surviving aircrew members have said they experienced some variation of this pattern, although many denied having experienced Symonds and Williams 'mid-tour slump,' and there were also many exceptions and mutations to their generalized findings:

> That increasing of tension generally did exist only for the first few (five or six) trips. After that, particularly if the initial trips had been "hairy," a feeling of invincibility developed and a little complacency set in. I suspect that complacency may have led to more than a few mishaps. That attitude continued and grew until the end of a crew's tour was in sight. At that point there was a complete reversal and a numbing tension took over and intensified until the final flight was completed.
>
> ~ Sid Philp[85]

Sid Philp's comment on a feeling of invincibility following from difficult initial combat operations is interesting, particularly as his own first mission was far from being uneventful:

> The first bombing raid that I took part in was on the 21st of January 1944; the target, Magdeburg. It occurred during the period that has come to be known as the Battle of Berlin. Our planned route took us east across the North Sea, then a feint towards Berlin before turning south to the target. The return trip was to be a beeline west over a heavily defended piece of real estate, across the Frisian Islands, then the safety of the North Sea and back to base. There was to be very little moon, but also very little cloud cover to hide in. The low murmurs from the veteran crews at briefing implied that this was not going to be a 'piece of cake.'
>
> There must have been a minor delay in take-off that night because I can recall all the *Halifax* aircraft lined up along the perimeter track with their engines cut, waiting for the Very pistol signal to take-off. I was pacing nervously in the dark alongside the aircraft when an unidentified officer approached me and made some inane, but supposedly comforting remark about the weather. I recall replying, using, in my nervousness, a flood of choice four-letter words. The officer then turned away without further remarks. Several days later, much to my chagrin, I met that officer again. He was the squadron padre!
>
> Our skipper that night was fairly new to the rest of us. Our first pilot had not returned from his initial 'second dicky' trip and we had flown only a few hours with this guy. This lack of joint training was to lead to some problems. It was only later that I discovered that I had been giving him 'True' courses to set on the dead reckoning (DR) compass and he had been setting them on the magnetic compass and was flying magnetic courses. The result was that we were constantly heading north of our planned route and our final leg south towards the target seemed to take forever. We were, of course, late in arriving over the target, which was well lit up by then.
>
> ... Shortly after we left the target area, we had our first fighter attack and the pilot attempted his first 'corkscrew.' This was a violent manoeuvre that was designed to make shooting deflection impossible and

to lose the stalker. Well, his attempt was so extreme that he put the aircraft into a spin. I can recall my navigation instruments floating around in front of me while I was suspended between my seat and my desk. Now, you weren't supposed to be able to pull a *Halifax* out of a spin, but somehow, our guy accomplished it. While we shook that first fighter, two others found us later and we again had to take evasive action, but now our skipper was more circumspect and the action was somewhat less violent. Before crossing the coast, we were coned by searchlights and were lit up like stage performers; at the same time we were hit fairly badly by ack-ack. One piece went right through the rear turret without touching the gunner; another piece ripped out some wiring next to the engineer; a third piece tore a ridge in the outside of the wireless operator's boot; and yet another spent piece landed on my desk. More evasive action let us out of that predicament and the crew got nary a scratch! However, our tanks received minor holes and we were losing petrol. We did make it back to England, but we had to make a landing at an emergency 'drome on the southeast coast. Just as we leveled off before touchdown, our engines cut due to lack of petrol. We rolled to the end of the runway and had to be hauled by a tractor from there.

I do not recall being frightened at any time while in the air and was able, I believe, to carry out my duties efficiently. However, once out of the kite and into a bus, I started to shake as though I had a severe chill. The shaking kept up until I arrived in the debriefing room and some clever soul, seeing my condition, handed me a mug of coffee with a very stiff shot of rum in it. I don't think any of the rest of the crew experienced the shakes then and I never did again. The next day we went out to the aircraft and counted 85 holes in it.[86]

It was perhaps understandable that surviving these early perils could have led to some form of crew over-confidence. However, for Murray Peden, the initial reaction to operations was quite different:

I cannot subscribe, from my own recollected experience, to the theory of three main phases in the level of stress from operational flying. I do recall that on our very first op, which was a 'Nickel' dropping leaflets at Montargis in France, I was very conscious that this was my first time over enemy territory, and I wondered anxiously how I would react to hostile action directed my way, most concerned that I should not panic and do something that would stamp me or my crew as less than press-on types. At age 19, it was the highest tension I'd ever had to endure. And it was acute.

Fortunately, the flak we saw that night was quite distant for the most part so that we by-passed that anticipated strain. It was still a new and tremendous strain to be flying at night in the enemy's ball park, knowing that at any moment a Ju 88 could sweep in on us and pound us with cannon and machine gun fire. The tension stemming from that knowledge one struggled to keep concealed in the background. Nevertheless it was there, as it was throughout one's whole tour...

Next we converted onto *Stirlings* and joined the squadron for the balance of our tour. First off, a new skipper had to fly two operations as second dickie with an experienced crew, from which he was supposed to derive the benefit of seeing how veteran pilots coped when Main Force hit a major German target. My first such flight came the same day we got to the squadron. I was hustled to briefing before I even had a chance to park my luggage in a hut. The target was Hanover, and I was to do the trip, my first operational flight in a *Stirling*, with a crew that had chalked up about 23 ops. They turned out to be a highly nervous and voluble lot, and their skipper, in my eyes, did not keep them under proper control. From a tension point of view, the trip started inauspiciously as far as I was concerned, first with the sight of a nearby *Stirling* on fire in the air, slowly sinking before our eyes to its doom on the ground, then, only moments later, with a near-collision between our own *Stirling* and one on a converging course my experienced skipper failed to see. It left me, the man under instruction, to seize the controls myself at the very last second and dive sharply, averting by the narrowest of margins the demise of two more *Stirling* crews. After a long and poorly carried out trip, highlighted by a glaring navigational error, we landed back at Chedburgh base, only to be vigorously strafed, seconds after we reached our dispersal, by an intruding Ju 88. It abruptly shot up a landing *Stirling*, then veered and whipped the terrain in front of it with long and shattering bursts of cannon and machine gun fire, all the while dropping a small flood of butterfly bombs, many of which exploded viciously as the German pilot swept by. I got up from pressing myself into the concrete during

Credit: RCAF photo

▶ Squadron Leader 'Reg' Lane in the cockpit of *The Ruhr Express*, the first Canadian-built *Lancaster* Mk.X to be ferried to England, August 1943.

this frightening display with my heart racing and feeling not at all sanguine about how easy it was going to be to soldier through a tour of 30 such operations...[87]

By late-1943, the sky over whatever portion of the Reich was hosting a visit from Bomber Command on any given night was witness to a pyrotechnic display of great intensity and variety. Along with all the ground fires, the bomb bursts, the flak, the searchlights, the target indicators (TIs) and other markers, in 1943, the Pathfinders temporarily started using route marking flares to aid the Main Force's journey to the target. However, the procedure, well intended, did more harm than good as it telegraphed the operation's primary flight path to the waiting German night fighters and flak. While the route illumination practice was soon temporarily discontinued,[88] the lesson was not lost upon the Germans. Shortly thereafter, flare shells fired from below and parachute flares dropped from above helped visually cue the German night fighters to their prey. For the pilots, there was no avoiding the observation of this frightening firework display in the target area, since they had to have total situational awareness to respond to directions from other crew members, and to scan the night skies at all times for threats. Murray Peden recalls the bomb run from a pilot's perspective:

> Part of the standard grist on most trips was that air-to-air combats would break out from time to time, all too often with the tell-tale flaring finish that marked the deaths of another bomber crew. All this

was but the lead-up to each trip's main event, the bombing run itself. At this point, close to the target, the bomber emerged from the precarious shelter of darkness and for five or more minutes flew toward and over the target in what was euphemistically called 'the area of illumination' centred over the city. Tom Paine, could he have looked ahead, might have thought his expression about these being the times that tried men's souls very apt. Heading straight and level with the bomb-doors open toward the best concentration of Target Indicators, one flew across a vast panorama studded with bursting flak in the air and bomb-bursts and raging fires on the ground. This progression through a nightmarish scene one made in the glare of a host of chandelier flares dropped by German fighters far above. On each occasion, I strove mightily to ignore these fearsome surroundings for what seemed an endless period, and to concentrate single-mindedly upon controlling the aircraft and responding delicately to the bomb aimer's directions for minor course corrections. Provided that one was not attacked by fighters, the bomb run was the supreme ordeal of the operation. A fighter attack, bringing you face-to-face with death, up real close, was worse. Even when the bombing run was uneventful – a classification we applied to it even when, on one occasion, we received some minor flak damage in the course of it – the welcome "Bombs gone!" from the bomb aimer was more than welcome. These bombing runs were not experiences I could look forward to without a trace of fear... not at any stage.[89]

Sid Philp also remembers arriving at a similar conclusion during the course of his first operation:

The only time the navigator was not busy was over the target area, since the bomb aimer was then in charge. That night I took the opportunity to take a peek at the target. My first sight was of the line of fighter flares along both sides of our track to the target. These were very bright flares, suspended on parachutes, that were designed to illuminate the bombers for the fighters. They gave the same appearance as when heading into a flare path for a night landing. Amongst the flares were puffs of bursting flak. Down below were the twinkling lights of bomb bursts and of myriad fires. Shooting up through it all were lines of flak tracer bullets. It was a beautiful and, at the same time, a frightening sight. I decided I had had enough beauty for one night and I crawled back down to my enclosed "office." I never again looked out at the target area...[90]

In summation, with respect to the stressful ordeal that constituted a wartime operational tour in Bomber Command, Dr. D. Stafford-Clark concluded:

> There *was* no single moment of security from take-off to touchdown, but often the sight of other aircraft hit by flak and exploding in the air, or plummeting down blazing to strike the ground in an incandescent wreck. The chances of any particular individual surviving his thirty trips alive, unwounded, and without having been forced down over enemy territory were generally accepted by the aircrew themselves as being one-in-five.[91]

LACK OF MORAL FIBRE

In the RAF, considerable emphasis was placed upon preventative treatment whenever possible. Returning crews were met with fringe amenities not normally available to the rank-and-file, including hot drinks, cigarettes, doughnuts, bacon-and-egg meals and post-operation spirits. Crews were encouraged to relax and to relate their experiences, with a view to venting some of the most immediate reactions to combat. Liberal leave policies were standard practice. However, for some of those in need of a respite, and for whom leave did not solve their anxieties, stronger measures were often required. These men were taken off flying duties for short periods, and then given additional food, warmth, drink and sedatives. The British strongly emphasized the value of uninterrupted sleep, and so, the administration of 'great whacking doses' of sodium barbital was not uncommon. In a large number of cases, this form of treatment was effective, since irrational fears and horrifying mental images were often quickly diffused.[92]

Cursory review suggests that nearly two-thirds of all Bomber Command's stress casualties were treated effectively by employing these methods at a local level.[93] For those who required more formal treatment, this was carried out at several major neuropsychiatric centres, although RAF psychiatric specialists were always in short supply at the time, and extensive periods devoted to psychotherapy or psychoanalysis would have been impossible burdens to place upon an unprepared system. Their fundamental goal was, obviously, to return as many airmen as possible to flying operations.

Yet, invariably, there was a very small minority of aircrew who could not prevail. Within the RAF during the Second World War, the Lack of Moral Fibre (LMF) designation was employed "... as a means of handling aircrew who would not or could not fly for reasons that were considered unjustifiable."[94] The LMF Memorandum, issued first in 1941 and then revised, in somewhat-clarified forms, in 1943 and again in 1945, targeted "...members of aircrews who forfeit the confidence of their commanding officers in their determination and reliability in the face of danger in the air, owing either to their conduct or to their admission that they feel unable to face up to their duties."[95] Aircrew who could not face the strain of operations were classified firstly as those who were medically fit, but who had forfeited their commanding officer's confidence without being subjected to exceptional operational stresses. A second category was reserved for those who were medically unfit solely on account of displaying nervous symptoms, but again, without having been subjected to exceptional stresses, while a third category covered anyone who was medically unfit and did not qualify for the first two categories.

Mild neurosis cases could be sent to the RAF Convalescent Depot Blackpool, or to the Officers Hospital Torquay, but the more severe cases were sent to a Not Yet Diagnosed Nervous/Neuropsychiatric (NYDN) Centre for treatment by specialists. However, Bomber Command generally advocated a harsh approach toward the treatment of neuropsychiatric (NP) casualties. Although some doctors favoured immediate release from the flying service if the problem appeared to be constitutional, or due to a faulty upbringing, and psychotherapy would not likely be successful, their Principal Medical Officer expressed the opinion that, "...temperamentally unsuitable members of aircrews... those lacking confidence... should be given no sympathy and should be dealt with by the Executive as early as possible."[96] Thus, the consequences of being branded LMF could be cataclysmic. And there is ample evidence to suggest that officers were treated more humanely than non-commissioned aircrew; again, a by-product of the British class system and the presumption, in some cases, that the lack of public school values would predispose NCOs to failure. John Lewis was asked if he had ever seen evidence of an LMF case during his long and distinguished operational service:

> We were all aware of the consequences of being convicted of LMF. We knew that punishment would be swift and severe; that you would be grounded immediately, stripped of your wings and rank badges, usually in a parade square ceremony before your entire squadron or wing. You might be allowed to remain in the air force on ground duties, but

▶ Wing Commander Bill Swetman, a gallant airman and popular leader, at the controls of his *Lancaster* while he commanded 426 (RCAF) Squadron in 1943.

Credit: DND PL28449

more than likely you would be sent home to Canada, dishonourably discharged and in disgrace. Once, on another station, I witnessed this punishment and the scene stays with me still. After it was all over and the parade had been dismissed, the young man continued to stand there, alone in the middle of the square, head bowed, eyes averted, absently picking at the strands of thread where his NCO stripes used to be. No one approached to offer him comfort.[97]

It is interesting to note that generally aircrew veterans held a compassionate attitude towards those who failed to *prevail*, but were ruthless with those who failed to *attempt*, or those who deliberately *avoided* the difficult missions.

Other distinguished veterans have offered thoughts about the LMF process that have been perhaps somewhat tempered by time, and also, how fear could gnaw away at a crew's self-confidence:

As for the LMF cases, I don't have the same attitude as I had during the war. Now I know about the great stress under which operational crews were living before and during raids flying over enemy territory, often aboard aircraft without any operable defences. I am not personally aware of any case of LMF in my own 426 Squadron during the time of my tour of operations. It is possible, however, that some crew members refused to carry on with operational flying.

Nevertheless, I now know enough to be able to understand that flying on German targets during the Second World War could induce enough fear in a crew member to drive him out of his mind and make him mentally sick. I have seen crews on board the bus that was taking us out to the dispersal to board our aircraft when we were going out on raids to Berlin who looked absolutely terrified. Their faces were as white as sheets! They seemed to be in a state of shock. I never did see crews that were petrified prior to taking off for a raid on Berlin come back from those raids. They were always reported missing...

~ Roger Coulombe
"The Berlin Kid"[98]

I came across a sad case of LMF during the war. A pilot I'll call "Billy" told me he felt he couldn't bring himself to take the bomber off with a full load. He thought he wasn't strong enough to pull it up off the runway. I tried to convince him it was just like any other time he flew off, that they were very good aircraft, and that he was a strong young man. It was all to no avail. How he got through the conversion unit flying those poor old aircraft, I don't know. He also must have done his two 'second dickie' trips. He said he had been lined up twice for an op when both times the trip was aborted for some reason, so he didn't have to go or to make any decisions. I forget what squadron he was with, or what happened when he went back to base after our talk, but after the war, I met a pal of his who told me Billy had been sent home LMF. One day, Billy went out hunting, and in climbing a fence, his rifle discharged, killing him. His pal didn't believe it was an accident, and neither do I. There were probably other factors involved, but since all kinds of young men were thrown into the service from all walks of life, glamorized at home, then traumatized when faced with combat, some compassion should have been shown. It might have been more productive if he had been reassigned to other duties, such as drogue pilot, or to Transport Command on an aircraft he thought he could handle. What a waste of a lot of training...

~ Jimmy Sheridan[99]

As was the case in other situations where RCAF personnel overseas experienced the occasionally-heavy, Draconian and class-conscious hand of RAF administrative policies, "...difficulties with the British LMF process became evident in Canada when the label of Waverer was applied to some RCAF airmen who clearly did not deserve it."[100] In a countering initiative, the RCAF, relying heavily upon its air force legal officers, drafted its own LMF policy in 1944, which emphasized the protection of individual rights and due process of law. "In adopting the creation of *clear and willful evasion of operational responsibility*[101] as a basis for judging the behaviour of aircrew, the RCAF regulations moved the LMF procedure away from the bureaucratic, operational and medical realms toward the political and legal arenas."[102] Although it was not promulgated until relatively late in the European air war, and it affected very few RCAF aircrew in terms of total percentages, this distinctly-Canadian policy signaled yet another victory for Canadian national pride and independence from British control.

Perhaps the last philosophical words on this subject from a veteran should fall to Murray Peden, whose distinguished wartime career and articulate reflections tend to put balance on the LMF policy:

> Remembering those who had carefully refrained from risking their precious hides, who had carefully refrained from bearing arms for their country, in any capacity, I always felt that LMF was a dirty label to fasten on someone who had volunteered for dangerous duty and had tried to carry out his commitment. The harsh treatment was necessary simply because the strain was so great. If there had been an easy and graceful way to abandon operational flying, many crews would have found the temptation hard to resist as their tours went on and the bloodshed continued.[103]

Although considerable effort has been expended in this brief study to assess the impact of the LMF policies, it would be misleading to place too much emphasis upon its relative importance overall. During the entire war, less than .2 percent of all Commonwealth aircrew were categorized as Lacking Moral Fibre, and even during some of the most arduous days of Bomber Command's operations, the calendar year between July 1943 and June 1944, less than .4 percent of aircrew members were even *identified* as being possible LMF cases.[104] This was, by any yardstick, a highly enviable record under extremely daunting conditions.

THE BALM OF INSPIRATIONAL LEADERSHIP

If the LMF policy was a hammer that helped generate the will to persevere during the bomber offensive, inspirational leadership was the velvet glove. Fortunately for Britain and the Dominions, there was no shortage of exceptional leaders in Bomber Command. The home islands produced Guy Penrose Gibson, VC, and also boasted the likes of Leonard Cheshire, VC, who led his men night after night over the most dangerous targets in inspirational example. By 1943, he had already completed two brilliant operational tours. His men would have followed him to hell and back, and frequently did just that. The Dominions produced 'Mick' Martin, Donald Bennett, and Dave Shannon from Australia, while Canada could point with pride to the likes of Bob Turnbull, 'Reg' Lane, 'Johnnie' Fauquier, Nelles Timmerman, Bill Swetman, and Joe Lecompte. Turnbull would end the war as a group captain and a 6 Group station commander, having already commanded flights and squadrons in distinguished overseas service covering nearly four years duration. Reg Lane flew three full tours of operations, one of only 24 RCAF members of Bomber Command to do so,[105] and he flew against virtually every vital enemy target in Europe. Johnnie Fauquier won, amongst other Commonwealth and foreign awards, the Distinguished Service Order (DSO) three times during three tours of operations, including service as the commanding officer of 405 Squadron, and a highly successful tour as commanding officer of 617 'Dambuster' Squadron late in the war, for which he voluntarily dropped rank from air commodore to lead the unit. Many people thought Fauquier was absolutely fearless. Instead, his bravery was reflected in the outstanding record he accumulated while he coped with fear. He once told a colleague: "A fellow who isn't afraid lacks imagination. And a guy who has no imagination can't be much of a combat pilot, and certainly never a leader."[106] Bill Swetman was cut from the same cloth, as Roger Coulombe recalls:

> When Wing Commander Crooks was killed over Peenemünde, he was replaced by a 23 year-old squadron leader who was then promoted to wing commander. His name was William 'Bill' Herbert Swetman, DSO, DFC, and he had already done one tour of operations flying *Wellington* and *Halifax* aircraft with 405 Squadron. He then completed a second tour of operations flying *Lancaster* Mark II aircraft with us as commanding officer of 426 Squadron. He was a very good, brave, and inspirational leader, and he didn't pick the easiest targets for himself, either. In fact, he participated in the Peenemünde raid the night his predecessor was killed in action. Actually, there

Credit: Halifax Restoration Team Trenton

▶ A typical late-war *Halifax* crew, this one from 434 'Bluenose' (RCAF) Squadron.

were no easy targets in Germany during 1943 and 1944. Swetman flew many raids on Berlin, although I don't know precisely how many, but he came on quite a few of them. So, I can certainly say Bill Swetman was an example of leadership and an inspiration for the pilots of his squadron. He was also a very trusted pilot. Air Vice-Marshal McEwen, the AOC of 6 Group, even flew with him as a 'second dickie' on a raid over a German city...[107]

~ Roger Coulombe

Yet another of the greatest examples of inspirational leadership within the RCAF Overseas came from a very high level. In its first year of operations, 6 Group lost 340 aircraft and the death toll would continue to rise, until a total of 814 group aircraft had been felled by war's end.[108] It is safe to say that 6 Group, like the rest of Bomber Command, experienced significant morale problems in 1943. Nonetheless, in February 1944, Air Vice-Marshal Clifford M. 'Black Mike' McEwen, mentioned above by Roger Coulombe, succeeded Air Vice-Marshal George Brookes as air officer commanding, and the fortunes of the group changed dramatically from that point in time. A dynamic, capable leader who had proven his mettle in the Great War as a distinguished fighter pilot, downing 27 enemy aircraft in the process, McEwen was an unrepentant advocate of arduous, realistic, and demanding training, as well as stern discipline.

No armchair commander, McEwen led fearlessly from the front, accompanying his crews on their toughest missions and against the explicit orders of Sir Arthur Harris, until Sir Arthur eventually 'lowered the boom' on McEwen and absolutely forbade any further operational flying by him, citing security issues associated with his high rank. However, knowing that their commander fully appreciated, even shared their dangers, the performance of the 6 Group crews soon became as good as any in Bomber Command, and better than most. "... McEwen's presence was soon taken for granted – he even became a good luck symbol. As the men saw it, when the man with the moustache was along, things were going to be fine. They felt drawn to this colourful airman who wanted to share their danger, and when ordered not to, could not sleep while his men were on a raid."[109]

Along with demonstrating a willingness to share their men's hardships and to provide sufficient rest and relaxation, the best combat leaders, and these included many worthy examples in the American camp as well, were able to provide some meaningful philosophy of life to their charges. It would appear that imbuing a sense of fatalism short of defeatism worked to a certain extent during the bomber offensive. Philip Ardery, a pilot, expressed it this way:

> It helped me to say to myself with complete calm: "You can't live forever. You have had a great deal in your life-span already, much more than many people ever have. You would not shirk the duty of tomorrow if you could. Go into it calmly, don't try too hard to live. Don't ever give up hope: never let the fear of death strike panic in your mind and paralyze your reason. Death will find you sometime, if not tomorrow. Give yourself a chance." And then I would remember that very appropriate sentence of Shakespeare: "Cowards die many times more before their deaths; the valiant never taste of death but once."[110]

Whatever the reasons, and there are many, the bomber offensive was a magnificent effort in the face of continued adversity, a true triumph of the human spirit. The prolonged, sustained fortitude of the crews that flew the operations was that rare form of bravery that Napoleon Bonaparte referred to as the Courage of the Early Morning.

▶ It took a lot of folks to man a wartime heavy bomber squadron.

Credit: DND PL42860

NOTES

1.   Sir Charles Webster and Noble Frankland, *The Strategic Air Offensive against Germany* (London: Her Majesty's Stationary Office, 1961), pp.201-202.
2.   Bill Sweetman, "The Avro Lancaster," in Jeffrey Ethell (ed.), *The Great Book of World War Two Airplanes* (New York: Bonanza Books, 1984), p.399.
3.   Mark W. Wells, *Courage in Air Warfare – The Allied Aircrew Experience in the Second World War* (London: Frank Cass, 1995), p.115.
4.   Ibid., p.161.
5.   Max Hastings, *Bomber Command* (New York: The Dial Press/James Wade, 1979), p. 214.
6.   Wells, p.116.
7.   J. Douglas Harvey, *Boys, Bombs and Brussels Sprouts* (Toronto: McClelland & Stewart, 1981), p.6.
8.   Pilot Officer David Oliver, a British Lancaster pilot, in Martin Middlebrook, *The Berlin Raids* (London: Penguin, 1988), p.318.
9.   Wells, p.28.
10.   Ibid., p.210.
11.   Richard Holmes, *Battlefields of the Second World War* (London: BBC Worldwide, 2001), p.199.
12.   Laurence Motiuk, *Thunderbirds at War - Diary of a Bomber Squadron* (Nepean, ON: Larmot, 1998), p.458.
13.   James H. Waugh, postwar questionnaire response, at <http://www.airforce.ca/wwii/ALPHA-WA.Two.html>, pp.45-46.
14.   Murray Peden, letter to author, dated 7 February 2001.
15.   Bruce Barrymore Halpenny, *Action Stations – Military Airfields of Yorkshire* (Cambridge: Patrick Stephens, 1981), p.109.
16.   Wells, p. 31.
17.   Ibid., p.115.
18.   Peden, letter to author, dated 7 February 2001.
19.   Bob Pratt, in *Warriors of the Night*, Part 2, (Video), (The Discovery Channel, 1999).
20.   "Airfields of Yorkshire," in *Flypast*, No. 207, October 1998, p.89. Further south at the Master Diversion Field RAF Woodbridge, another 1200 wartime recoveries were made utilizing FIDO. Murray Peden, *A Thousand Shall Fall* (Toronto: Stoddart, 1988), p.408.
21.   John Terraine, *The Right of the Line – The Royal Air Force in the European War 1939-1945* (London: Hodder and Stoughton, 1985), p.33.
22.   John Searby, *The Bomber Battle for Britain* (Shrewsbury: Airlife Publishing, 1991), p.81.
23.   Peden, *A Thousand Shall Fall*, p.414.

24. Paul Nyznik, "Pathfinder!", in *Airforce*, Vol. 21, No. 1, Spring 1997, p.8.

25. Bert Houle, in David L. Bashow, *All the Fine Young Eagles* (Toronto: Stoddart, 1996), p.144.

26. Martin Caidin, *Black Thursday* (New York: E.P. Dutton, 1960), p.80.

27. Holmes, p.197.

28. Some British aircraft, especially the *Lancaster* and the *Stirling*, had very small hatch doors. While the American B-17 *Flying Fortress'* hatch doors were approximately 30" x 30", the *Lancaster's* was only 22" x 22", and was particularly difficult to find in the dark. "Operational research statistics showed that about 50 percent of Americans successfully bailed out of damaged aircraft. In contrast, only about one-quarter of British airmen made it safely out of *Halifaxes* and *Stirlings*." Wells, p.54. In the *Lancaster*, the *only* recommended egress point was the small nose hatch, particularly difficult to find in the dark. Additionally, for those wondering, the main crew door on the right hand side of the *Lancaster's* aft fuselage was not considered viable as an emergency escape location, since it was located directly in front of the horizontal stabilizer, and there was too much risk of the crew member striking it upon exiting the aircraft. However, negotiating the entire length of a stricken and frequently out-of-control *Lancaster*, including clambering over that formidable wing spar, was problematic at best. Just over one-in-ten *Lancaster* rear gunners survived if the aircraft was destroyed by enemy action. Bill Sweetman, "The Avro Lancaster," in *The Great Book of World War Two Airplanes*, p.396.

29. Holmes, p.197.

30. Kenneth McDonald, letter to author, 25 August 2000. Ken McDonald remained in the RAF after the war, rising to the rank of group captain and adding an Officer of the Order of the British Empire (OBE) to his DFC. On completion of military service, he returned to Canada.

31. Lieutenant-General (ret'd) Reg Lane, telephone interview with author, 25 January 2002.

32. While the photographic proof of an individual crew's bombing was considered an essential part of post-operation analysis in order to determine the amount of destruction meted out to the target, it also served other purposes. First, it constituted proof that the crew had bombed the target area and had not 'wavered' in pressing home their attack. Second, in a more upbeat vein, it allowed the authorities to recognize and acknowledge particularly accurate bombing with respect to the designated aim point(s). This was manifested in the awarding of "Target Tokens," certificates signed by the appropriate group commander and presented to deserving crews, who had obtained particularly good aiming point photographs.

33. Holmes, p.200.

34. Jimmy Sheridan, letter to author, dated 20 September 2000.

35. Peden, *A Thousand Shall Fall*, p.412.

36. Richard Overy, *Bomber Command 1939-1945* (London: HarperCollins, 1997), p.204.

37. Robin Neillands, *The Bomber War – The Allied Air Offensive against Nazi Germany* (New York: The Overlook Press, 2001), p.368.

38. Ibid.

39. Violent crimes against the aircrew appeared to occur most frequently in the open countryside, committed predominately by irate villagers or NSDAP (Nazi Party) officials. In contrast, those apprehended by soldiers, particularly those of the *Luftwaffe*, were usually safeguarded, and *most*, although not *all* crews captured in the urban areas were not abused, which, considering that the cities generally were the primary targets of the bombing, seems rather curious. Ibid, p.369.

40. When the news of the deaths was presented to the prisoners of *Stalag Luft III*, and the question was asked as to how many of the escaping prisoners had been merely *wounded* while escaping, the German authorities were at a loss for an answer. Apparently, those responsible for the crimes did not consider that eventuality. *Stalag Luft III*, at <http://www.elsham.pwp.blueyonder.co.uk|gt_esc|>, p.18, accessed 17 February 2004.

41. In all, 72 Germans were placed on a wanted list for the murders. "Of the 72 on that list, 21 were eventually tried, found guilty, and executed. Nine more received prison terms ranging from ten years to life; ten had forestalled the investigation by committing suicide and a further ten were either acquitted or had charges against them dropped. Twenty-two could not be traced, were either found to have been killed in the last stages of the war or just disappeared; some of them, as was established, into Russian prison camps from which they never returned. Squadron Leader Jack Bushby, RAF, "After the Great Escape," re-printed in *Airforce*, Vol.18, No. 2, July 1994, p.6.

42. Ed Carter-Edwards, *Canadians Who Served with the Halifax Bomber Recollections*, Trenton, ON: Halifax Memorial, RCAF Museum.

43. Greenhous *et al.*, *The Crucible of War*, p.565.
44. Brereton Greenhous and Hugh A. Halliday, *Canada's Air Forces 1914-1999* (Montreal: Art Global, 1999), p.100.
45. Ibid.
46. Roger Coulombe, letter to author, dated 23 October 2000.
47. Hastings, p.215.
48. Readers should note that the author has not been unable to verify Mr. Hastings's "notorious for indifference" categorical comment with any other reputable source, nor that 6 Group behaviour was in any *measurable* way different from other groups under the direction of a Master Bomber. Ibid., p.163.
49. As quoted in Ibid., p.215.
50. However, a significant number of senior RAF officers still did refer disparagingly to the men from the Dominions as "Colonials;" a term which had been out of vogue since British Prime Minister Joseph Chamberlain's Imperial Conference of 1897, marking the Diamond Jubilee of Queen Victoria's 60th year on the throne. At this conference, Chamberlain proposed the idea of a Commonwealth or Imperial Federation, with Britain at the helm of like-minded nations, who had now graduated from being "Colonials" to "Imperials."
51. Charles P. Symonds and Denis J. Williams, *Psychological Disorders in Flying Personnel of the Royal Air Force* (London: His Majesty's Stationary Office, 1947), p.53.
52. James Sheridan, letter to author, dated 24 October 2000.
53. Jim Northrup, letter to author, dated 18 August 2000.
54. Roger Coulombe, letter to author, dated 23 October 2000.
55. Howard B. Ripstein, letter to author, dated 21 November 2000.
56. Ron Cassels, *Ghost Squadron* (Winnipeg, MB: Ardenlea Publications, 1991), p.48.
57. Halpenny, p.3.
58. Greenhous et al., *The Crucible of War*, p.226.
59. J. Douglas Harvey, *The Tumbling Mirth – Remembering the Air Force* (Toronto: McClelland and Stewart, 1983), p. 68.
60. Howard B. Ripstein, letter to author, dated 21 November 2000.
61. Roger Coulombe, letter to author, dated 23 October 2000.
62. Sid Philp, letter to author, dated 16 August 2000, previously sent to Mr. David Brown, 21 January 1994.
63. Reg Patterson, letter to author, dated 7 November 2001.
64. Greenhous *et al.*, *The Crucible of War*, p.526.
65. Wells, p.125.
66. Overy, p.149.
67. Terraine, p.522.
68. Ibid., p.523.
69. Having said this, as the war entered its closing months during the post-*Overlord* period, some adverse war news, as it affected Bomber Command, appears to have been deliberately withheld from the British public.
70. M. Middlebrook and C. Everitt released *The Bomber Command War Diaries: an Operational Reference Book*, in London in 1985.
71. Kenneth McDonald, letter to author, dated 25 August 2000, previously sent to Michael M. LeBlanc, 13 June 1994.
72. At the same time, the Pathfinders mandated a continuous tour of 45 sorties. Terraine, p.527. Since almost all PFF crews had previous operational experience, the number of sorties flown prior to joining 8 Group was supposed to have been applied to the required total. That said, this policy does not appear to have been applied with any degree of consistency. Of interest, it was generally felt that PFF faced the highest loss rates of all. However, that was not always the case. John Lewis, distinguished Canadian navigator veteran of PFF recalls: "Between 18 November 1943, my first op with 405 (Squadron), and 19 May 1944, my 24th, the squadron sent out 311 Lancs and lost 11, a rate of 3.53 percent. Bomber Command, during the same period, detailed 13,313 aircraft, lost 749, a rate of 5.62 percent." John Lewis quoted in Paul Nyznik, "Pathfinder," in *Airforce*, Vol. 21, No. 1, Spring 1997, p.10.

73. A very important caveat to this policy was that the 30 sortie first tour requirement could be waived by group and squadron commanders if they were satisfied that the individuals involved had carried out their duties satisfactorily and were in need of a rest from operations. Terraine, p.523.

74. In the words of John Searby, DSO, DFC, a very distinguished PFF group captain, "The battering we received over the North German Plain cost us more than a thousand aircraft and between seven and eight thousand lives. Berlin wasn't worth it." Greenhous *et al.*, *The Crucible of War*, p.785. This is hyperbole, although only in a sense. In the course of the nineteen dedicated raids against "Whitebait," the command code-name for Berlin, during the period 23 August 1943 - 31 March 1944, Bomber Command would lose 625 aircraft and crews, and at least a further 80 would crash in Britain with heavy loss of life. However, during the same period, the Command carried out 36 major raids against other important German industrial targets. In all, 1578 aircraft were posted missing from the 55 cumulative raids of the period, for a loss rate of 5 percent, which was also the equivalent of *twice* the front line strength of Bomber Command at the time. Martin Middlebrook, "Bomber Command - The Turning Points," in *Flypast*, No.207, October 1998, pp.50-51.

75. Symonds and Williams, p.49.

76. Ibid., p.44.

77. Ibid., p.45.

78. D. Stafford-Clark, "Morale and Flying Experience", originally published in the *Journal of Mental Science*, reprinted in Alan W. Mitchell, "Bomber Crews Were Men with a High Quality of Courage," in *Gaggle and Stream - Magazine of the Bomber Command Association of Canada*, August 2002, p.8.

79. Don Charlwood, *No Moon Tonight* (Sydney: Goodall, 1990), p.77.

80. D. Stafford-Clark, in Alan W. Mitchell, "Bomber Crews...,"p.7.

81. Halpenny, p.49.

82. Wells, p.47.

83. Caidin, p.87.

84. Symonds and Williams, p.61.

85. Sid Philp, letter to author, dated 29 August 2000.

86. Sid Philp, letter to author, dated 16 August 2000, previously sent to Mr. David Brown, 21 January 1994.

87. Murray Peden, letter to author, dated 7 February 2001.

88. It would re-appear later, in very distinctive and specialized formats, as the nightly operations assumed more and more complexity, including diversion or "spoof" raids. Also, specialty flares or markers were used to designate when to initiate or cease specialty operations, such as the use of *Window*.

89. Murray Peden, letter to author, dated 7 February 2001.

90. Sid Philp, letter to author, dated 16 August 2000, previously sent to Mr. David Brown, 21 January 1994.

91. D. Stafford-Clark, in Alan W. Mitchell, "Bomber Crews...," p.7. This was certainly true for some peak periods of the bomber offensive. However, *generally* speaking, the crews would fare much better during the last calendar year of the war.

92. Wells, p.77.

93. Ibid.

94. Allan D. English, *The Cream of the Crop - Canadian Aircrew 1939-1945* (Montreal & Kingston: McGill-Queen's University Press, 1996), p.81.

95. Quoted in Ibid., p.84.

96. Quoted in Ibid., p.88.

97. John Lewis, quoted in Raul Nyznik, "Pathfinder!", *Airforce*, Vol. 21, No. 1, Spring 1997, p.9.

98. Roger Coulombe, letter to author, dated 23 October 2000.

99. James Sheridan, letter to author, dated 24 October 2000.

100. English, p.128.

101. Author's bold and italicized type.

102. English, p.128.

103. Peden, p.416.

104. Greenhous *et al.*, *The Crucible of War*, p.787.

105. Amazingly enough, several Canadian airmen would actually complete *four* operational tours in Bomber Command. Two known cases were Glenmore Ellwood, from Portage la Prairie, Manitoba,

and James R. Dow, from Winnipeg. Both men attained the wartime rank of squadron leader and both were awarded the DSO as well as the DFC and Bar. Ellwood served as a Pathfinder with 405 Squadron where he flew on seven of the Berlin raids, then later became Johnnie Fauquier's navigator on 617 Squadron. He passed away in 1999. *Airforce*, Vol. 23, No. 2, Summer 1999, p.59. James Dow was, along with other operational tours, a bomb aimer with 635 Squadron, and he was in sustained action from late-1941 until late-1944. He passed away in 2000. <http//www.airforce.ca/wwii/ALPHA-DI. html>.

106. A.R. Byers (ed.), Reader's Digest, *The Canadians at War 1939-1945* (Westmount, QC: The Reader's Digest Association of Canada, 1986), p.285.

107. Roger Coulombe, letter to author, dated 23 October 2000.

108. Byers, p.285. Although many 6 Group aircraft would be lost after the first year of operations, the number of sorties generated was *much* greater thereafter, and the concomitant loss rate was *much* less.

109. Ibid.

110. Philip Ardery, *Bomber Pilot* (Lexington, KY: University Press of Kentucky, 1978), p.93.

Chapter Three

THE BALANCE SHEET
~
THE COSTS AND THE GAINS
OF THE BOMBER OFFENSIVE

Many survivors have paid a high price in lost health and happiness, made worse by the denigration of their efforts by critics ranging from the morally fastidious, through those who supported the campaign until they saw what it had done and then wished to distance themselves from it, to those with a political axe to grind. Like the firestorms that were its most dreadful expression, condemnation of the bombing campaign has fed upon itself until the flames of cant and the smoke of hypocrisy have obscured its many accomplishments; not least the saving of countless Allied soldiers' lives.

~ Richard Holmes
Battlefields of the Second World War

Critics of the bomber offensive frequently argue that the materiel and human cost of the campaign far overshadowed the gains, and that the resources dedicated to it could have been more effectively utilized elsewhere. They have argued that the combat manpower could have been better used in the other fighting services, especially the army during the gruelling campaign in northwest Europe, and industry could have been used to produce more weapons for these fighting services. However, proponents of this line of thought assume that the weight of effort expended upon the bombing campaign was inordinately high. Richard Overy maintains that it was actually rather modest. "Measured against the totals for the entire war effort (production and fighting), bombing absorbed 7 percent, rising to 12 percent in 1944-45. Since at least a proportion of bomber production went to other theatres of war [and to other commands – D.B.], the aggregate figures for the direct bombing of Germany were certainly smaller than this. Seven percent of Britain's war effort can hardly be regarded as an unreasonable allocation of resources."[1] Further, although some significant infantry shortages were experienced in 1944, they never reached an extremely critical overall level and were eventually rectified. With respect to materiel, none of the services was conspicuously wanting for

▶ By 1944, the majority of Germany's industrial cities were significantly the worse for wear.

Credit: DND PL42655

anything by 1943, and the British effort was thereafter bolstered by substantial North American war production.

THE DOWN SIDE

Much of the criticism of the bombing campaign has focused upon the human cost, the unquestionably heavy loss rates endured by Anglo American aircrews, 81,000 of whom forfeited their lives aboard 18,000 downed aircraft from the Eighth Air Force and Bomber Command alone.[2] However, these losses need to be placed in perspective, especially when compared to the 20-27 million war dead suffered by the Soviet Union alone. Nonetheless, the human cost of the campaign, discussed some depth in Chapter One, was formidable.

During the war, Bomber Command's 125,000 airmen[3] flew 364,514 sorties over Europe,[4] and the majority of the command tonnage was dropped from the summer of 1944 until the cessation of hostilities. To put the total campaign in perspective, by VE Day and from the commencement of hostilities, 955,044 tons of bombs had been dropped by the command upon Germany, Italy, enemy occupied territory, and targets at sea. Approximately 74 percent of the total tonnage was delivered after 1 January 1944, and 70 percent of the total after 1 July 1944, from which time forward the Bomber Command loss rates were greatly reduced.[5] In round figures, 48,000 tons were dropped upon European targets up until the end of January 1942, an additional 42,000 tons by year's end, another 158,000 tons in 1943, and the balance thereafter. Of the totals dropped on the European Axis powers during the war, 68.8 percent fell upon the Reich itself, 30.19 percent upon the enemy occupied territories, 0.94 percent upon Italy, and 0.07 percent upon targets at sea.[6] "If the bombing of Germany had little effect on production prior to July 1944, it is not only because she had idle resources upon which to draw, but because the major weight of the air offensive against her had not been brought to bear. After the air war against Germany was launched on its full scale, the effect was immediate."[7]

There were periods of time when the odds against aircrew survival were particularly daunting. For example, with respect to the Canadian 6 Group's Handley Page *Halifax II/V* operations between March 1943 and February 1944, the average monthly loss rate was 6.05 percent per operation, producing a mere 16 percent survival rate.[8] Between August 1943 and March 1944, the group's Avro *Lancaster II* loss rate averaged 5 percent per operation, producing a concomitant 21 percent survival rate.[9] During the group's first year of operations, for those flying Vickers *Wellingtons* between January and October 1943, the loss rate averaged 3.6 percent, producing a survival rate of 34 percent.[10] That said, the February 1944 decision by Harris to restrict the Merlin-powered *Halifax II/V* squadrons from operations over Germany, due to service ceiling limitations during a period of brisk operational tempo, undoubtedly saved many aircrew lives. An earlier decision to relegate Bomber Command *Wellington* squadrons to predominantly *Gardening* (mining) operations during the summer and early autumn of 1943 similarly eased the haemorrhaging in that community.[11]

There is also no doubt that the particular time at which aircrew members commenced their operational tours significantly affected their chances of survival. Given a period of intense operational tempo, it was not unusual for a crew to complete an operational tour within three calendar months, a common occurrence during the last year of the war. However, if, for example, those three months fell within the confines of the Second Battle of the Ruhr, which took place from March to July 1943, or the Berlin raids, which occurred from November 1943 to March 1944, individual crew odds of survival were much less than for those who commenced operations later in 1944, after a state of relative air superiority had been achieved. That said, the later rates graphically illustrate how enormous the bombing weight of effort was during the final nine months of the war under increasingly favourable circumstances, and they mitigate somewhat the dreadful earlier statistics.

THE CONTRIBUTIONS TO VICTORY OF THE BOMBER OFFENSIVE

So much for the losses. What of the gains? First, the gains were not only those directly attributable to the bombing, such as the actual destruction of targets, but they also constituted a host of indirect benefits brought on as adjuncts to the bombing. In Richard Overy's words:

> From [renowned economist John Kenneth] Galbraith onwards the view has taken root that the only thing that Bomber Command did, or was ordered to do, was to attack German cities with indifferent accuracy. The Bombing Surveys devoted much of their effort to measuring the direct physical damage to war production through city bombing. This has produced since the war a narrow economic interpretation of the bombing offensive that distorts both the purposes and nature of Britain's bombing effort to an extraordinary degree.[12]

While part of the bombing effort was to be directed at Germany's home front military and economic structures if the nation first attacked civilian targets in an indiscriminate manner, very large portions of the overall effort were directed at many other targets for which the command's aircraft were needed. Again, as Overy mentions, not even half the command's total wartime dropped bomb tonnage was dedicated to the industrial cities.[13] Also, during the latter stages of the campaign, even attacks against industrialized cities were frequently tactical rather than strategic, conducted in support of the advancing Allied land armies. For much of the first four years of the war, support for the naval war comprised a significant portion of the command's overall effort, while for much of 1944, it was extensively used in support of the invasion of northwest Europe. Additionally, command aircraft were used for reconnaissance, for propaganda missions, for electronic warfare and deception operations, for support to Occupied Europe's resistance movements, and, for humanitarian aid and mercy missions towards the end of hostilities. Bomber Command was a true 'Jack-of-all-trades,' and it required the full resolution of its commanders not to become excessively and repeatedly diverted from its primary mandate, due to all the competing demands upon its limited resources.[14] That said, and with the benefit of '20/20 hindsight,' while Arthur Harris was undoubtedly correct in his assessment of the need for a broad application of area bombing during the early years of the campaign, his dogged rejection of the so-called 'panacea' targets later in the war appears to have been somewhat myopic. As we now know,

Albert Speer and others dreaded timely follow-on efforts to the highly successful 1943 attacks on the Ruhr dams, Hamburg,[15] and the ball-bearing industry, and they believed that such a concentration of effort at the time would have been cataclysmic for the Reich. Similarly, an earlier and more dedicated application of effort against the enemy's oil resources, which pitted the Commander-in-Chief Bomber Command against the Chief of the Air Staff, *might* have brought the European war to a somewhat earlier conclusion. But such is the fog of war, and Arthur Harris sincerely believed he was following the correct course and was utilizing his command to inflict the most damage under the circumstances presented to him. And the course he chose, the targets he elected to pursue, perhaps at the cost of others more viable, were certainly not without merit or justification. The wisdom of hindsight needs to be tempered with the perceptions of the day. Furthermore, Harris was firmly convinced from an early stage of the bombing campaign that frequent, concentrated repeat visits to specific targets would incur prohibitive losses to Bomber Command.

The bombing offensive was also seen as a way to avoid the carnage of stagnated land warfare, exemplified by the *abattoir* that the Western Front had become during first three years of the Great War. "For Britain, with its small population and the lack of a large standing army, a small force of specialized volunteers was arguably a more effective way of mobilizing British manpower than the development of a large and inexperienced ground army."[16] Also, all the great early airpower theorists of the pre-Second World War period, Guilio Douhet, William "Billy" Mitchell and Viscount Trenchard, had espoused the primacy of offensive air operations, the relative invulnerability of the bomber, and the comparative fragility of civilian morale. The bomber offensive was very much in lockstep with Britain's overall peripheral strategy, which meant a war of long-term economic attrition and opportunism against the Germans, as opposed to a directly confrontational war of mass and concentration. The bomber offensive was, in fact, the epitome of unconventional, guerrilla warfare, and thus in keeping with Britain's overall strategic plan.

Further, the command made possible a combat initiative that was deemed vital, not just for the damage it would cause the Third Reich, but for the galvanizing of both British and global support. It certainly affected American and Commonwealth opinion, as well as that of potential allies and enslaved nations, telegraphing British resolve to forcefully press home the fight against the tyranny of Nazism, alone if necessary. Its very prosecution assured Britain a pivotal say in the conduct of the war. It also did wonders for home front morale,

Credit: DND PL30780

▶ A 431 'Iroquois' (RCAF) Squadron *Halifax III* attacking a V 1 rocket launching site in the French countryside, 25 June 1944.

bolstering the British public in a time of great need for reassurance and hope. This evidence of commitment was never more important than after the German invasion of the Soviet Union during the summer of 1941. The bombing offensive constituted a second front, a significant source of relief to the beleaguered Soviets when no other offensive action was realistic or even possible. Later, bombing's contributions would become a prerequisite to the successful invasion of northwest Europe; "...an independent campaign to pave the way for a combined arms invasion of Hitler's Europe."[17] From April until September 1944, the majority of Bomber Command's activities were conducted in lockstep with the preparation, execution, and aftermath of the invasion through Normandy. And in the wake of this effort, the command would deal decisive blows to the enemy's transportation and petroleum resources, effectively paralyzing the Third Reich in its final hours.

The total defeat of Germany's air force, through direct attacks upon production facilities, airfield and support installations on the ground, and a highly successful war of attrition in the air, constituted a pivotal contribution to winning the war. Of the overall bombing offensive, Albert Speer, Hitler's Minister for Armaments and War Production, said: "As far as I can judge from the accounts I have read, no one has seen that this was the greatest lost battle on the Germans' side."[18]

And what of the *specific* direct and indirect effects of the bombing? The latter were in ways much more damaging to the Axis war effort, and while engineers speak of a Law of Unforeseen Advantages, many of these indirect benefits were anticipated, if not deliberately orchestrated. That said, the direct damage was also highly significant and both the direct and indirect results of the bombing will now be discussed in depth.

THE OIL AND TRANSPORTATION CAMPAIGNS

Once relative air superiority had been attained over northwest Europe by the middle of 1944, the Allied air forces exploited this turn of events in a series of concentrated and systematic attacks against the German synthetic oil industry and transportation systems. The attacks on both these resources contributed significantly to the final collapse of the Reich. By way of example, German domestic oil production plummeted from 673,000 tons in January 1944, to 265,000 tons in September, and aviation fuel was temporarily reduced to 5 percent of needs.[19] Since nothing was more germane to the collapse of the German armed forces than the irrevocable defeat of its air power, the effective grounding of the *Luftwaffe* constituted a knockout punch. The campaign against the synthetic petroleum plants, the refineries, and the oil fields was the most effective means of rendering the *Luftwaffe* impotent. The overall shortage of aviation gasoline adversely affected flying training from as early as 1942, producing a concomitant serious degradation in the quality of flight school graduates. The specific output of aviation fuel actually fell from 195,000 tons in May 1944, to 35,000 tons by mid-summer, and to a paltry 7000 tons by September 1944. Although stockpiled resources kept the *Luftwaffe* flying after a fashion throughout the summer, by autumn, shortages were acute. This had to be a bitter irony for Germany's air leaders, for it came at a time when the air industries had achieved a new peak in fighter production, completing 3133 of these combat aircraft in September alone. Along with making this production increase in conventional-type aircraft of little military significance, the limited availability of low-grade fuels, which could only be used in high-performance turbojet aircraft, was one reason that a jet force could not be fielded in time to become a significant, widespread threat to the Allies. As a broader, over-arching result, the Eighth and Fifteenth Air Forces, working in concert with Bomber Command, destroyed virtually all of Germany's coke, ferroalloy and synthetic rubber industries, 95 percent of its fuel, hard coal and rubber capacity, and 90 percent of its steel capacity.[20] And while it is true, as was the case with aviation fuel, that a certain amount of stockpiling of raw materials

Credit: DND PL144305

▶ A night bombing raid on Nuremburg, 27/28 August 1943.

meant that these results were not forecast to impact production to a *massive* extent until the latter half of 1945, during the autumn of 1944, when Bomber Command's attacks upon the industrial cities were being resumed in earnest, virtually no-one in authority anticipated that the European war would draw to a close as early as the spring of 1945. As it materialized, the impact was still highly significant. And while various contemporary sources, including German accounts, state that Bomber Command's area bombing contributed between 20 percent and 31 percent[21] of the direct aircraft production losses, and between 35 percent[22] and 55 percent[23] of armoured vehicle production losses, many more losses were incurred while the Germans were attempting to distribute the finished products under near-continuous heavy air attacks. At any rate, the point is moot. Without fuel to convey the aircraft aloft or to roll the tanks into battle, they were useless.[24]

The loss of oil production was also felt in many other ways. In August 1944, the final run-in time for aircraft engines was cut from 2 hours to

½ hour. For lack of fuel, pilot training, previously cut down, was further curtailed. Through the summer, the movement of German *panzer* divisions in the field was hampered more and more seriously as a result of losses in combat and mounting transportation difficulties, together with the fall in fuel production. By December, according to Speer, the fuel shortage had reached catastrophic proportions. When the Germans launched their desperate counteroffensive on December 16, 1944, their reserves of fuel were far from sufficient to support the operation. They counted on capturing Allied stocks. Failing in this, many *panzer* units were lost when they ran out of gasoline.[25]

At this juncture of the war, Arthur Harris may have, in hindsight, exercised faulty judgment in not mounting a more enthusiastic and focused campaign against the oil resources, since he still put considerable emphasis upon the bombing of the industrial cities. That said, the counter-oil campaign was decisive, if arguably prolonged, due to concentration upon other interests. However, a number of industrial cities hit by Bomber Command during this phase included significant damage to oil and related targets. The results were on occasion significantly more successful than the daylight bombing of the Americans, due to a high degree of experience and accuracy with the blind-bombing aids *Oboe* and *H2S*, the Air Position Indicator (API), the Group Position Indicator (GPI) and the improved Mark XIV gyro stabilized automatic bombsight (SABS). The blow dealt was decisive; it just may have taken longer to deliver, due to a perception of conflicting priorities between the Anglo-American camps.

> ...the systematic air raids of the fall of 1944 once again throttled traffic and made transportation, this time for good, the greatest bottleneck in our war economy.
>
> ~ Albert Speer[26]

Prior to the war, Germany possessed a world-class railway system that was very capable and well maintained, and it was complemented by an equally formidable inland waterway system, well adapted to the movement of bulk material to and from the industrialized Ruhr. However, the railroad system became increasingly overburdened due to the industrial dispersion necessitated by the bombing, and this dispersion required the construction of considerably more railroad infrastructure, which was highly susceptible to concentrated air attacks. While the German transportation system did not become a priority target until very late in the war, "... the effects of the heavy air attacks beginning in September of 1944 were felt at once and were clearly apparent in the general traffic and operating statistics of the *Reichsbahn*... the heavy attacks of September and October produced a most serious disruption in railway operations over the whole of western Germany."[27] Concurrently, successful attacks on waterway targets devastated industrial traffic on the Rhine and the north German canals, causing the vital Ruhr district to suffer heavy declines in throughput. By way of example, the Dortmund-Ems Canal, from October 1944 until March 1945, could average only 12 percent of the throughput attained during the previous year.[28] Due to the concentrated attacks of September and October, the supply of critical components to virtually all vital war production elements was severely impacted, and reserves were virtually exhausted by November and early December. Most dramatic was the near-total curtailment of hard coal supplies to the Ruhr. "The consequences of the breakdown in the transportation system were probably greater than any other single factor in the final collapse of the German economy...most of the chaos which gripped the German economy was traceable directly or indirectly to the disaster which overtook the transportation system."[29] The loss of transportation infrastructure stymied the flow of basic raw materials, components, and semi-finished products, and also severely limited the distribution of finished products.

It is true that priority attacks upon the transportation system came in measure too late in the war for their *full* impact to be felt upon the German armed forces at the fighting fronts. "By the end of the war, however, it had so paralyzed the German industrial economy as to render all further war production virtually impossible. It had, moreover, removed the foundation of the civilian economy, suggesting the inevitability of eventual collapse under continued air attack."[30]

THE INDIRECT EFFECTS OF THE BOMBING CAMPAIGN

Throughout Germany in 1944 alone, approximately 800,000 workers were engaged in essential repair work solely attributable to the bombing, especially to factories and to modes of communication. An additional 250,000 - 400,000 personnel were required to provide the necessary equipment, resources, and services to effect the repairs. Thus, a tremendous amount of available manpower was diverted from other essential employment to the reconstruction effort.[31] Furthermore, industrial reconstruction itself was often subjected to push-pull meddling from the highest levels, breeding further manpower wastage. Albert Speer noted that Hitler was very shaken by the destruction of valuable historic buildings, particularly theatres. "Consequently, he was likely to demand that burned-out theatres be rebuilt immediately. Several times I tried to remind him of other strains on the construction industry."[32]

The bombing of the industrial cities forced the policy of decentralized production, and it placed additional burdens and vulnerability upon the transportation and communication networks, as well as the diversion of resources from new construction efforts. It was highly disruptive to industrial firms that had been deliberately and extensively *centralized* to operate at maximum efficiency. Decentralization or industrial dispersal also demanded a greater spreading of and reliance upon a very limited pool of skilled labour. This dilution of skill and experience in turn resulted in a sharp decline in the quality of weapons produced. Supervisory shortages also resulted in significantly more industrial sabotage from an increasingly unwilling press-ganged and slave labour force. It denied the Germans the ability to operate a rational, efficient, highly centralized industrial war effort, which would have permitted much higher levels of output.[33] With respect to the aircraft industry alone:

> Existing production schedules were disrupted and dilution of management supervision made itself felt. In the end, it increased the load on its overburdened transportation system and, when attack was concentrated on transportation, the final assembly plants lacked the necessary sub-assemblies and components. The policy of dispersal was then revised in favour of concentration underground, but it was too late.[34]

The frenzied production pace, aided and abetted by the bombing, led to significant quality control issues and greatly reduced worker productivity. Shortages of skilled labour and strategic materials, production interruptions, plant damage, slipshod construction, and even sabotage all led to declines in end-product quality. Nowhere was this more evident than in the aircraft engine industry, where power plant reliability generated major morale problems in the *Luftwaffe*, especially amongst the inexperienced fighter pilot cadre.

THE EFFECT UPON ENEMY MORALE

Yet the night bombing campaign's greatest contribution to the winning of the war was precisely what Harris claimed and the conventional wisdom has so often discounted. The 'area' bombing attacks did have a direct and palpable effect on the morale of the German

Credit: DND PL32218

▶ A very accurate raid against the *Luftwaffe* base at Volkel, Holland, 3 September 1944.

population, and the German leadership, in response to that impact, seriously skewed Germany's strategy. Recent scholarship in the Federal Republic indicates that as early as the summer of 1942, the night bombing campaign was affecting German attitudes. In 1943, the heavy bombing caused a dramatic fall off in popular morale.[35]

As the foregoing words of American military historian Williamson Murray emphasize, the bombing's impact upon enemy morale was significant. However, it was unrealistic to expect that in an extreme police state such as the Third Reich, a popular uprising and overthrow of the Nazi regime would ensue. Still, the cumulative effects of the bombing, especially the bombing by night, were intensely demoralizing. And once the Allies had legislated the ruination of enemy morale, particularly that of the industrial work force, as an overt war aim, regular intelligence reports reinforced the views of senior Allied commanders that this war aim was being fulfilled. In fact, as early as the summer of 1940, British intelligence sources in neutral Switzerland reported the impact of the still-minimal bombing upon enemy morale as follows: "A Swiss recently returned from Germany states there is some labour unrest in the Ruhr owing to the fact that workers are doing 12 hour shifts a day and fail to get a proper night's rest owing to aerial attacks."[36]

One of the most beneficial of an early series of Bomber Command raids, and one frequently underestimated in terms of its significance, was the bombing of Berlin on the nights of 30/31 August and 4/5 September 1940. While the damage was not extensive, the raids generated considerable public resentment. Adolf Hitler was goaded into switching his bombing priorities to a retaliatory campaign against London and other British cities, just when the campaign against Fighter Command's airfields and command and control facilities was proving decisive. There is little doubt that this emotional decision by Hitler, soon echoed by Göring, aided in the survival of both Fighter Command and the British nation at one of their moments of greatest vulnerability.

Richard Overy, along with many others, believes the Allied bombing was severely disruptive to German society. Throughout the war, nearly nine million citizens were evacuated from the German cities, which not only dramatically reduced the potential work force, but also placed incredible strains upon infrastructure to provide shelter, nourishment, and other essential consumer goods to all the displaced persons, further diverting resources from the war industries. Worker efficiency in areas directly threatened by the bombing suffered considerably; long, exhausting hours were spent in cramped air raid shelters or cellars. Absenteeism increased, and by 1944, it averaged almost four full working weeks per worker annually in the Reich. By way of example, at the Ford works in Cologne on any given day in 1944, at least one-quarter of the work force was absent. When the numbers documenting the unparalleled levels of productivity of German industry during 1944 are brought forward, one has to wonder what they would have been had the Germans not been faced with a near-constant threat of death from the air. Much of the production was generated by slave labourers dragooned from the occupied territories, and they worked in atrocious conditions. This work force was never more than two-thirds as productive as free German workers, nor were they motivated to improvement beyond the spur of terror. A significant amount of the late-war increased industrial output is explained by the fact that Germany was deliberately working nowhere close to full war capacity for the first three years of the Second World War. Along with vast suffering, the bombing placed a very definite ceiling on German productivity, even given a state of total war.

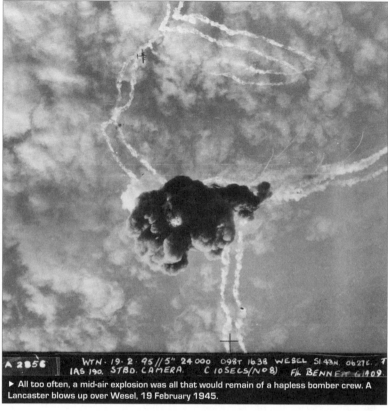

Credit: DND PL144292

> All too often, a mid-air explosion was all that would remain of a hapless bomber crew. A Lancaster blows up over Wesel, 19 February 1945.

When Albert Speer took the helm as Armaments and War Production Minister in February 1942, the nation was only producing three percent more of these products than in peacetime, and Adolf Hitler was adamant that the military endeavours of the Third Reich would not interfere with the consumer industries. Hitler expected a *Blitzkrieg* win in the Soviet Union, and he launched this precursor to what would eventually become Total War on the foundation of a peacetime economic and industrial output. Until the German defeat at Stalingrad in February 1943, German industry generally was only working one ten-hour shift each day. Thereafter, Total War was declared, and manufacturing policy changed to accommodate three shifts and a '24 and 7' operation, accommodating a largely-involuntary work force of 2,500,000 prisoners and at least 1,500,000 foreign workers drawn in from the occupied territories, all of them augmented by an additional estimated 7,500,000 slave labourers.[37] It is difficult to conceive of just what the Germans would have been able to accomplish, had they *not* been forced into a very demanding industrial decentralization program, had they *not* been forced to honour the bombing threats through so much bolstering of their homeland defences, had they maintained uninterrupted use and control of their production facilities, and had they maintained unimpeded use of their very diversified transportation networks.

As the bombing intensified, there were profound political ramifications to Speer's industrial policies. Hitler and his cronies lost confidence in him and began to blame him for all the nation's economic ills. Himmler became increasingly involved in economic matters and began running Speer's system at gunpoint, which in turn de-motivated many Germans.[38]

> Bombing appreciably affected the German will to resist. Its main psychological effects were defeatism, fear, hopelessness, fatalism and apathy. It did little to stiffen resistance through the arousing of aggressive emotions of hate and anger. War weariness, willingness to surrender, loss of hope in a German victory, distrust of leaders, feelings of disunity, and demoralizing fear were all more common among bombed than among un-bombed people... The disruption of public utilities in a community did much to lower the will to resist. Especially significant was the disruption of transportation service; it was the most critical public utility for the morale of the civilian population. Electricity was next in importance among the utilities, then water, then gas. A vital blow to the morale of a bombed community was the destruction of school and recreational facilities for children. This necessitated the evacuation of school children. Parents were doubly affected by such evacuation because they suffered not only the burden of family separation but also the possible loss of the moral guidance of their children to the Nazi Party.[39]

The highest German authorities were very concerned with home front morale throughout the bombing campaign. Albert Speer paraphrased Hitler on 8 March 1943 as follows: "Hitler repeatedly explained that if the bombings went on, not only would the cities be destroyed, but the morale of the people would crack irreparably."[40] To maintain a feel for the pulse of the nation's morale, the Germans fielded an extensive intelligence service, and the Official Morale Reports this service provided demonstrate that "...in official German eyes the air war was of crucial importance in the struggle for popular support of the Nazi regime... These accounts consistently assert that air attacks were undermining morale and producing defeatism..."[41]

Credit: DND PMR 93-293

▶ Some of the inevitable casualties of war. At least these Canadian airmen have identifiable graves.

Propaganda, a keystone of the Third Reich, was used as a means of stimulating morale and it permeated everything in German day-to-day life. However, "...bombing had much to do with the final discrediting of propaganda, because it brought home to millions of Germans the tangible proof of Allied air power – indisputable proof completely at odds with the familiar Nazi propaganda."[42] Surveys done after the war indicate that only 21 percent of the Reich's citizens regarded German information provided during the war as reliable, while 54 percent regarded it as being "completely unreliable."[43]

It is perhaps appropriate that Germany's foremost conjuror of public opinion, Joseph Goebbels, should have the final word on the impact of the bombing upon German morale. These brief excerpts from his 'twelfth-hour' personal diaries belie the public 'spin' on the bombing woven throughout the war by the German Propaganda Ministry:

12 March 1945

The air terror which wages uninterruptedly over German home territories makes people thoroughly despondent. One feels so impotent against it that no one can now see a way out of the dilemma. The total paralysis of transport in West Germany also contributes to the mood of increasing pessimism among the German people.[44]

15 March 1945

Not only our military reverses but also the severe drop in the German people's morale, neither of which can now be overlooked, are primarily due to the unrestricted enemy air superiority.[45]

31 March 1945

The political attitude of the people west of the Rhine was very bad. They had been demoralized by the continuous enemy air raids and are now throwing themselves into the arms of the Anglo-Americans, in some cases enthusiastic-ally, in others at least without genuine resistance.[46]

This lack of resistance in the German urban areas at the 'twelfth hour' of hostilities undoubtedly hastened the German surrender, and, based upon previous experiences, saved many late-war casualties on both sides through a reduction in difficult and bitter house-to-house fighting.

> A real importance of the air war consisted in the fact that it opened a Second Front long before the invasion of Europe. That front was the skies over Germany. The unpredictability of the attacks made the front gigantic. Every square metre of territory we controlled was a kind of front line and because the attacks were both by day and night, it required a 24 hour state of continuous readiness.
>
> ~Albert Speer[47]

In recent years, a number of eminent German historians and political scientists have reversed a widespread and popular German stance that the area bombing was ineffective. Doctor Horst Boog, who served as Chief Historian of the German Office of Military History, spoke at a Symposium on the Strategic Bomber Offensive, held at the RAF Staff College at Bracknell in the United Kingdom in March 1993, and undertook to dispel two persistent myths concerning area bombing and German civilian morale:

> He said: "Let me give you some recent views about the... bombing. The judgment that the British area attacks were ineffective can no

longer be supported. For a proper assessment we have to look at in-direct effects. Had there been no bomber offensive things in Russia might have developed differently." He also notes that over a million men were now on the AA guns. They would have served their coun-try's war effort better in Russia, or in factories.

Doctor Boog also dispels the myth of continued high morale under bombing. He defines morale as, "The will to continue to work for the war effort." But he makes the point that the people were prisoners of the Nazi regime. "Their political surveillance system meant doing what one was told and not shirking in the presence of others." He says, "morale was certainly weakened, as recent studies have revealed, and especially in cities suffering heavy attacks."[48]

German historian Götz Bergander has drawn a significant distinction between *private* morale and *war* morale in the Third Reich. Bergander maintains the former was never broken, because this constituted the will to live, "... based upon personal, family and vocational aspirations and generating inventiveness, stubbornness and the desire to assert oneself. The latter, reflected in people's ability to think about future prospects, was, on the other hand, severely dam-aged – much more than first thought."[49]

In reality, the air raids on cities and industry shook the foundations of the war morale of the German people. They permanently shattered their nerves, undermined their health and shook their belief in vic-tory, thus altering their consciousness. They spread fear, dismay and hopelessness. This was an important and intentional result of the stra-tegic air war, of this warfare revolution.[50]

TIE-DOWN OF RESOURCES FOR DEFENCE OF THE REICH

Very little credit has been given for the vast numbers of personnel and copious amounts of equipment that remained tied down in Germany in defence of the industrialized cities, nor to those personnel required to repair the damage done by the bombing. Speer acknowledges that many new and promising battlefield technological improvements had to be shelved in order to produce additional anti-aircraft weaponry, and that half the electronics in-dustry was engaged in producing radar and communications equipment for the defence of the Reich. A third of the precision optics industry was required to produce gun sights for the flak batteries, which frequently left German field forces critically short of their own needs.[51] *Reichmarschall* Hermann Göring positioned nearly nine thousand of the formidable and versatile 88 mm flak guns within the Fatherland; guns and operators which could have doubled the German defences against Soviet tanks on the *Ostfront*. By 1944, there were 14,489 heavy flak guns deployed in the west, while a further 41,937 light guns were similarly deployed to augment the heavier weapons.[52] Anti-aircraft shells consumed one-fifth of all ammunition produced. *Feldmarschall* Erhard Milch, the Quartermaster-General of the *Luftwaffe*, said that within the Reich, nearly 900,000 men, along with a significant number of women and children, were employed in the anti-aircraft forces alone by 1944.[53] With respect to aircraft operations, from September 1942 until January 1943, the *Luftwaffe* was tasked to keep the beleaguered German garrison at Stalingrad supplied and to provide combat air support against a tightening Soviet noose. However, due to the need to honour the bomber offensive in the West, along with other *Luftwaffe* commitments, coupled with the renaissance of the Soviet air forces, this proved to be an impossible task. The resultant loss of the entire German 6th Army in February 1943 was therefore at least partially attributable to Bomber Command's efforts to that point of the war. By January 1944, 68 percent of Germany's day and night fighter forces were dedicated to facing the Anglo-American bomber threat, leaving only 17 percent of these forces for the Eastern Front after other needs were accommodated.[54] By October 1944, the percentage of fighter aircraft retained in the Reich would balloon to 81 percent.[55] These formidable apportionments slowly but inexorably starved the German field armies of essential air support. Again, by 1944, German bomber aircraft accounted for only one-fifth of all aircraft production, due to the paramount albeit long-delayed acknowledgment of the overriding need for fighters.[56] Thus, without the Allied bombing, German forces at the fighting fronts would have had much greater aerial support and protection, and Allied forces on all fronts would have been much more exposed to German aerial bombardment.

There were a significant number of unpredictable diversions of effort produced by the bombing, although German war policy itself is as much to blame for the ultimate success of the bomber offensive. When *Generaloberst* Wever, the *Luftwaffe's* first Chief of Staff, died in 1936, Germany lost its most fervent advocate of the need for its own long-range strategic bomber fleet.

Instead, it geared its bomber production to medium and short-range types to be used in conjunction with land forces employing dynamic, short-term *Blitzkrieg* tactics. A truly strategic, independent bombing force would have laid all the industrial targets within the United Kingdom open to attack from the air, as well as a multitude of vulnerable Soviet power stations and industrial complexes, the majority of which had been relocated to the east of the Ural Mountains by 1943. It would also have posed a significant long-range threat to Allied shipping convoys in the North Atlantic. However, lack of extended planning, underestimation of enemy capabilities, and conflicting war priorities brought about by different needs for different war theatres all played a part in dooming the development and production of a viable long-range strategic bomber until Allied bombing had forced fighter priorities upon German aircraft production. Bureaucratic ineptitude, high-level bickering, sycophantic pandering to the frequently-contradictory, meddlesome, unrealistic, and inappropriate war guidance of Adolf Hitler himself, as well as an extreme shortage of strategic materials, further stymied any such direction of effort.

From 1944 onwards, Germany was, of necessity, devoting the bulk of its aircraft production capabilities to day and night fighters, consisting largely of obsolete models and technologies, for the defence of the Reich. The strategic and administrative decisions that were made in 1940 and 1941, and even earlier, with respect to bomber fleets and air tactics, effectively sealed Germany's fate and guaranteed permanent air inferiority for the rest of the Second World War. German air strategy, rather than being *proactive* and *unpredictable*, became *reactive* and almost totally *predictable*, due in no small measure to the Allied bombing.[57]

Approximately 70,000[58] aircrew members of the *Luftwaffe* were either killed or reported missing during the Second World War, and while they destroyed roughly 70,000 enemy aircraft on all fronts, they lost between 62,500 and 100,000 of their own machines in the process.[59] Many of the losses were fighter aircraft and fighter pilots, waging a hopeless battle of attrition, the majority of them in defence of the homeland. From the British camp, of the 8655 Bomber Command aircraft that went down over the Reich, Italy and Occupied Europe, approximately 6000 were attributable to air-to-air combat during the bombing offensive.[60] Nearly 1800[61] *Luftwaffe* night fighter aircrew, a very small portion of the larger *Luftwaffe* fatal casualty total, lost their lives during these predominantly-nocturnal engagements.[62]

SOME SINISTER THREATS CONTAINED

One of the most significant effects of the bombing was that it goaded Hitler into striking back in a wasteful and inefficient retaliation campaign, embodied in the V-weapons program. This massive industrial diversion consumed the equivalent of 24,000 additional fighter aircraft for the *Luftwaffe*, and neither the V 1 nor the V 2 proved decisive. Also, the program squandered the nation's technical capacities, for it meant that much more promising technologies, such as the Me 262 jet fighter, the Type XXI and Type XXIII U-Boats, new acoustic torpedoes, and the surface-to-air *Wasserfall* missile had to be given much less priority in terms of both intellectual and material commitment.[63] In the words of Albert Speer, from the end of July 1943 onwards, "...our tremendous industrial capacity was diverted to the huge missile known as the V 2... the whole notion was absurd."[64] Further, the 1944 campaign against the V 1 launch sites, coupled with the earlier (albeit costly) Bomber Command raid on the rocket development centre at Peenemünde on 17/18 August 1943, and in October upon the V 1 manufacturing site at Kassel, effectively blunted the limited impact of these weapons. Had they been available in quantity on D-Day, the effects of the bombs raining down upon the embarkation ports and the massed invasion fleet could have been catastrophic for the Allies. The Me 262 could potentially have been a war-winner for the Germans. However, it was slightly delayed in its service debut, due to Hitler's insistence that it be produced as one of the retaliation weapons, namely as a *Blitz* bomber, before it was approved belatedly for production as a fighter during the winter of 1944. More serious was the delay, necessitated by the pursuit of other priorities at least partially generated by the bombings, in addressing the technological shortcomings of the jet's engines. Had the aircraft been mass-produced as a fighter even six months earlier, its impact upon Allied bomber formations could have been cataclysmic. In short, the bombing campaign generated unforeseen technological responses conducted at breakneck pace, and helped encourage the German executive branch towards desperate solutions forged by passionate aims of retribution versus cold, methodical, and logical action.

Had Germany not been so diverted by the bombings and been free to mobilize its manpower and technological resources in a total war environment, chemical, biological, and even atomic weapons might well have been in store for the Allies. And based upon the Nazi track record, although their use was certainly somewhat moderated by fear of reprisals in kind, there is considerable evidence to suggest that the German authorities had no scruples with respect

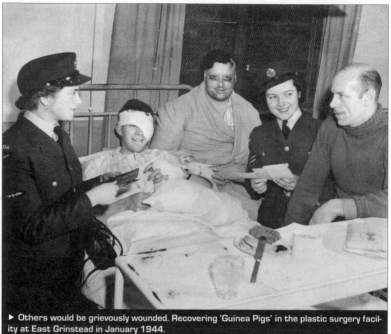

▶ Others would be grievously wounded. Recovering 'Guinea Pigs' in the plastic surgery facility at East Grinstead in January 1944.

Credit: DND PL26206

to their employment in acts of desperation, had they been widely available and deliverable. Concerning atomic weapons, the Germans were not particularly focused in that direction after the autumn of 1942, although their development remained a continuous worry for the Allies. As to whether Hitler would have had any moral reluctance to use them, Albert Speer's words are interesting: "I am sure that Hitler would not have hesitated for a moment to employ atom bombs against England."[65] And how, in Speer's opinion, did the bombing affect the pursuit of a focused German atomic program? "The increasing air raids had long since created an armaments emergency in Germany which ruled out any such ambitious enterprise. At best, with extreme concentration of all our resources, we could have had a German bomb by 1947."[66] Specifically, the wholesale evacuation of much of the Kaiser Wilhelm Institute for Physics research facility's infrastructure from the Dahlem suburb of Berlin to Haigerloch in the Black Forest, due to intimidation generated by the Berlin air raids, undoubtedly forced considerable delays and confusion upon the German atomic program and disrupted its focus.[67]

Furthermore, the curtailment of the V 2 program in the spring of 1945 was perhaps a more fortuitous event for the Allies than is broadly realized.

Specifications were already 'in the works' for an advanced version of the rocket known as the A 10, which was to use the V 2 as its second stage, and it would have had a trans-Atlantic reach. Had Germany been able to put together an atomic weapon program to meld with this delivery capability, the results could have been cataclysmic for the Allies. However, the bombings, the persecution of significant Jewish scientific talent, the widespread multiplicity of duplicating research programs, all of which were competing for Hitler's favour instead of working together, collectively conspired to stagnate German atomic weapons development. Further, the Germans had failed to separate U 235, the essential fissile element, on a *large* scale by August 1944, even though they had by then succeeded in manufacturing uranium oxide, a core material for atomic weapons. Still, in the view of the Alsos Team of Allied atomic specialists that thoroughly ransacked Germany at the close of the war, the Germans were years away from producing an atomic weapon at the same time the Allies were nearing successful completion of their own.[68]

With respect to biological warfare, recent research has determined that Germany was ready to deploy a foot-and-mouth bacteriological virus against Britain during the final months of the war. Successful tests were conducted in 1943 over Russian terrain against reindeer, but there was no guarantee that lagging German bomber and delivery system capabilities, due to the skewed concentration on fighter development necessitated by the bombing, were up to dispensing the material accurately.[69] The dispersal of chemical agents was constrained similarly by problems associated with effective delivery. The deadliest nerve gas of the day, Tabun, was manufactured in quantity at Dyhernfurth on the Oder River late in the war. Considered ten times more lethal than Phosgene, which was, until then, rated the most lethal war gas, 15,000 tons of Tabun were produced before the Soviets overran the production facility in 1945. However, all the finished products had been fitted into different host munitions and removed from the production facility prior to Soviet occupation. At war's end, nearly a half-million artillery shells and more than 100,000 aircraft bombs filled with Tabun were found in German arsenals, but their availability proved to be too late to orchestrate a delivery campaign, and subsequently they were destroyed by the western Allies. Other German nerve gas agents were called Sarin and Soman. The former, a quantum leap over Tabun in terms of lethality, proved to be exceptionally difficult to manufacture. Competing priorities and technological problems associated with its delivery delayed the emergence of Sarin, although over 7000 tons of it had been stockpiled by the end of the war. However, had the time, the will, and the wherewithal remained to effectively field the gas, the Sarin stockpile would have been enough to kill all the occupants of at least thirty cities the size of Paris. Soman, an even more potent agent, was never developed beyond the laboratory.[70]

THE MINING CAMPAIGN REAPS HUGE DIVIDENDS

Other Bomber Command 'diversions' contributed significantly to the war effort. The mining campaign was particularly successful in denying the use of the western Baltic to the Germans for transit and training. Late in the war, the influence of *Grossadmiral* Karl Dönitz upon Hitler was significant, particularly after Hermann Göring had fallen into disfavour. Bomber Command had mined the shallow waters of the western Baltic very effectively, which then made retention of the eastern Baltic of paramount importance to the *Kriegsmarine*. However, the eastern Baltic was more difficult for bombers to reach, and the region's deeper waters also rendered mines less effective. In order to retain sea control of the area, Dönitz maintained that the Germans needed to hold the Courland Pocket in western Latvia, and also the Gulf of Danzig, Memel, and East Prussia. Hitler agreed completely with Dönitz's assessment and concurred that loss of the region would paralyze the *Kriegsmarine*, particularly its U-Boat operations. That said, in a late-war conference, *Generaloberst* Heinz Guderian proposed that the forces in Courland, Memel, and East Prussia be evacuated in order to provide troops to counter the impending Red Army spring offensive. Nonetheless, based upon the influence of Dönitz, Hitler vetoed Guderian's proposal, and this effectively tied down forty German divisions, or a third of the forces available to fight the approaching Red Army. As it transpired, these tied-down forces effectively contributed virtually nothing to the 'twelfth-hour' defence of the German homeland, and protection of U-Boat operations in the eastern Baltic was also by then a moot point. In the words of the Australian journalist and historian, Chester Wilmot:

> The history of the Second World War affords no more striking example of the interplay of naval, air and land power, or of the interrelation of the Eastern and Western Front or, for that matter, of the grotesque miscalculations and wild hopes that governed Hitler's strategy. Because the German Air Force was unable to protect the U-Boat bases and training waters in the western Baltic, the German Army was obliged to hold the eastern Baltic against the Russians so that the German Navy might build up a new U-Boat fleet capable of inflicting a severe defeat on the Western Allies, and especially on the

hated British, whose refusal to capitulate in 1940 had made inevitable that war on two fronts, which had already destroyed most of Hitler's empire and was in the process of destroying the Third Reich.[71]

NO RESPITE FOR THE U-BOATS

In terms of direct effects of the bombing war against the *Kriegsmarine*, Sir Arthur Harris made the point that Bomber Command destroyed six German capital ships by either bombing or mining, in comparison to only four sunk during the entire war by the Royal Navy. Further, Bomber Command's Official History recorded that the command, working in conjunction with the American heavy bomber fleet, destroyed at least 207 German submarines during construction or in port after completion.[72] At the end of 1943, Dönitz held forth the promise of a reincarnated, invincible *Kriegsmarine*, spearheaded by a fleet of formidable new U-Boats. These submarines, which incorporated many technological improvements to enhance survivability and combat effectiveness, were scheduled for initial delivery in the autumn of 1944. Ultra-high-speed radio transmitters, more sophisticated acoustic torpedoes, rubber-coated hulls to complicate radar detection, as well as *schnorkel* underwater breathing devices and significant augmentation of the onboard batteries to allow the boats to remain submerged for protracted periods of time were just some of the improvements incorporated into these formidable new weapons. However, other industrial diversions, brought on in no small measure by the bombings, delayed production of the new boats. "First Brest, then Lorient saw the start of a long series of bombing raids which also greatly affected the civilian population, and the Germans soon realized the need to build shelters for personnel and equipment. To effectively protect the submarines themselves, it was necessary to produce solid bunkers... The accelerated construction of the U-Boat pens at Hamburg was a direct result of the bombing of the sheltered U-Boat bases in France."[73] Due partially to this enormous diversion of economic effort, production of the new variants was not given a high priority until the spring of 1943, by which time the Battle of the Atlantic effectively had been lost for Germany. The 'blue-water' Type XXI and its much smaller littoral-operating cousin, the Type XXIII, could perhaps have made a difference had they been brought on line two years earlier. Capable of formidable ranges underwater, the performance characteristics of both types were outstanding, and they promised much better prospects for attacking Allied shipping and evading the escorts than did the conventional U-Boats. Both required only a minimal daily time at *schnorkel* depth to keep their batteries charged, thus making detection extremely

Credits: DND PL42542

Credits: DND PL42536

▶ Reap the Whirlwind. Two views of the ruined city of Cologne, 1945.

difficult. But the spectre of bombing vulnerability had perpetuated a decision in the summer of 1943 to build these submarines in inland factories as modules,[74] and then transport those modules to coastal facilities for rapid final assembly.

However, the modular production produced delays brought on by improper fit-ment between the individual sections, and the reliance upon transportation of the modules to the final assembly points was also affected by the bombing.

> The failure to achieve the objectives was mainly caused by organiza-tion troubles, faulty design and bad workmanship. It was particularly annoying when sections did not fit to each other because the specified tolerances were exceeded. All these took place mainly in the first half of 1944 and it was fixed in the second half of the year. At that time, however, the Allies realized the danger and started regular bomb-ing raids, particularly on shipyards and water transport installations needed for transportation of massive Type XXI sections.[75]

Direct bombing delayed construction even further, such that only two Type XXIs and six Type XXIIIs were fully ready for combat by 1 May 1945; the date when 381 Type XXIs and 95 Type XXIIIs had been planned for delivery.[76] On top of the construction delays, the constant mining of the Baltic from the air inhibited the extensive training required on the new boats, delaying still further their introduction to service. Albert Speer elaborates upon the effects of the bombing: "We would have been able to keep our promise of delivering forty boats a month by early in 1945, however badly the war was going otherwise, if air raids had not destroyed a third of the submarines at the dockyards."[77] For all the aforementioned reasons, hardly any of the new boats were operational at war's end, although their success in a few engagements demonstrated great promise. However, it was once again a case of 'too little, too late...'[78]

PAVING THE WAY FOR INVASION

The strategic bombing campaign made possible a direct invasion of north-west Europe in the summer of 1944. The lodgement in Normandy was a direct result of the generalized destruction of the German industrial and eco-nomic war machine, particularly the German air force, prior to the actual inva-sion. The secondment of Bomber Command and the Eighth Air Force from April until September 1944 to Supreme Headquarters Allied Expeditionary Forces (SHAEF) under General Eisenhower resulted in a significant deple-tion, destruction, and disorganization of the *Luftwaffe*, as well as the enemy's rail communications, prior to the invasion. In its immediate wake, these for-mations provided highly extensive direct tactical support for the land cam-paign. Bomber Command was particularly zealous in its pursuit of rail targets, attacking over one hundred of them prior to D-Day. Since much greater accuracy was possible in 1944, by June, most of the 37 rail centres assigned to Bomber Command were either destroyed or heavily damaged. These efforts, coupled with the destruction of the Seine River bridges the week prior to the invasion, rendered effective German reinforcement virtually impossible. Air superiority then secured the flanks of the lodgement area after the landings, and concomitant attacks on oil production facilities significantly further handicapped both the German army and the *Luftwaffe*.

Along with attacking other major military targets in France, Bomber Command dropped some 14,000 tons of high explosives on the Atlantic Wall fortifications during the prelude to the landings, including 5000 tons of explosives on the defending beaches themselves.[79] After the ground forces were ashore, the command continued its attacks on rail and military targets, including successful efforts against the ports of Le Havre, Boulogne, Brest, Calais, St. Malo, and Cap Gris Nez. Most of France had been cleared of the enemy when Eisenhower handed control of Bomber Command back to the RAF on 16 September 1944. However, the command continued to support the land armies in a tactical sense whenever called upon to do so, including during the late-war push into Germany. The words of Joseph Goebbels bear testimony: "... the enemy is afraid of severe casualties but, as soon as he meets resistance, he calls in his air force which then simply turns the area of resistance into a desert."[80]

THE GERMAN CIVILIAN TRAGEDY IN PERSPECTIVE

With respect to collateral casualties within the Greater German Reich, various sources estimate that approximately 410,000 civilians were killed due to Allied bombing. However, to this number one must add 23,000 non-military police and civilians attached to the German armed forces, 32,000 foreigners and prisoners of war, and 128,000 displaced persons, which brings the total to approximately 593,000 non-combatants. A further 60,000 Italians need to be added to this total within the context of the European Axis states. An additional 486,000 people were wounded or injured by the bombing within the Greater German Reich alone. However, while these are large numbers, they pale in comparison to the genocide perpetrated upon the peoples of Eurasia by the Germans and their proxies. In counterpoint, Great Britain lost roughly 65,000 civilians to aerial attack, approximately 43,000 of whom perished during the Blitz of 1940-1941.[81] Total wartime German armed forces losses were approximately 3.8 million killed.[82] With respect to the stated Allied war aim of de-housing the civilian work force, 3,370,000 dwellings in the Reich were destroyed by the bombings, and 7,500,000 persons were made homeless.

The civilian loss of life from the bombing has, in Richard Overy's words, "…occasioned the most bitter recriminations of all against the bombing strategy. It is something that Bomber Command survivors take seriously and have thought about deeply."[83] That said, he argues that the British executive no longer felt obliged to act in self-restraint after the German bombing of Warsaw and Rotterdam during the war's opening months, and that the tens of thousands of British deaths during the Blitz and the later Baedeker Raids on British cities other than London "…made redundant any further discussion about the rights and wrongs of bombing targets with the risk of civilian casualty."[84] Those who see fit to challenge the morality of the area bombing in particular should bear in mind that a far greater travesty would have been to allow the moral obscenity that was the Third Reich to prevail unchecked.

Readers also need to bear in mind that bombing conducted for the purpose of lowering enemy morale was not the exclusive purview of Bomber Command. In Chapter One, we covered the American attitudes and policies with respect to area bombing, as practiced *generally* in *Operations Thunderclap* and *Clarion,* and *particularly* at Dresden and Berlin. Major-General Frederick L. Anderson Jr. was the commanding general of the American Eighth Bomber Command within the parent Eighth Air Force for most of the combined portion of the European air war. With respect to the isolated, late-war American bombing of mainly smaller urban centres, General Anderson noted that while such operations were not expected in themselves to shorten the war, "…it is expected that the fact that Germany was struck all over will be passed on, from father to son, thence to grandson, (and) that a deterrent for the initiation of future wars will definitely result."[85] In an extension of this argument, British author Keith Lowe, in his highly acclaimed 2007 release entitled *Inferno: The Destruction of Hamburg, 1943,* maintains, along with others, that the experience of this specific bombing, and the subsequent campaign against the German cities, eventually knocked militarism out of the German people. Current German attitudes with respect to participation in foreign military operations certainly reinforce this point.

As the late-war evidence of Nazi atrocities mounted, best exemplified by the overrunning of the death camps and the institutionalized murder committed therein, there developed a significant Allied hardening of sentiment, for right

GEBT MIR FÜNF JAHRE
UND IHR WERDET
DEUTSCHLAND NICHT
WIEDER ERKENNEN
ADOLF HITLER

GIVE ME FIVE YEARS &
YOU WILL NOT
RECOGNIZE GERMANY
AGAIN

Credit: Author's collection

▶ Sign posted in rubble-strewn streets of Mainz, Germany, close to the war's end.

or for wrong, to bring the German people so completely to their knees that they would never again contemplate bringing another holocaust down upon the world. This was reflected in the partial tactical use of strategic bombers during the push through Germany in the closing weeks. If a German urban area resisted and generated Anglo-American casualties resulting from house-to-house fighting, such as had occurred at Ortona, Italy, and elsewhere in the advance across northwest Europe, it was normally shelled and bombed into rubble. However, those centres that acquiesced peacefully were normally spared further destruction. For the most part, similar courtesies were not extended during the Soviet advance, and German citizens were quite aware of the distinction being exercised by the western Allies.[86] These actions served to reinforce the point that no citizen of the Third Reich was immune *to* or exempt *from* the bombing, and that further armed resistance was futile. The deliberate demoralization of the enemy undoubtedly helped shatter the German will to resist, hastening the capitulation of German forces in the western urban centres, and thereby saving many lives, both Allied and Axis.

THE MORAL ISSUE

As Richard Overy has recently postulated, perhaps the most important point to take from study of the moral argument for the bombing campaign is *why* the two major participating democracies ultimately "…[engaged] in forms of total war that abandoned altogether the moral high ground they had tried to occupy in the 1930s."[87] The reasons are not particularly complex. First, the British, who were the first of the two "great democracies" to abandon that moral high ground, were also the first to engage the Axis forces, and they had been provided with many prior examples of indiscriminate area bombing by Germany, including Warsaw in 1939, Rotterdam, London, and many other British cities in 1940, then Belgrade, Yugoslavia, and additional British urban centres in 1941 and 1942. Area bombing was really the only viable offensive tool available to the British at the time, and it served due notice to friends and foes alike that Britain could, and would, fight back. It provided offensive relief to the Soviets when no other form of concentrated, sustained attack upon the enemy was yet possible. Further, while the premises upon which the bombing was conducted, along with some elements of its execution, may, in hindsight, appear somewhat flawed, substantial and repeated feedback from intelligence sources inside the Third Reich indicated that the bombing was scoring telling blows. Much of this rationale was still applicable after the United States entered the war. Further, the Americans were exerting pressure upon their British partners to conclude the European war as expeditiously as possible, and then to turn their combined attentions against the Japanese in the Pacific theatre. The Americans also learned, both through association with the British and from their own combat experiences, that their own bombing forces were also, in reality, blunt instruments of destruction with little true precision bombing capabilities. This, in spite of the long-fostered, mythological public stance that they could precisely 'drop their bombs in a pickle barrel' with the Norden bombsight. Much of the present-day abhorrence of the wartime area bombing strategy has been generated and inflamed by the current propensity for viewing the campaign through the lens of *today's* technological capabilities. While existing 'smart' weapons can surgically gut a specific room in a building without figuratively 'rattling the china' in an adjacent room, such technology simply was not available during the Second World War.

During the war's closing months, the Germans waged an extremely effective propaganda campaign against the bombings. It was channeled through the neutral countries to various Allied news agencies, and it highlighted, among other things, the bombing of Dresden in February 1945. The 'disinformation' embedded in these communiqués included grossly inflated casualty figures of up to 1000 percent.[88] The bombing of Dresden has become the *cause célèbre* of all those opposed to the bombing offensive, but was the city a mere casualty of war, or was it a highly legitimate military target? In fact, early in 1945, far from being just an innocent and beautiful baroque urban centre subjected to wanton destruction by the Allies, Dresden was an armed camp, a vital communications, transportation, and staging hub for German forces fighting on the Eastern Front, and host to scores of factories engaged in highly significant war production work, including that accomplished by the massive Zeiss-Ikon complex, by far the largest single employer in the city. And it had been a very long time since Zeiss-Ikon had manufactured anything as innocuous as a holiday snapshot camera. Along with Zeiss-Ikon, Dresden played host to the Siemens glass plant, the Seidel & Naumann industrial complex, and a Shell refinery. Other facilities embedded in the residential suburbs, as was the custom in Berlin and other major urban centres, were factories producing engines for *Junkers* aircraft, radar, and other electronic components, fuses for anti-aircraft shells, gas masks, cockpit components for *Messerschmitt* fighters, an arsenal, and a poison gas factory. "These war factories employed somewhere in the region of 10,000 people – 1500 of them in the fuse factory alone – so it can hardly be maintained that Dresden made only a small contribution to the German war effort."[89] The 1944 handbook to the German Army High Command's Weapon Office itemized 127 factories in the city of Dresden that were engaged in industrial war work, and an authority at the Dresden City Museum has recently categorized the list as being "...very incomplete."[90] By that time, most of Dresden's pre-war industrial activities, which had largely been related to leisure and luxury goods, had been converted to war-related production tasks. For example, Seidel & Naumann had switched from sewing machines to armaments; Richard Gäbel & Company, from manufacturing marzipan and waffles to torpedo components; J.C. Müller Universelle-Werke, from cigarette-making machines, to machine guns, aircraft parts, searchlights, torpedo components, and directional equipment made by 4000 workers, many of whom were foreigners from the occupied territories. And the list of war industrial enterprises goes on and on...[91] The picturesque city centre, the *Altstadt*, contained the Central Telegraph Office, the Main Police Headquarters, a power station, one of the Siemens factories, and a significant military transport headquarters. Perhaps most importantly, Dresden was also a major rail hub and junction point, as well as a key nodal point in the German postal and telegraph network, and, consequently, it constituted a critical location for the military with respect to transportation and communications. Three major rail stations and the Friedrichstadt marshalling yards were all located a mile or less from the *Altstadt*, and both the north-south and east-west axes of the German state railway system ran directly through the city, which controlled rolling stock over more than 3000 miles of track. By late-1943, the Dresden railway directorate employed a total of 128,000 workers. "It was the hub connecting the two major rail lines between Berlin and Leipzig and accordingly was a troop concentration area. There was therefore no logical reason – other than its distance from Lincolnshire – for it to have been exempt from air attack."[92] It was, in short, a legitimate transportation and communications target, the kind that had been receiving priority attention from the Anglo-American bombing forces for many months. And although Dresden was a city of great beauty and cultural significance, it was also one of the most ardently pro-Nazi and zealously anti-Semitic cosmopolitan centres in the Third Reich, and it had enthusiastically embraced the German National Socialism movement from its outset. *Gauleiter* Martin Mutschmann, the senior Nazi party official, provincial governor, and defence commissioner in Dresden, was particularly brutal and relentless in his persecution of local Jews and other "undesirables." A significant number of Dresden's citizens took their behavioural cues from the *Gauleiter*'s cruel example.[93]

Readers will also recall from Chapter One that Dresden was bombed to assist the Soviets in their own combat endeavours, as they were then conducting major offensive operations approximately 100 kilometers to the east of the city. Once the war was over and Dresden had fallen behind the Iron Curtain, it was not to the Soviets' advantage to trumpet this bombing request to the new world order, since the ideological polarities that characterized the subsequent Cold War had hardened very quickly. Today, there are those who continue to condemn the bombing. One of the most prominent recent examples is the British philosopher Anthony C. Grayling, who has actually gone as far as to imply a 'moral equivalency' between the Allied strategic bombing campaign and the 9/11 attacks on the United States. Part of the problem, this writer believes, is a widespread current propensity to view historical decisions and the actions that resulted from those decisions through the filtering lens of present day sensitivities. History can only be judged properly from within the context of the times during which it occurred. Hindsight, as the saying goes, invariably benefits from 20/20 clarity.

As to the frequently advanced argument, fatuous at best, that the Second World War was 'Hitler's war', and that 70 million Germans wanted no part of it, those

Credit: Halifax Restoration Team Trenton

▶ A Canadian *Halifax* crew and their fetching pinup nose art in a happy wartime moment.

attitudes were not much in evidence when Nazi legions were having their way with most of Eurasia during the first three years of the war. Nor is that argument of any consolation to the ghosts of the millions who were systematically exterminated in the death camps and elsewhere. Lost in much of the debate is the fact that Nazism was a thoroughly repulsive and evil force bent upon world domination, enslavement, and mass genocide. It needed to be stopped quickly, and by whatever best means were believed to be available at the time.

Public opinion surveys from the war confirm widespread support for the bombing.[94] Neither politicians nor historians of the period challenged the policy extensively at the time, and while British authorities maintained staunchly

that civilian casualties were nothing but "... an unfortunate by-product of attacks on industrial areas, there is little reason to believe that the general public
would have complained had it been otherwise."[95] Further, there was very little
questioning of the morality of the bombing during the war, and what little that
did occur came primarily from isolated British religious leaders. In the spring
of 1941, the Bishop of Chichester, George Bell, and Doctor Cosmo Lang, the
Archbishop of Canterbury, both felt that the still-embryonic policy of bombing non-combatants should not be allowed to prevail. However, most British
clerics supported the bomber offensive through its various stages of development. "'Often in life there is no clear choice between absolute right and wrong;
frequently the choice has to be made of the lesser of two evils,' wrote Dr. Cyril
Garbett, the Archbishop of York, '...and it is a lesser evil to bomb a war-loving
Germany than to sacrifice the lives of thousands of our own fellow-countrymen...
and to delay delivering millions now held in slavery.'"[96] Garbett then went on
to argue compellingly in favour of Allied use of air power to bring the conflict
to a swift, successful conclusion. These views were published in *The Times* on
25 June 1943, and they had, by then, the unequivocal approval of Lambeth Pal-
ace, home of the Archbishop of Canterbury.[97] Indeed, William Temple, who
succeeded Cosmo Lang as the Archbishop of Canterbury, echoed Garbett's
stance in favour of the bomber offensive, and Lang would also do so eventually.
Temple, reluctantly, and yet with total conviction, concurred that the bombing
was a necessary evil in a world far from perfect. In December 1942, he wrote
opponents of the area bombing policy in part: "The worst of all things is to fight
and do it ineffectively. Therefore, while I agree with you [that] strategic consideration cannot stand alone, it [the bombing] becomes very nearly decisive
for our conduct."[98] Only Bishop of Chichester George Bell, in terms of prominent British religious leaders, remained a consistent critic of the area bombing
policy. Downstream of his initial objections, in February 1943, Bell urged the
House of Lords to resist the War Cabinet's decision to further area bombing.
And again on 9 February 1944, he demanded that the House of Lords put an
end to such bombing, an opinion that, according to the House of Lords official
website, "... received very little support at the time, and no support at all from
the Government."[99]

Finally, Martin Middlebrook offers the following opinion: "A country fighting
for its very existence cannot afford to have strict boundaries of morality in the
means by which it saves itself. It is sheer humbug to suggest that the use of
bombers at this time was wrong when it was touch and go whether Britain
survived at all."[100]

CHAPTER THREE

THE LEGAL ISSUE

Even the German camp has long acknowledged that, moral issues aside, the area bombing policy as it was conducted during the Second World War was entirely legitimate. During the war, Eberhard Spetzler was a legal staff officer in the *Luftwaffe*. Post-war, when he was a professor of law at the University of Göttingen, Spetzler opined:

> Since there are separate rules for land and sea warfare and none was ever signed for aerial warfare, the Rules for Land Warfare cannot be applied to strategic bombing. Article 25 clearly states that it is meant to protect civilians during the physical conquest of their land. Bombers do not occupy enemy territory, they only destroy it. For a city to be protected by Article 25, it must not have any defences. Fighters attacking bombers over their target must be considered [to be] defending the city.[101]

In point of fact, although the Red Cross Convention on the Protection of Civilians in Wartime was agreed upon in Stockholm in August 1948,[102] it was never formally ratified, and the matter has only been fully legislated against since 1977 in the wake of the Vietnam War, when the First Protocol to the Fourth Convention expressly forbade deliberate military attacks upon civilians. And it should be emphasized that this particular legislation was made possible largely by significant technological advances with respect to weapons delivery, which have, for the most part, rendered area bombing unnecessary.

The widespread damage resulting from the fire raids on Rostock and Lübeck in March and April of 1942 was candidly and appreciatively reported to the British public at the time, as it was in the Dominions. For example, in far-away Ottawa, none other than the Canadian Prime Minister Mackenzie King recorded similar sentiments. He noted in his diary that the Germans were the ones who had first embarked upon an indiscriminate bombing policy.[103] While B.K. Sandwell, the liberalist editor of *Saturday Night* worried about the moral toll it would take upon the aircrews themselves, in the end, he had to side with the policy:

> The defeat of Germany can only be brought about by killing Germans, and if the object of these raids is to kill Germans... it is a perfectly proper object. The blood of such innocent persons as these is

not upon us... The whole German people brought upon themselves whatever calamities may issue for them out of this war, when they put themselves under the kind of government which was bound to make such a war ultimately inevitable. It is our unavoidable task to make Germany suffer.[104]

Other Canadian national papers echoed Sandwell's opinions:

In its editorial of 31 May 1943, the *Toronto Telegram* declared that, while bombing undoubtedly meant "misery and death for the people of the Axis nations... it is better that they should be blotted out entirely than that the world should be subjected to the rulers they have tolerated so long, and there are many who hold that they must be made to know in full the horrors of war, if a new war is to be avoided." The *Winnipeg Free Press*, meanwhile, had already belittled the few who demanded limitations on bombing because they were asking "air crews still more to endanger their own lives so that they may perhaps save the lives of workers in industrial war facilities or living in the immediate neighbourhood of those targets."[105]

AREA BOMBING AND THE JAPANESE WAR

Not the least of the wartime contributions of the Allied bombing campaign in Europe was that its success inspired a similar late-war campaign against the industrial cities of the Japanese home islands. The strategic area bombing of Japan, conducted by the American Twentieth Air Force in 1944 and 1945, destroyed an area thirty times greater in size than did the two atomic weapon releases at Hiroshima and Nagasaki in August 1945. Ironically, when high-level daylight bombing with high explosives proved ineffective and costly early in the campaign, the Americans borrowed a page from Bomber Command's operational notebook by conducting a series of night raids at relatively low level using incendiaries. The success of this area bombing was due to the unfettered use of those incendiary weapons against highly inflammable targets. In reality, the loss of 250,000 Japanese lives, the wounding or injuring of a further 500,000, and the destruction of 40 percent of the buildings in 66 industrialized cities had brought Japan to the brink of surrender prior to the atomic bomb drops on 6 August and 9 August respectively.[106] And yet, based upon the evidence of the fierce determination to resist an Allied invasion of the home islands, perhaps best exemplified by the sacrifice of 2530 Japanese Navy aircrew members[107] and at least as many Army aircrew[108] on *Kamikaze* missions directed against Allied shipping, the last of which took place on the day of the cessation of hostilities, 15 August 1945, the Allied executive was greatly concerned about the blood cost to *both* sides, should an invasion of the Japanese home islands prove necessary. Winston Churchill elaborates:

> We had contemplated the desperate resistance of the Japanese fight-ing to the death with Samurai devotion, not only in pitched battles, but in every cave and dugout. I had in my mind the spectacle of Oki-nawa Island, where many thousands of Japanese, rather than surren-der, had drawn up in line and destroyed themselves by hand grenades after their leaders had solemnly performed the rite of *hara-kiri*. To quell the Japanese resistance man by man and to conquer the country yard by yard might well require the loss of a million American lives and half that number of British – or more if we could get them there: for we were resolved to share the agony.[109]

Indeed, the Japanese War Cabinet, the military clique under the control of the Prime Minister, General Hideki Tojo, was bound and determined to commit the Japanese people to mass suicide, calling for the sacrifice of up to 100,000,000 Japanese to repel the Allied invasion of the home islands.[110] The area bombing of Japan had certainly dealt a debilitating blow to the Japanese war industries, and the remaining factories were on the verge of collapsing for want of com-ponent parts and damage to infrastructure. And yet, in July 1945, since the Japanese aviation industry was still capable of producing over 1000 military aircraft per month,[111] many hundreds of warplanes were still available for home defence,[112] and there was no shortage of suicidally-inspired pilots available and willing to substitute courage for technological inadequacy and dive their air-craft into a massed Allied invasion force. Further, "Orders went out that every Japanese man between the ages of 15 and 60 and all women aged 17 to 40 would meet the invaders at beaches with sharpened bamboo poles. Allied peace feel-ers were rejected."[113]

Although it was a difficult decision for the Allies, the two atomic drops, with the concomitant loss of an additional 150,000 Japanese citizens, com-bined with a rapidly-worsening war situation, largely precipitated by the area bombing of the industrial cities, but also influenced undoubtedly by the 'twelfth hour' entry of the Soviet Union into the Pacific war, coupled with Allied absolution of the emperor with respect to responsibility for the prosecution of the war, persuaded the Japanese that further resistance was pointless. Defending against the massed fleets of formidable, heavily-protected B-29 *Superfortresses* was difficult enough, but the atomic drops on Hiroshima and Nagasaki convinced them that they were powerless to defend the *entire* nation from the high and fast-flying, singly-penetrating B-29s that could be bombing anywhere in the nation, 'the ultimate shell game,' to draw an analogy. This underscoring of the futility of further resistance spared the Japanese people from the obligation of being killed to the last available fighting man and woman. Therefore, strategic bombing undoubtedly ultimately prevented many casualties, both Allied and Japanese, by eliminating the need for an armed invasion of the Japanese mainland, the costs of which, measured by any yardstick, would have been horrific.

It is perhaps appropriate that the area bombing policy's most dedicated champion, Sir Arthur Harris, should have the last word on the moral justification of command policy. Readers will recall that in 1942, in one of his most famous newsreel speeches of the war, he reminded his audience that it was the Nazis who had "...sown the wind," and that, in return, they would "...reap the whirlwind."[114] His words were, to say the least, prophetic. And ultimately, any short-fall to expectations of what the bombing campaign could accomplish cannot be laid at the feet of Sir Arthur Harris. Rather, Robin Neillands believes that, unlike the later atomic drops upon Japan, Harris simply did not have the weapon to devastate Germany in a manner that would concomitantly crush the German will to resist. Furthermore, Neillands believes,

> ...[that Harris] was also hindered throughout his campaign by a classic piece of military miscalculation, a failure by the Allied Combined Chiefs of Staff to maintain the aim. The aim of Bomber Command operations, apart from the time they began in 1939, was *to carry the war to the heart of the enemy homeland.* That was what the strategic bomber was *for,* and no one in authority disputed this. "There is one thing that will bring him [Hitler] down, and that is an absolutely devastating, exterminating attack by heavy bombers on the Nazi homeland. We must be able to overwhelm him by these means, without which I do not see a way through." Thus wrote Winston Churchill in 1940,[115] and throughout the war, the Directives that landed upon Harris's desk continued to press this point on him. Harris needed no such urging; what he needed was more aircraft and a free hand. Instead, there was a failure, at all levels, to maintain the intention and carry it through.

The main failure lay in not providing Bomber Command with the wherewithal to carry out this declared intention; it was not the fault of Air Chief Marshal Harris. From the earliest days of the war there was a continual diversion of bomber strength, with aircraft and crews sent to North Africa and Italy, to Coastal Command and to the Far East. This steady drain prevented Harris from ever achieving the size of force he needed to carry out the instructions he was given.[116]

A FEW CLOSING THOUGHTS

Bomber Command played an essential part as a guarantor of Allied victory during the Second World War. It provided an offensive tool that took the fight to the enemy when none other was available, and it gave the citizens of the Allied nations hope and pride while it did so. It provided Britain and the Dominions, through its very prosecution, a political dimension by which it could influence the conduct of the war. It demanded a significant diversion of German resources away from the Eastern Front, thereby aiding the USSR in its part of the combined struggle. It struck substantial and unrelenting blows against enemy morale. It threw Germany's broader war strategy into disarray, and it generated a loss of German air superiority, along with doing much significant damage to the Reich's war industrial base. It made the way safer for an Allied re-entry into northwest Europe in 1944, and it effectively stymied German economic mobilization and technological development in many areas. While a great human price was paid for these accomplishments on both the combatant sides, in relative terms, the losses incurred to the Anglo-Americans were small when compared to those suffered elsewhere, such as in the USSR. And the overall cost was relatively low as a percentage of the total war effort, considering the gains that were realized.

> Although the air war was only a part of an enormous conflict that swept over Europe, it did prove decisive in helping the Allies achieve victory, since it played an indispensable role, without which the Anglo-American lodgment on the continent and the final defeat of the Third Reich was inconceivable.
>
> ~ Williamson Murray[117]

What bombing (in part) did – both area and precision – was to act as a constant source of attrition for most industrialists, interrupting transport flows, hitting small component factories, attacking gas, electricity and power supplies. Many of these were not critical but the important thing was their cumulative effect.

~ Richard Overy[118]

NOTES

1.   Richard Overy, *Bomber Command 1939-1945 - Reaping the Whirlwind* (London: HarperCollins, 1997), p.200.
2.   Mark K. Wells, *Courage and Air Warfare* (London: Frank Cass, 1995), p.2.
3.   Of note, Robin Neillands appears to be the only reputable author who cites 110,000 versus 125,000 as the total number of aircrew who flew with Bomber Command during the war years, nor does Neillands cite his source. Sir Arthur Harris and a host of other distinguished sources, including Richard Holmes, all use the 125,000 figure. Further, if the Neillands total number is correct, then the overall fatal loss rate for Bomber Command climbs from 45 percent to 51 percent. Robin Neillands, *The Bomber War - The Allied Air Offensive Against Nazi Germany* (New York: Overlook Press, 2001), p.379.
4.   Sir Arthur Harris, *Bomber Offensive* (London: Collins, 1947), p. 267, and Overy, *Bomber Command*, p.202.
5.   Overy, *Bomber Command*, p.209, and John Terraine, *The Right of the Line - The Royal Air Force and the European War 1939-1945* (London: Hodder and Stoughton, 1985), p.537.
6.   Overy, *Bomber Command*, p.209.
7.   Franklin D'Olier *et. al.*, *The US Strategic Bomb Survey-Overall Report-European War-September 30, 1945*, (Washington: US Government Printing Office, 1945), p.71.
8.   Embedded within this statistic are even more chilling ones. By way of examples, between 11-13 May 1943 and 21-25 June 1943, 6 Group's missing rate rose to 11.5 percent, and on the night of 12/13 May, on a raid to Duisburg, to 13.3 percent. Also, *Halifax* losses from mid-December 1943 to mid-January 1944 averaged 9.8 percent. Brereton Greenhous, Stephen J. Harris, William C. Johnston, and William G.P. Rawling, *The Crucible of War 1939-1945 ~ The Official History of the Royal Canadian Air Force - Volume III* (Toronto: University of Toronto Press, 1994), pp.671, 681.
9.   Ibid., p.681.
10.   Ibid., p.683.
11.   During the (generalized) period of the Battle of Berlin, "... 1081 crews failed to return from 24,754 night bombing sorties (4.36 percent), mining cost just twenty-one of 2078 sorties (1.01 percent). No. 6 Group Analysis of Results, DHist 74/250, in Ibid., p.788.
12.   Overy, *Bomber Command*, p.183.
13.   To be precise, it was 430,747 tons dropped out of 955,044 total, or 45.1 percent. <http:/www. nucleus.com/twright/bc-stats/html>, accessed 23 September 2003.
14.   Overy, *Bomber Command*, p.184.
15.   And similar surges of effort to the Hamburg raids of July-August 1943 on other industrial centres.
16.   Overy, *Bomber Command*, p.185.
17.   Ibid., p.191.
18.   Albert Speer, "Spandau: The Secret Diaries," in The Bomber Harris Trust, *A Battle for Truth* (Agincourt, ON: Ramsey, 1994), p.64.
19.   Overy, *Bomber Command*, p.191.
20.   Edward Jablonski, *America in the Air War* (Alexandria, Virginia: Time-Life Books, 1982), p.142.
21.   Overy, *Bomber Command*, p.191.
22.   Ibid.
23.   Jablonski, p.142.
24.   E.L. Homze and H. Boog, *The Luftwaffe* (Alexandria, VA: Time-Life Books, 1982), p.161.

25. D'Olier *et al.*, p.39.

26. Albert Speer, *Inside the Third Reich* (New York: Galahad, 1970), p.224.

27. D'Olier *et al.*, p.60.

28. Ibid., p.61

29. Ibid., p.62.

30. Ibid., p.65.

31. Overy, *Bomber Command*, p.192.

32. Speer, *Inside the Third Reich*, p.299.

33. Overy, *Bomber Command*, p.197.

34. D'Olier *et al.*, p.19. Specifically, Germany's planned underground factory program, which constituted over 48 million square feet of floor space to accommodate the manufacturing needs of the aircraft industry, tanks, vehicles, V-weapons, ships, other weapons, machine tools, other supplies, and projects specifically for the SS, had only been completed to the extent of 13,396,200 square feet, at tremendous cost in diversion of economic effort, by the end of the European hostilities. Overy, *Bomber Command*, p.215.

35. Williamson Murray, *The Luftwaffe-Strategy for Defeat* (Secaucus, NJ: Chartwell, 1986), p.223.

36. Memo No. 529 (Special Distribution and War Cabinet from Switzerland), dated 28 July 1940, in Public Record Office (PRO) Premier 3/11/1, p.35.

37. Dudley Saward, *Bomber Harris-The Authorized Biography* (London: Cassell, 1984), pp.162-163.

38. Overy, *Bomber Command*, p.197, and Richard Overy, *A Presentation to the Symposium on the Strategic Bomber Offensive, 1939-1945*, RAF Staff College Bracknell, 26 March 1993.

39. D'Olier *et al.*, pp.96-97.

40. Speer, *Inside the Third Reich*, p. 262.

41. D'Olier *et al.*, p.97.

42. Ibid., p.98.

43. Ibid.

44. Joseph Goebbels, *Final Entries 1945* (New York: Putnam's, 1978), p.117.

45. Ibid., p.149.

46. Ibid., p.299.

47. Albert Speer, "Spandau: The Secret Diaries," in The Bomber Harris Trust, *A Battle for Truth*, p.64.

48. Burke Cahill, member, Canadian Committee for the Study of World War II, letter to Director General History, National Defence Headquarters, circa 2000, at <http://www.blvl.igs.net/~jlynch/bharis60.html> , p.4, accessed 14 September 2003.

49. Henry Probert, *Bomber Harris - His Life and Times* (Toronto: Stoddart, 2001), p.337.

50. Götz Bergander, quoted in Ibid., p.338.

51. Speer, *Inside the Third Reich*, pp.278-279.

52. Overy, *Bomber Command*, p.197.

53. The Bomber Harris Trust, *A Battle for Truth*, p.65, and Overy, *Bomber Command*, p.213.

54. Overy, *Bomber Command*, p.197.

55. Ibid., p.214.

56. In fact, even *Luftwaffe* bomber commanders had long argued for a concentration on fighter production, far earlier than it actually occurred.

57. Murray, p.225.

58. Matthew Cooper, *The German Air Force 1933-1945* (London: Jane's, 1981), p.377. Also, between 1 September 1939 and 28 February 1945, the last date for which reliable figures exist, *Luftwaffe* fatalities included 44,065 aircrew killed and another 27,610 missing or captured. Alfred Price, *A Pictorial History of the Luftwaffe 1933-1945* (London: Ian Allan, 1969), p.59.

59. Homze and Boog, p.170.

60. Most of the remaining losses were attributed to anti-aircraft artillery fire (flak).

61. Cajus Bekker, *The Luftwaffe War Diaries* (London: MacDonald,1967), p.380.

62. Specifically, the German night fighter arm accumulated a wartime total of 6048 air-to-air victories, 215 during day operations and 5833 at night. Of the latter total, only 1041, or one-sixth, were gained over the Eastern Front. Gebhard Aders, *History of the German Night Fighter Force 1917-1945* (Stuttgart: Motorbuch-Verlag, 1978), p.239. *Nachtjagdgeschwader* I alone accounted for 2318 victories, measured against 676 fatal aircrew casualties. Werner Held & Holger Nauroth, *The Defense of the Reich* (New York: Arco, 1982), p.219.

63. Overy, *Bomber Command*, p.201.

64. Speer, *Inside the Third Reich*, p.365.

65. Ibid., p.227.

66. Ibid., p.229.

67. Antony Beevor, *The Fall of Berlin 1945* (New York: Viking, 2002), p.139. On 24 April 1945, Soviet troops reached Dahlem and the Kaiser Wilhelm Institute for Physics the following day. Along with various pieces of useful equipment, NKVD troops found "...250 kilograms of metallic uranium; three tons of uranium oxide; twenty litres of heavy water." Ibid., pp.324-325. Further, related work was being conducted at a plant in Stassfurt in northern Germany, where an Allied team led by John Lonsdale, head of security for the Manhattan Project, found a cache of bomb materials on 17 April 1945. Specifically, the team discovered about 1100 tons of ore, some in the form of uranium oxide. This team, known as the Alsos Mission, additionally rounded up several prominent German atomic scientists in the region within a week, including Werner Heisenberg and Otto Hahn. Anahad O'Connor, "John Lonsdale," *The Scotsman*, Monday, 8 September 2003, at <wysiwyg://14/http://www.news.scotsman.com/obituaries.cfm?id=989462003>, accessed 24 October 2003.

68. John Keegan, *The Second World War* (New York: Penguin, 1989), p. 582.

69. Nazis Planned to Use Virus Against Britain," in *The Times*, Monday 12 March 2001, at <wysiwyg://3http://www.the.times.co.uk/article02-97518,00.html>, accessed 16 October 2003.

70. Brian J. Ford, *German Secret Weapons: Blueprint for Mars* (New York: Ballentine's, 1969), pp.106-110, and *Forgotten Battles: The Weapons: Tabun Nerve Gas*, at <wysiwyg://19/http://www.geocities.com/pentagon/bunker/335/germweps/tabun.html>, accessed 12 November 2003.

71. Chester Wilmot, *The Struggle for Europe* (London: Wordsworth, 1998), p.620.

72. Noted in Martin Middlebrook, *The Nuremberg Raid* (London: Penguin, 1973), p.312.

73. Jan Heitmann, "Destroying the Hamburg U-Boat Pens," in *After the Battle* (London: Battle of Britain International, 2001), Volume 111, pp.30-31.

74. Speer, *Inside the Third Reich*, p.273.

75. *U-Boat-The Elektroboats-Getting Ready*, at <http://uboat.net/technical/electroboats3.htm>, accessed 14 December 2003.

76. Ibid.

77. Speer, *Inside the Third Reich*, p.274. To elaborate further upon the air raids, on the night of 8/9 March 1945, 312 Bomber Command aircraft dropped 983 tons of bombs on Hamburg, inflicting heavy damage upon the Blohm & Voss shipyard and also destroying boats at the Howaldswerke yard. On 31 March, 469 aircraft dropped 2217 tons, inflicting more severe damage on the Howaldswerke facility. Again on 9 April, 17 specialty *Lancasters* bombed Hamburg's Fink II pens with fifteen five-ton *Tallboys* and two ten-ton *Grand Slams*, causing serious damage to the pens themselves, as well as the neighboring barracks, boiler houses, storage houses and workshops. The night prior to this impressive day raid, 440 Main Force bombers had dropped 1481 tons on the Hamburg port facilities. Heitmann, pp.34-35.

78. Only Type XXIIs U 2511 and U 3008 were operational by the end of hostilities. Robert Hutchinson, *War Beneath the Waves* (London: HarperCollins, 2003), p.104.

79. Overy, *Bomber Command*, p.88.

80. Goebbels, p.298.

81. Holmes, p.215.

82. Overy, *Bomber Command*, p.202, and Bekker, p.386.

83. Overy, *Bomber Command*, p.202.

84. Ibid.

85. Public Record Office documents, as quoted in Richard Norton-Taylor's "Allied Bombers Chose 'Easy' German Targets," in *The Guardian*, Thursday 23 August 2001.

86. In spite of all their pious, post-war posturing, particularly with respect to Dresden, the Soviets made no attempt whatsoever to spare the Reich's civilians from bombing or shelling. In fact, quite the opposite constituted the norm.

87. Richard Overy, *Are We Beasts? A review of The Fire: The Bombing of Germany 1940-1945*, by Jörg Friedrich, and *Inferno: The Destruction of Hamburg*, by Keith Lowe, in *Literary Review*, March 2007, at <http://www.literaryreview.co.uk/overy_03_07.html>, accessed 7 March 2008.

88. The German propaganda ministry's communiqués to the neutral press agencies in the wake of the Dresden raids instantly sensationalized them by claiming as many as 200,000 – 250,000

fatal casualties. Probert, p. 320, and Group Captain Peter W. Gray, "Dresden 1945 – Just Another Raid?" in *Royal Air Force Airpower Review*, Vol.4, No.1 (Spring 2001), p.8. Among those who, either knowingly or unwittingly, propagated the 'top end' casualty rates was British journalist David Irving in his book *The Destruction of Dresden* (London: Kimber, 1963). Mr. Irving, by his own admission, possessed no academic credentials in history. He was, in fact, a university dropout. In the book, he electrified audiences worldwide by providing a "best estimate" of 135,000 fatal casualties, which he compared directly to 71,379 fatalities incurred at Hiroshima. The book, which included some very graphic photographs to accompany the inflated casualty figures, engendered broad-scale revulsion against the Allied wartime bombing policy, "...and [it was] not extinguished when Mr. Irving himself admitted his error in 1966 in a letter to *The Times*; in this, he quoted a report of the Dresden area police chief, of whose authenticity he said there was no doubt, giving a death toll of 25,000 dead and 35,000 'missing.' [This was reputed to be the best information then available that could be extracted from East Germany, meaning that Dresden's ordeal was roughly on the same scale as that of Hamburg in July 1943. D.B.]. Mr. Irving, '...[having] no interest in promoting or perpetuating false legends,' hastened to publish this. Sharp and special criticism of the Dresden attack nevertheless continues, some of it far from temperate, and clearly fuelled by nuclear disarmament issues which have nothing to do with history." Terraine, p. 678. Given Mr. Irving's denial of the Holocaust and his subsequent conviction on related issues by an Austrian court, a judicious dollop of healthy skepticism is probably in order when examining both his revised statistics and his motives for advancing some of his 'evidence' in the first instance. However, the fact that in recent years he has been roundly and broadly discredited is largely irrelevant. Once his initial assessment, buttressed by other intemperate, non-objective evaluations of the raids had been advanced, the proverbial 'genie was out of the bottle,' and it still remains difficult to find objective treatments of the Dresden raids. However, the report unearthed by the Dresden police chief's office, mentioned by Irving, which was put together in early March 1945, assessed Dresden's death toll at approximately 25,000, with several thousand more fallen in all probability buried in the rubble. The additional figure of 35,000 'missing' quoted by Irving is extremely misleading, as this number was probably based upon the chaotic displacement of citizens that prevailed in the wake of the raids. "Earlier reputable estimates of casualties varied from 25,000 to more than 60,000, but historians now view around 25,000-35,000 as the likely range [Götz Bergander, *Dresden im Luftkrieg: Vorgeschichte-Zerstörung-Folgen* (Munich: Wilhelm Heyne Verlag, 1977), and Richard J. Evans, *The Bombing of Dresden in 1945: Falsification of Statistics*, at <http://www.holocaustdenialontrial.org/evidence/evans005.asp#5.2d>], with Dresden historian Friedrich Reichert pointing toward the lower end of it" [Friedrich Reichert, *Verbrannt bis zur Unkenntlichkeit – Die Zerstörung Dresdens 1945* (Dresden: Dresdener Museum, 1994). ...According to official German report *Tagesbefehl* (Order of the Day) No.47 ("TB47") issued on 22 March [1945] the number of dead recovered by that date was 20,204, including 6865 who were cremated on the *Altmarkt*, and the total number of deaths was expected to be about 25,000.[Paul Addison & Jeremy A. Crang (eds.), *Firestorm: The Bombing of Dresden* (London: Pimlico, 2006), p.194; Frederick Taylor, *Dresden: Tuesday, February 13, 1945* (New York: HarperCollins, 2004), p.424; and Richard J. Evans, <http:www.holocaustdenialontrial.org/evidence/evans005.asp#5.2d> and <Http://www.holocaustdenialontrial.org/trial/defense/evans/520dv>.] Another report on 3 April [1945] put the number of corpses recovered at 22,096 [Addison and Crang, p.75]. The municipal cemetery office recorded 21,271 victims of the raids were buried in the city cemeteries, of which 17,295 were placed in the *Heidefriedhof* cemetery (A total that included the ashes of those cremated at the *Altmarkt*). These numbers were probably supplemented by a number of additional private burials in other places. [Addison and Crang, p.75] A further 1858 bodies of victims were found during the rebuilding of Dresden between the end of the war and 1966. [Taylor, last page of Appendix B, p.509]. Since 1989, despite extensive excavation for new buildings, no war related bodies have been found. [Ibid.]. The number of people registered with the authorities as missing [at the time of the raids] was 35,000, around 10,000 of which were later found to be alive." <http://en.wikipedia.org/wiki/Bombing_of_Dresden_in_World_War_II>, pp.4,10, accessed 18 March 2008. However, the loss of life in the Dresden raids was considerably higher than in many other bombing raids, and one of the contributing factors undoubtedly was the lack of preparation for the effects of aerial attack by the city's *Gauleiter* Martin Mutschmann, since the local Nazis did not expect the city to be bombed. Ibid., p.3. Worthy of note, on 2 October 2008 in *Der Spiegel*, Frederick Taylor further observed: "Now, more than 60 years later, it seems we must lower our estimates. After four years' work, an impressive commission of German historians [including

the renowned Dr. Horst Boog – DB] this week filed its report on this issue, and it seems that even the lowest figure so far accepted may be an overestimate. Drawing on archival sources, many never previously consulted, on burial grounds and scientific findings – including street-by-street archaeological investigations – plus hundreds of eyewitness reports, the 'Dresden Commission of Historians for the Ascertainment of the Number of Victims of the Air Raids on the City of Dresden on 13/14 February 1945' has provisionally estimated the likely death toll at around 18,000 and definitely no more than 25,000." <http://www.spiegel.de/international/germany/0,1518,581992,00.html>.
89. Neillands, p.352.
90. Taylor, p.148.
91. Covered and referenced in depth in Bashow, pp. 336-388, and Notes 15-25.
92. Gray, p.7, and Taylor, pp.62-75, 148-153, 155, 161 (direct quote).
93. Gray, p.7.
94. Wartime polling with respect to the bombing was rather frequent. Some representative examples follow:

Canada - 11 November 1942 - "Do you approve or disapprove of bombing Germany's civilian population? Of Italy's? Of Japan's?" (Canadian Intellectual Property Office [CIPO])

National Total	Germany's	Italy's	Japan's
Approve	57%	51%	62%
Disapprove	38%	44%	34%
Undecided	5%	5%	4%

Hadley Cantril (ed.), *Public Opinion 1935-1946* (Princeton: Princeton University Press, 1951), p.1068.

Great Britain - December 1943 - "How do you feel about the bombing?" (Only one answer per respondent allowed) (British Information Protection Office [BIPO])

Satisfaction, getting some of their own medicine, keep it up.	47%
We are justified in doing it. It is a necessity.	17%
Dislike bombing but necessary under present circumstances.	16%
Sorry for the kids and old people but it's necessary.	3%
They should bomb only industrial plants and communications.	2%
I am against bombing.	7%
Miscellaneous.	6%
No answer; don't know.	2%

Ibid.,p.1069.

Great Britain - December 1943 - "What do you think are likely to be the effects of the bombing of the German cities?" (Only one answer per respondent allowed) (BIPO)

Upsets German morale.	40%
It will shorten the war.	24%
Smash war industries.	10%
Bombing will win the war.	3%
Bombing alone will not win the war.	3%
Germans will retaliate.	2%
Miscellaneous.	9%
Don't know.	5%

Ibid., p.1069.

95. Greenhous *et al.*, p.726.

96. David Ian Hall, *Arguments For and Against the Strategic Bomber Offensive: The Contrasting Views of Wing Commander T.D. (Harry) Weldon and RAF Chaplain L. John Collins*, An essay presented by Doctor Hall of Linacre College, University of Oxford, for the Bomber Harris Trust Essay Competition, 30 June 1997, p.10.

97. Ibid.

98. Ibid.

99. <http://www.parliament.uk/about/visiting/exibitions/bishop_bell.cfm>.

100. Middlebrook, *The Nuremberg Raid*, p.314.

101. Eberhard Spetzler, *Luftkrieg und Menschlichkeit* (Göttingen, Germany: NP, 1956), quoted in Hermann Knell, *To Destroy a City* (Cambridge, MA: Da Capo Press, 2003), pp.326-327.

102. Ibid., p.329.

103. Greenhous *et al.*, p.727.

104. B.K. Sandwell, *Saturday Night*, Editorial, 13 June 1942, p.13.

105. "Few Will Object to Continuance of Allied Raids," in *Toronto Telegram*, 31 May 1943; and "Bombing Civilians," in *Winnipeg Free Press*, 27 April 1943, both transcribed in Greenhous *et al.*, p.728.

106. Hew Strachan, *European Armies and the Conduct of the War* (London: Routledge, 2001), p.188.

107. Statistic transcribed by author during visit to Japanese Navy *Kamikaze* memorial at the naval museum of the Japanese Maritime Self-Defense Force Officer Candidate School, Etajima Japan, 16 July 2002.

108. Masatake Okumiya, Jiro Horikoshi, and Martin Caidin, *Zero* (New York: ibooks, [1956], 2002), p.354.

109. Winston Spencer Churchill, *The Second World War*, Volume 2 (New York: Time-Life Books, 1959), p.561.

110. Statistic transcribed by author from the Hiroshima Peace Museum, Hiroshima Japan, 15 July 2002. The War Cabinet, apparently figuratively, was calling for the sacrifice of every Japanese man, woman, and child, if necessary, to repel the invaders from the west, since the *total* population of Japan, as late as April 1947, was just over 73 million persons.

111. Okumiya *et al.*, p.362.

112. Ibid., p.378.

113. Jablonski, p.169, and Peter Jennings and Todd Brewster, *The Century* (New York: Doubleday, 1998), p.276.

114. Quoted in Overy, *Bomber Command*, p.202.

115. Minute to Lord Beaverbrook, Minister of Aircraft Production, July 1940. Quoted in Neillands, p.301 and Note 7.

116. Neillands, p.301.

117. Quoted in Murray, p.234.

118. Overy, *A Presentation to the Symposium on the Strategic Bomber Offensive 1939-1945*, p.19.

About the Author

Lieutenant-Colonel (ret'd) David L. Bashow has written extensively in books and select periodicals on a variety of defence, foreign policy, and military history topics. His published books have been well received by academics and general readers alike, and most have achieved bestseller status. In 2004, he retired from military service after a long career as a Canadian Air Force fighter pilot, a senior staff officer, and a military academic. His flying time includes nearly 2400 hours in the CF-104/F-104G *Starfighter*, and he is a graduate of the USAF/GAF Fighter Weapons School and the US Navy's Topgun School at the postgraduate level. In 2002, he was appointed an Officer of the Order of Military Merit, and he has also received the U.S. Meritorious Service Medal. Dave has also received commendations from both the Canadian Forces and the United States Air Force for saving aircraft in extreme emergency conditions. He is currently Editor-in-Chief of the *Canadian Military Journal* and an Associate Professor of History at the Royal Military College of Canada. Prior to *None but the Brave*, his most recent book was entitled *No Prouder Place ~ Canadians and the Bomber Command Experience 1939-1945*, and it represents more than five years of scholarship and research. It has received outstanding reviews and it is now in its second printing.

GLOSSARY

BEM .... British Empire Medal.

Bumerang .... German device used to detect *Oboe* transmissions.

CBE .... Companion of the Order of the British Empire.

Chastise .... Air attack on the Ruhr dams, May 1943.

Clarion .... American operation to disrupt German communications and morale by widespread bombing and fighter attacks, February 1945.

Corkscrew .... Manoeuvre for evading enemy air attack in a bomber.

Corona .... Counterfeit orders or commands transmitted by radio to German night fighters.

Crossbow .... Bombing campaign associated with attacks on V-weapon launch sites, 1944.

Dartboard .... Jamming measure used against German fighter communications.

DFC .... Distinguished Flying Cross.

DFM .... Distinguished Flying Medal.

Donnerkell .... German device for detecting *Oboe*-equipped aircraft.

Drumstick .... Jamming of German fighter radio control channels.

DSO .... Distinguished Service Order.

Dudelsack (Bagpipes) ..... Device for jamming British radio and wireless transmissions.

Dunkelnachtjagd .... The German "dark night fighting" system, at the heart of which were the giant *Würzburg* detection, height-finding, and gun-laying radars, which were a quantum leap over the relatively primitive *Freya* radars.

Düppel .... Strips of metallic foil air-dropped to confuse enemy radar, counterpart known as *Window* to Allied forces.

FIDO .... Fog dispersal for runways by using a double row of gasoline-fed burners.

Fishpond .... Airborne radar for warning Bomber Command crews of nearby enemy aircraft.

GLOSSARY

Flamme .... German device for homing on IFF and *Mandrel* transmissions.

Flensburg........................ German electronic device to direct night fighters to *Monica*, *Mandrel*, and *Piperack* transmissions.

Freya .... German early warning radar.

Freya-Halbe .... Device to negate the effect of *Mandrel* on Freya.

Gardening .... Mine-laying operations in enemy waters.

Gee .... British radio aid to navigation utilizing three ground transmitting stations.

G-H .... Allied blind bombing device. *Oboe* in reverse.

Giant Würzburg............. German early warning radar permitting fighter controllers to track night fighters and their targets.

Gisella .... German attack on Bomber Command airfields, March 1945.

Gomorrah .... Concentrated incendiary operations against Hamburg, July-August 1943.

Grocer............................ Another RAF device for jamming German AI radars.

H2S................................ Airborne ground mapping radar aid to navigation and target identification.

H2X............................... American version of *H2S*.

Heinrich .... German device for jamming *Gee* transmissions.

Helle Nachtjagd............. German air defence system of searchlights used to highlight enemy bombers for flak (anti-aircraft artillery) and night fighters.

Himmelbett .... "Bedspring in the Heavens," the German air defence system that eventually extended from Denmark to the middle of France. It used radio communications to integrate early-warning and interception radar facilities, searchlight and flak batteries, fighter control stations, and fighter squadrons. Also known as the Kammhűber Line, after its founder, General Kammhűber.

Laubfrosch..................... German device for detecting *H2S* emissions.

Lichtenstein................... German Airborne Intercept (AI) radar.

LMF ....Lack of Moral Fibre.

Mammut .... Another German early warning radar.

Mandrel.......................... Radio jamming saturation of German early warning system.

MBE...............................Member of the Order of the British Empire.

Millennium .... The first RAF 1000-bomber raid, conducted against Cologne, May 1942.

Monica .... British electronic device for warning bomber crews of approaching enemy night fighters.

Naxburg .... German ground-based radar used for tracking *H2S* transmissions.

Naxos .... A German electronic device used for homing on *Monica*.

Neptun .... A late-war German AI radar.

Nickeling........................ Propaganda leaflet raids.

OBE ....Officer of the Order of the British Empire.

Oboe.............................. British electronic blind bombing device, used by the Pathfinders for target marking.

Perfectos .... British electronic device that triggered German IFF equipment.

Piperack .... British airborne device used for jamming German AI radars.

Pointblank..................... Bombing directive by Joint Chiefs of Staff downstream from the Casablanca Conference (January 1943) for the bombing priorities of the Combined Bomber Offensive, specifying the destruction of the German Air Force, June 1943.

Schräge Musik................ "Hot" or "slanted" jazz music. The German name applied to the upward-firing cannon systems mounted extensively on German night fighters.

Shiver .... Jamming device used against *Würzburg* GCI radars.

SN2................................ German AI radar.

Spanner.......................... An early German infra-red airborne target detection device intended to home in on the hot exhaust gas emissions of Allied bomber engines.

GLOSSARY

Thunderclap .... An operation originally planned as a massive air attack on Berlin designed to hasten the German surrender. First proposed in August 1944, but not executed in its planned form.

Tinsel .... The jamming of German fighter radio communications and control channels.

Ultra .... Signals intelligence derived from penetration of the German *Enigma* cipher machines.

Village Inn .... British tail-mounted, rearward-looking radar warning device.

Wasserman .... German early-warning radar.

Whitebait .... Code name for the 1943-1944 Bomber Command raids on Berlin.

Wilde Sau .... "Wild Boar," German "freelance" night fighters.

Window .... Strips of metallic foil cut precisely to the wavelengths of enemy radars, air-dropped in bundles to confuse those radars with a saturation of false electronic "echoes." Also called "chaff."

Würzburg .... German ground-controlled interception radar.

Index

INDEX

INDEX

Ripstein, Howard 92
Roosevelt, Franklin D. 22

Sandwell, B.K. 156, 157, **166** *notes*
Searby, John **116** *notes*, **119** *notes*
Shannon, David 113
Sheridan, Jimmy 78, 88, 111, **117** *notes*, **118** *notes*, **119** *notes*
Short *Stirling* 6, **22** *caption*, **26** *caption*, 27, 64, 66, 67, 105, **117** *notes*
Sinclair, Archibald 12, 19, 41, 42, 47, **55** *notes*, **56** *notes*, **58** *notes*, **59** *notes*
Singleton, John 19, **56** *notes*
Singleton Report 19
Speer, Albert 31, 33, 125, 126, 129, 130, 134, 135, 137, 138, 141, 142, 147, **161-163** *notes*
Spetzler, Eberhard 156, **166** *notes*
Spitfire (see "Supermarine *Spitfire*")
Standard Beam Approach 69
Stirling (see "Short *Stirling*")
Superfortress (see "Boeing B-29 *Superfortress*")
Supermarine *Spitfire* 39
Supreme Headquarters Allied Expeditionary Forces (SHAEF) 23, 24, 29-31, 147
Swetman, Bill *colour insert*, **58** *notes*, **110** *caption*, 113, 114
Symonds, Charles P. 87, 100-102, **118** *notes*, **119** *notes*

Target Tokens **117** *notes*
Tedder, Arthur 31, 43, **59** *notes*
Tempest (see "Hawker *Tempest*")
Temple, William, **57** *notes*, 155
The Report on the Bombing of Germany (see "Singleton Report")
Thompson, Les 67
Timmerman, Nelles 113
Tizard, Henry **56** *notes*
Tojo, Hideki 158
Tour of Operations vii, 26, 27, 63, 85, 89, 90, 99, 111, 113
Transportation Plan (Transportation Campaign) 30, 33, **57** *notes*, 127
Trenchard, Hugh 1, 2
Turnbull, Bob 113
Twining, Nathan 25

United States Army Air Force (USAAF) ix, xi, 21, 23, 25, 29, 31, 32, 36, 37, 38, 43, 44, **57** *notes*
United States Strategic Air Force (USSTAF) 25, 30, 34, 36

Vickers *Wellington* vii, *colour insert*, 5, 85, 113, 123

Waugh, Jimmy 65, **116** *notes*
Waverer 112
Wellington (see "Vickers *Wellington*")
Wells, Mark **56** *notes*, 64, **116** *notes*-**119** *notes*, **161** *notes*
Western Air Plans 4
Wever, Walther 139
Whitebait **119** *notes*, **172** *gloss*
Whitley (see "Armstrong-Whitworth *Whitley*")
Williams, Denis J. 87, 100, 101, 102, **118** *notes*, **119** *notes*
Wilmot, Chester 144, **163** *notes*
Yalta Conference 41, 43